POLITICAL ECONOMY
AND FREEDOM

G. Warren Nutter

G. WARREN NUTTER

POLITICAL ECONOMY AND FREEDOM

A COLLECTION OF ESSAYS

———

Edited by Jane Couch Nutter

Foreword by Paul Craig Roberts

LibertyPress

INDIANAPOLIS

Liberty*Press* is a publishing imprint of Liberty Fund, Inc., a foundation established to encourage study of the ideal of a society of free and responsible individuals.

The cuneiform inscription that serves as the design motif for our endpapers is the earliest known written appearance of the word "freedom" (*ama-gi*), or liberty. It is taken from a clay document written about 2300 B.C. in the Sumerian city-state of Lagash.

Library of Congress Cataloging in Publication Data

Nutter, G. Warren, 1923–1979
    Political economy and freedom.

    Bibliography: p.
    Includes index.
    1. Economics—Addresses, essays, lectures. 2. Laissez-faire—Addresses, essays, lectures. 3. Liberty—Addresses, essays, lectures. 4. United States—Economic conditions—1945–   —Addresses, essays, lectures. 5. Soviet Union—Economic conditions—1918–   —Addresses, essays, lectures. 6. International relations—Addresses, essays, lectures.

I. Nutter, Jane Couch. II. Title.
HB171.N86 1983   330   82–48106
ISBN 0–86597–024–6
ISBN 0–86597–025–4 (pbk.)

10 9 8 7 6 5 4 3 2 1

Contents

PART THREE

Foreword

G Warren Nutter was born on March 10, 1923, in Topeka, Kansas. He earned his bachelor's, master's, and doctoral degrees at the University of Chicago in the 1940s, taught at Yale, and moved to the University of Virginia in 1956, where he was chairman of the economics department during most of the 1960s. During 1969–1973 he was granted a leave of absence from Virginia to serve as assistant secretary of defense for international security affairs.

I met Warren for the first time in the classroom in 1961 where he taught me price theory, not as formal pyrotechnics—though he could do that too—but as analysis of how the market grapples with the choices posed by reality. The University of Virginia in the early 1960s had a highly innovative economics department, probably unique in its strong emphasis on political economy.

Nutter established his reputation by making enduring contributions to price theory, comparative economic systems, and industrial organization. He was more than a first-class technician, however; he was a committed scholar with a deep faith in the contribution that ideas and knowledge could make to the betterment of society. As a political economist in the classical sense, he studied the "science for building the good society," that good society being the one that "maximizes use of voluntary agreement in organizing social activity."

A concern for the central issues of his time characterized Nutter's empirical studies. In the late 1940s, it was widely believed by economists as well as by the general public that industries in the United States were becoming increasingly concentrated and dominated by monopolies and oligopolies; that competition is not a "natural" state and therefore inexorably develops into a system of monopoly. In *The Extent of Enterprise Monopoly in the United States, 1899–1939,* Nutter in-

vestigated the facts and found that there had been no increase in concentration in the forty years covered by his study, except for industries
operating under government control or supervision. In this work he first
demonstrated the characteristics that were to typify all his empirical
works: meticulous collection and recording of data and a unique insight
into their interpretation.

In the late 1950s and early 1960s there was worldwide interest in the
performance of the Soviet economy, which was then believed to be
capable of continuously generating growth rates that, by existing standards, were very high, thus lending support for the argument that a
centrally planned economy could outperform a market system over the
long run. One of the conclusions of Nutter's massive study *Growth of
Industrial Production in the Soviet Union* was that the rate of growth of
Soviet industry, while significant, was not remarkable when considered in the long term or when compared to the record of the United
States in similar stages of development. Nutter also showed that the
official index of Soviet industrial output substantially exaggerated its
growth. But, perhaps more importantly, he found that the rate of
growth was slowing down. Although his conclusions provoked much
controversy and he had few defenders at the time, history has vin-
dicated his findings.

Nutter considered the growth of government to be perhaps the most
ominous development since World War II, and his monograph *Growth
of Government in the West,* while clearly only a framework for a
massive study, was the outcome of that concern.

Since his own scholarly interests transcended narrow boundaries,
Nutter was skeptical about the imperialistic stretching of economic
techniques and terminology, as if they could explain all human experience. From time to time he would remind economists that the economy
developed without them and performed better before they got their
hands on the management of it. He also took economists to task for
claiming too much on the basis of narrow behavioral assumptions.

The theme of *process* pervades this volume. In the second essay,
"Economic Aspects of Freedom," Nutter tells us: "At base, there is
no difference between what a society does and how it does it. The
means are what count, not the ends, if indeed ends have any meaning
independent of means." In Essay 28 he writes:

> . . . results are no more ideal than the processes through which they are
> achieved. This is the age-old problem of whether ends justify means, and
> the answer implicit in American political ideals is that they do not. Indeed,
> it is the process of discussion and deliberation leading to consent that

forms the philosophical core of our traditional political system, the assumption being that the right process generates, by definition, the best possible results.

Insight about *process* provided the philosophical basis for Nutter's dedication to free markets, to limited government, and to standing by one's friends and allies.

Warren Nutter knew that the mathematical finery of economists often hid a lack of substance. All economists should come to terms with the message of "Economic Welfare and Welfare Economics" (Essay 5). Here he is the warrior in combat over fundamental principles, bravely going to the heart of things: "I am challenging the vision of the problem, the mode of analysis, the outlook of economists."

Nutter believed that the "Pareto optimum" condition (the state of the economy where no one can be made better off without making someone else worse off) "cannot be defined independently of the path through which it is to be approached. . . . In the course of trying to move toward the optimum, the economy moves the optimum itself." How, he asks economists, do you measure a caterpillar as it changes into a butterfly? Since an economy *changes* at least as much as it *grows,* "an appraisal of performance that takes no account of this fact is bound to be misleading if not irrelevant."

Professors are used to erasing their diagrams and equations from the blackboard, thus creating the world anew, starting over from scratch. But in the real world there is no eraser. In Essay 5, Nutter says:

> Economists must, first of all, grasp the fact that where an economy goes depends on how it gets there. There are no practical alternative policies that will lead to the same state of affairs. Once any significant economic decision is made, it leaves its imprint on society, and conditions can never be restored to their original configuration. . . . We must therefore give up any notions we may have of casting the economy as a whole into a preconceived structure.

Nutter was convinced that no amount of deliberate social control can ensure "the optimum growth path" for the economy because "the nature of the problem is altered in the process of solving it."

Nutter's work had just as many necessary lessons for the statesman who spurns process and prizes outcome. All sorts of delusions and tragedies result. For example, in Essay 31:

> Much is said in official statements and the press of the great strides toward peaceful relations that have already been made in such agreements as the one on the status of Berlin. But those agreements have been reached

because the West has acceded to positions consistently and persistently advanced by Soviet diplomacy in the postwar period.

Warren Nutter could say a lot in very few words. Anyone surprised or dismayed by developments in Latin America can find a one-sentence explanation for the failure of our foreign policy in Essay 28: "It became popular to treat military control as the cause rather than the consequence of this weakness [of democratic institutions], and the remedy seemed to be for us to do what we could to weaken military elements in those countries."

"Nothing," Nutter tells us in Essay 30, "will diminish our ability to wield a stabilizing influence in world affairs so much as a well-deserved reputation for infidelity and unreliability in time of trouble." Those who learn the lessons he taught can carry on the fight.

Nutter was not altogether pessimistic about the outcome of the fight. He never accepted the "inevitable." In the last paragraph of the first essay, he sets a tone

> . . . of hope rather than expectation, for there is little in the momentum of unfolding history to comfort those who cherish freedom. What is there to prevent the fraction of income taxed by government from rising to half, three-quarters, and more? There is a hope, and it is this: having become so impressed with the fact that freedom is not everything or the only thing, perhaps we shall put that discovery behind us and comprehend, before it is too late, that without freedom all else is nothing.

Nutter was convinced that our economic and foreign policies had to be based in our heritage of freedom. To be successful, our policies must communicate openly to the people an affirmation of our principles —something that it is difficult to get the modern sophisticate raised on a diet of skepticism to do. But without faith in our principles, leaders are forced into secrecy and manipulation, and their policies fail by arousing the distrust of the people. To the pragmatist this may sound too profound, to the skeptic too dogmatic, and to the realist too naive. To Warren Nutter, the pragmatist flounders among principles, the skeptic distrusts them, and the realist discards them. Having seen the alternatives, Nutter was not afraid of principles.

Paul Craig Roberts

Paul Craig Roberts holds the William E. Simon Chair in Political Economy at The Center for Strategic and International Studies of Georgetown University in Washington, D.C.

Introduction

Economists have long enjoyed the reputation, not wholly unwarranted, of practicing the dismal science. They are so regarded by fellow intellectuals as well as the general public, and one important reason is the narrow view economists take of the human race and its behavior. I speak, of course, of the concept of economic man, which encompasses something more than Scrooge but a good deal less than the typical human being.

To the economist, man is nothing but a choice-making animal for whom all goods—that is, all things of value—are measurable and substitutable, the one for the other. Hence, man is an animal most happy in the marketplace, merrily exchanging wares with others till all maximize bliss. Differences in values are resolved through voluntary exchange, since getting more of anything makes it worth less.

When challenged to justify this narrow vision of man, the economist rightly points to the market and says: "Look, my theory works. Ergo man is an economic animal." He is justly proud of the fact that he has a theory of value that works.

So far so good. But the economist is prone to becoming dizzy with success and venturing into other scholars' backyards, bringing his theories with him. He wants to do good everywhere, whether asked or not, and he tries to do so by tidying up the other social sciences. And so he eagerly reconstructs other disciplines in the image of economics and people in the image of economic man.

These remarks were given at a panel discussion of the National Association of Manufacturers in December 1974.

Political science is the favorite hunting ground, and we are therefore blessed with a growing number of economic theories of politics. According to this way of thinking, all social problems have the same cause: a discrepancy in measurable and substitutable values. Hence all social problems are resolvable by friendly compromise in which each contestant gives a little and gets a little. Everything will work out as it does in the marketplace if we just set up the right structure of property rights and rewards.

Now I have long been uneasy about this rather arrogant economic imperialism that is practiced by some of my esteemed colleagues, and I bring it up today because businessmen, being immersed as they are in the market, can easily slide into the same bad thinking habits. After all, that's the way it goes in business: everybody has his price.

Well, the world is bigger than the marketplace, and many valuables are simply not marketable. The concept of the economic man works to explain markets because most people behave that way most of the time. But some behave differently all the time, and all do some of the time. Otherwise, why do we have wars, hot and cold?

No theory of social behavior is complete unless it allows for the passion of the mob, the zeal of the martyr, the loyalty of the palace guard, the insatiability of the egomaniac. For that reason, the really serious problems of society will never be explained or resolved by the economics of politics.

The principal problems of the day are at root not economic but social, ethical, and political. We are a people in search of a cause.

PART ONE

1

Freedom in a Revolutionary Economy

I

Times change. When my townsman Thomas Jefferson journeyed to Williamsburg in May 1779 and shortly afterward took up residence in the palace as governor, Virginia was at war. Strange things were happening in the economy, and they were to become stranger over the ensuing two years of Jefferson's stewardship. Inflation was rampant, goods were requisitioned, property was impressed, salt rationed, hoarding declared a crime, and exports put under embargo. Short of arms, Virginia launched an abortive project to produce them in a state arsenal. If price and wage controls were not widely or vigorously applied, it was in spite of constant urgings by the desperate Continental Congress to do so. The lessons of experience were simply too compelling: wherever and whenever price and wage fixing had been tried in the new states fighting for independence, it had brought nothing but great economic mischief.

As we assemble here today in Williamsburg on the eve of the bicentenary of our republic, we may be grateful for one important difference in the times: we are not now at war. In that respect, times have changed.

This essay, which was originally given as a lecture at the College of William and Mary, Williamsburg, Va., in February 1974, is reprinted from *America's Continuing Revolution: An Act of Conservation* (Washington, D. C.: American Enterprise Institute, 1975), pp. 183–201. It was also published in *The American Revolution: Three Views* (New York: American Brands, 1975), pp. 91–122.

This is not to say that the harsh measures resorted to in the revolutionary war were normal for the colonial period as well. Quite the contrary. Under the British policy of "salutary neglect," in force until 1763, the colonial economy had been largely spared the mercantilist imprint of the age. "Plenty of good land, and liberty to manage their own affairs their own way," Adam Smith observed, "seem to be the two great causes of the prosperity of all new colonies."[1] But why, he wondered, had progress been so much more rapid in the English colonies of North America than in other European colonies throughout the world? The answer was not to be found, he thought, in a richer or more abundant soil, but rather in institutions that enabled the English colonists to make better use of the plentiful resources at their disposal.

These were, first, political. As Smith put it:

> In every thing, except their foreign trade, the liberty of the English colonists to manage their own affairs their own way is complete. It is in every respect equal to that of their fellow-citizens at home, and is secured in the same manner, by an assembly of the representatives of the people, who claim the sole right of imposing taxes for the support of the colony government.[2]

But there was more. Plenty of good land meant not only abundant resources but also, in a less literal sense, the elbowroom needed by a new social order if it was to discard those vestigial institutions that had stifled progress for so long under the established order of things. A case in point was land tenure itself, which could be freed from the bonds of primogeniture and entail in the absence of an entrenched nobility or similar aristocracy. The new society could, when permitted by the mother country, strike out in new directions and prosper accordingly.

The contribution of the mother country was, in Adam Smith's eyes, strictly that of a mother.

> In what way, therefore, has the policy of Europe contributed either to the first establishment, or to the present grandeur of the colonies of America? In one way, and in one way only, it has contributed a good deal. *Magna virum Mater!* It bred and formed the men who were capable of atchieving [*sic*] such great action, and of laying the foundation of so great an empire; and there is no other quarter of the world of which the policy is capable of forming, or has ever actually and in fact formed such men. The colonies owe to the policy of Europe the education and great views of their active and enterprising founders; and some of the greatest and

---

[1] Adam Smith, *The Wealth of Nations* (New York: Modern Library, 1937), p. 538.
[2] Ibid., p. 551.

most important of them, so far as concern their internal government, owe to it scarce anything else.[3]

The cultural flow did not, of course, cease with the founding of the colonies. The book from which I have quoted—*The Wealth of Nations*—was, for one thing, published the same year as the Declaration of Independence. And then there was James Watt's invention of the steam engine scarcely a decade before. This remarkable confluence of ideas laid the foundation for a revolutionary society. All at once, it seems, there sprang forth this congenial triad: a novel concept of representative government, a science of economics, and an industrial technology, each revolutionary in its own right and exponentially so when combined together.

These ideas had their proximate origin in two amazingly small circles of minds, one located in the incipient United States and the other in Scotland. Though no Virginian can gladly resist the temptation to do so, I will not dwell on the American circle, so well known to us as our Founding Fathers. And, as far as the Scottish circle is concerned, the only point I wish to make here is that Smith and Watt were once colleagues at the University of Glasgow.

John Rae, Smith's biographer, describes their relation in this way:

> There is nothing in the University minutes to connect Smith in any more special way than the other professors with the University's timely hospitality to James Watt; but as that act was a direct protest on behalf of industrial liberty against the tyrannical spirit of the trade guilds so strongly condemned in the *Wealth of Nations,* it is at least interesting to remember that Smith had a part in it. Watt, it may be recollected, was then a lad of twenty, who had come back from London to Glasgow to set up as mathematical instrument maker, but though there was no other mathematical instrument maker in the city, the corporation of hammermen refused to permit his settlement because he was not the son or son-in-law of a burgess, and had not served his apprenticeship to the craft within the burgh. But in those days of privilege the universities also had their privileges. The professors of Glasgow enjoyed an absolute and independent authority over the area within college bounds, and they defeated the oppression of Watt by making him mathematical instrument maker to the University, and giving him a room in the College buildings for his workshop and another at the College gates for the sale of his instruments. In these proceedings Smith joined, and joined, we may be sure, with the warmest approval. . . .

[3] Ibid., p. 556.

Watt's workshop was a favourite resort of Smith's during his residence at Glasgow College, for Watt's conversation, young though he was, was fresh and original, and had great attractions for the stronger spirits about him. Watt on his side retained always the deepest respect for Smith, and when he was amusing the leisure of his old age in 1809 with his new invention of the sculpture machine, and presenting his works to his friends as "the productions of a young artist just entering his eighty-third year," one of the first works he executed with the machine was a small head of Adam Smith in ivory.[4]

Respect for Smith was hardly confined to Watt or Scotland, for *The Wealth of Nations* migrated easily and widely abroad, finding an eager audience in many parts and certainly on our shores. Our Founders were familiar with this great work in one way or another, some more than others.[5] Alexander Hamilton, Tench Coxe, or whoever wrote the renowned *Report on Manufactures* paraphrased Smith at length and quoted him verbatim at one point, though without acknowledging the source.[6] Deliberations at the Constitutional Convention reveal a much wider group acquainted with the emerging science of economics.

Passage of time has caused differing verdicts to be rendered on the originality, rigor, and consistency of Smith's masterpiece, but history leaves no doubt about its massive impact and significance. Its genius derived from the molding together of fragments of evolving economic thought into a synthetic whole, masterfully applied to familiar situations in a way that revealed a coherent system for organizing social activity not easily envisaged before and destined to capture the imagination of thoughtful leaders ready to grasp revolutionary ideas. It, like the Declaration and the ensuing Constitution, struck a spark in receptive timber. Social thought was not to be the same afterward as before.

Ideas do have consequences, dependent on the historical conjuncture into which they are thrust, and this was a propitious time for exciting ideas. The political thinkers and leaders who arose in those formative years of our republic were, of course, influenced by many things: vested interests and personal ambition as well as idealism and ideology; conventional wisdom and prevailing institutions as well as radical thought; the sheer momentum of affairs as well as rational calculus. So

---

[4] John Rae, *Life of Adam Smith* (New York: Augustus M. Kelley, 1965), pp. 73–74.

[5] See William D. Grampp, *Economic Liberalism* (New York: Random House, 1965), vol. 1, pp. 128 ff., 154.

[6] See Edward G. Bourne, "Alexander Hamilton and Adam Smith," *Quarterly Journal of Economics* 7 (1893–94): 328–44.

was the electorate whose consent was sought and needed to launch the new society. Those who easily discern a simple order in history, an uncomplicated nexus of cause and consequence, may single out one or another factor as the dominant force shaping the course of events in those times, but not I. Such sweeping interpretations of history obscure more than they reveal. Opportunities and constraints are the stuff of history, together with chance, reflective thought, and choice. And none of these elements flows mechanically and predictably from the nature of man, custom, institutions, or any other readily identifiable single source. History is instead the product of all these interacting forces mutually influencing each other. My only object, then, is to give revolutionary ideas and sober reflection their due in this singular epoch.

When the delegates assembled for the Constitutional Convention, there was good reason in circumstances of the time for their attention to be drawn to the related issues of strengthening government at the national level and of "regulating commerce," a term that had roughly the same meaning then as "economic policy" has today. Prosperity had not spontaneously emerged in the wake of independence, contrary to great expectations before the fact. Instead of prosperity, there was depression, aggravated in no small measure by the confused and con- founded government of the Confederation. Experience in dealing with these troubles was modest from all points of view: influential leaders were in their thirties; conscious economic policy on the part of government—in London as well as at home—had a history of scarcely more than a score of years; and precedents for the envisaged new order were lacking altogether. Imagination and vision were bound to assume commanding importance.

Wherever and however they acquired their economic vision, the makers of the Constitution deliberately gave wide berth to the economy of the nation being formed, reserving only a restrained guiding hand for government. In saying this, I am mindful of the persistent controversy over how much power the prevailing constitution makers intended to bestow upon the government of the Union. On this score, however, I find quite persuasive the case made by William Grampp, eminent historian of economic liberalism.

Concentrating on the eleventh-hour efforts at the Convention to expand the economic role of the federal government, Grampp notes that

> what is interesting is that the proposals—all of them controversial, almost provocative—should have been made only a few days before the con-

vention adjourned, when unanimity was urgently needed and when many delegates were trying heroically to find compromises that would produce it. Proposals such as that made by Madison [to empower the federal goverment to charter corporations] had been made earlier in the convention. That they were made again so near the time [of] adjournment suggests that their advocates were making a last great effort to write broad economic powers into the Constitution. Perhaps they prevailed upon Franklin in the belief that his great authority would be decisive. But they were defeated. . . . The very extensive powers proposed by Randolph, Morris, Franklin, Hamilton, and Madison were reduced to the limited provisions of Section 8 of Article I, which include the power to tax, borrow, regulate commerce, pass uniform bankruptcy laws, coin money, establish post offices and post roads, and grant patents.[7]

The limits thus established take on significance when compared with the traditional economic powers of the age, which, as Grampp observes,

can be deduced from the controls which the governments of France and England exercised or tried to exercise during the period of mercantilism, from the sixteenth to the middle of the eighteenth century: the fixing of prices, wages, and interest rates, prohibitions of forestalling and engrossing, regulating the quality of goods, licensing of labor, programs to increase the population, sumptuary control, monopoly grants and other exclusive rights, incorporation, state enterprise, and the control of foreign trade and finance including the protection of domestic industries. The convention considered only four: monopoly and other exclusive rights, control of foreign trade, state enterprise, and sumptuary control. The last two were rejected. The granting of monopoly rights was restricted to patents and copyrights. The control over foreign trade was left in an ambiguous state, except for the prohibition of export taxes. Although not made explicit, the Constitution allowed some power to increase the population, because the Federal government could offer free land as an inducement to immigration.[8]

Good often issues more from powers denied to government than from those granted, and this was surely the case as far as economic development over our republic's first century is concerned. None of the prohibitory provisions of the Constitution was to take on greater significance than the one forbidding individual states to erect barriers to

---

[7] Grampp, *Economic Liberalism*, vol. 1, pp. 106–8.

[8] Ibid., pp. 108–9.

commerce among themselves. Making trade free within an internal market that was to expand to vast proportions permitted the nation to indulge, for example, in recurrently restrictive tariffs, as the politics of a good century and a half seemed to dictate, without serious hindrance to economic progress. Our great market was to lie at home in a free-trade area larger than the world has yet experienced anywhere else. Our Founders could hardly have foreseen that this would happen, but they must have had a conceptual vision—no matter how crude it might seem to those passing judgment today—of the broad benefits that would ensue from internal free trade. Otherwise, why bother to write this strict prohibition into the Constitution?

While such specific sentiments of the time are rather easily discerned, the underlying social philosophy is more elusive, defying simple description in the ideological vocabulary of today. Liberalism will hardly do as a description if only because slavery was accepted by most and extolled by many. Nor can we speak of a democratic ideal in the modern sense, since democracy—either as then comprehended or as since manifested—was specifically rejected in favor of republicanism, a quite different concept of representative government as Irving Kristol so elegantly clarified earlier in this series.[9] Individualism is perhaps the term that best captures the essential spirit of the time and at once implies the complex of derivative values: liberty for the citizen—which is to say, the person deemed competent and responsible —to make his own decisions; power for the citizen, mainly in the form of private property, to realize his potential; humanitarian concern for the less fortunate and incompetent; and equality of all citizens before the law and of the electorate within the polity.

II

If the thinker-turned-statesman had his moment at the founding of the republic, it was to be the practitioner pure and simple—the doer, the man of action—who was to dominate the scene for at least the next century, when pragmatism became America's watchword. The individualistic spirit found expression in the world of affairs, not in philosophic reflection, as each citizen was swept up in the excitement of his workaday world—his farm or business, his trade or profession, his

[9] Irving Kristol, ''The American Revolution as a Successful Revolution,'' in *America's Continuing Revolution*, pp. 3–21.

public or private life. The nation, it would seem, was too busy enjoying the fruits of progress to ponder its causes, and theory emerged from practice. Political thought issued from practicing politicians, and economic thought—interestingly—from practicing jurists.

Economists, such as there were, were either special pleaders or academic amateurs. In his classic essay on early American economic thought, the late Frank Fetter wondered: "why did the fertile and original conceptions which sprang, as it were, spontaneously from the new environment in America, not come to fruition in a constructive and more lasting system of American economic thought?" He found much of the answer to lie in "partisanship, which blocks the path to disinterested scientific effort whenever personal prejudices and pecuniary or class interests are affected by the application of any kind of theory to practical problems."[10]

The consequence—and, in turn, reinforcing cause—was lack of a learned profession of economics. As Fetter observes:

> It is a remarkable fact that during the whole period before 1870 there was not a single so-called political economist who had received the minimum amount of special training demanded today for the practice of law, or of medicine, or for the pursuit of the natural sciences. All were trained primarily in some other field: theology, moral philosophy, literature, languages, law, practical politics, journalism, business, or some branch of natural science. In political economy they were all self-trained amateurs, who, as it were, happened to wander into this field. If the study of the more exact sciences were pursued only by men with such dominant motives and such unspecialized training, little scientific progress could be expected.[11]

I leave it to others to judge whether the absence of trained economists made us better or worse off in this first century of sweeping economic development. However that may be, the fact is that there was no body of qualified scholars, skilled in critical thought, to observe the unfolding economy, issue commentary, formulate general principles, apply them to problems of the time, and advise on policy. Instead it was the law, issuing from acts and cases, that was to shape a framework for the economy, articulate its principles, and guide policy.

The propelling legal philosophy of the era conceived the purpose of law to be, in Roscoe Pound's words, "a making possible of the max-

---

[10] Frank A. Fetter, "The Early History of Political Economy in the United States," in James A. Gherity, ed., *Economic Thought: A Historical Anthology* (New York: Random House, 1965), p. 489.

[11] Ibid., pp. 489–90.

imum of individual free self-assertion.'' Or, as James Willard Hurst has put it more concretely:

> We continually experienced the tangible accomplishments of individuals, small groups, and local effort, with a heady sense of living in a fluid society in which all about him all the time one saw men moving to new positions of accomplishment and influence. Our background and experience in this country taught faith in the capacities of the productive talent residing in people. The obvious precept was to see that this energy was released for its maximum creative expression.[12]

At the same time, those who made and interpreted the law were not slaves to some sterile dogma of laissez faire. Far from it. As Hurst reminds us, this was no ''Golden Age in which our ancestors—sturdier than we—got along well enough if the legislature provided schools, the sheriff ran down horse thieves, the court tried farmers' title disputes, and otherwise the law left men to take care of themselves.'' There was no reluctance to legislate positively ''where legal regulation or compulsion might promote the greater release of individual or group energies.''[13]

But the pervasive spirit of the law, whether it invoked or restrained the power of government, was individualistic. It was normal that ''the years 1800–1875 were, then, above all else, the years of contract in our law.''[14] Subject to the restrictive doctrines of consideration and residual authority of the state to refuse enforcement, the thrust of the law was to encourage voluntary exchange and association. The legal system was responding to the burgeoning scope of the market and in turn stimulating further expansion, in a process of interaction similarly experienced in England at an accelerating pace during the eighteenth as well as the nineteenth century. It was, in fact, an English jurist who, with typical facility, gave classic expression to the legal philosophy dominant in our first century.

> If there is one thing more than any other which public policy requires, it is that men of full age and competent understanding shall have the utmost liberty of contracting, and that contracts, when entered into freely and voluntarily, shall be held good and shall be enforced by courts of justice.[15]

---

[12] James Willard Hurst, *Law and the Conditions of Freedom in the Nineteenth-Century United States* (Madison, Wis.: University of Wisconsin Press, 1956), p. 7.

[13] Ibid.

[14] Ibid., p. 18.

[15] Sir George Jessel, M.R., in *Printing and Numerical Registering Co. v. Sampson* (1875), as cited in Hurst, *Laws,* p. 12.

In a word, contract was king, a sovereign precept demanding obedience from subservient legal principles. No wonder the courts and legislatures were so busy elaborating and defining property rights and liabilities, sweeping away vestigial restrictions on alienation, erecting an intricate structure of commercial law, and creating the corporate person with its full range of appendages and paraphernalia.

The spirit of the time may be fairly interpreted as enthusiasm for venture, viewed as the source of prosperity and progress. Consequently, the law leaned over backward not to hinder the entrepreneur, not to hold him unduly responsible for incidental harm flowing from venturesome activity. It was as if ''nothing ventured, nothing gained'' had become the literal creed of the age. For, as Hurst points out:

> The insistence on a showing of criminal intention [in any case involving liability] amounted in effect to a presumption in favor of the independence of individual action. The middle-nineteenth-century rationale of the law of negligence, in tort, reflected the same basic value judgment. Expansion of economic energies brought men into closer, more continuous relations in situations increasingly likely to yield harm. Nonetheless, at first the law emphasized the social desirability of free individual action and decision. Liability in tort should normally rest on a showing of fault on the actor's part; action at one's peril was the exception. Hence the burden lay on the injured person to show reason why the law should intrude its force to shift some of the burden of loss onto the one who caused injury.[16]

This attitude no doubt appears strange to a generation accustomed to the rhetoric of Ralph Nader and the Sierra Club. I have dwelt on these legal presumptions of the last century neither to extoll nor to disparage them, but to stress their importance as a manifestation of the social ethic of the time. Who is to bear the burden of proving what, and why? The presumptive answers given to these questions say more about a society's conception of the good life than any list of good intentions, no matter how long.

In the matter-of-fact world of our first century, freedom took on concrete meaning in the marketplace, and it worked. A continent was settled, a nation built, and prosperity persistently augmented. The portentous questions of slavery and preservation of the Union might overhang the political scene, but the grand passion was economic development, and the object of the love affair was the market, the creature of free enterprise and exchange.

---

[16] Hurst, *Laws*, p. 19.

III

So it was at least on the surface, but something happened on the way to our second century. There was, first, the torment of the Civil War, which probably served more to arouse the social conscience than to soothe it. Yet, the slaves freed and the Union preserved, the economy hardly paused before plunging into the era of bigness, surely the culmination of a less abrupt historical process.

What had been happening on the economic front was a revolution in transport, the spanning of the continent by railroad, creating a truly national market and opening the way for big business, big finance, and all the other forms of bigness. The individualistic spirit was bound to be put under severe stress as gigantic voluntary associations, the very creatures of contract, assumed a corporate and depersonalized nature basically in conflict with the principle of free individual choice. Tocqueville had already been impressed in the 1830s by the remarkable ability of American private enterprise to mobilize large sums for grand ventures, but he noted that "what most astonishes me is not so much the marvelous grandeur of some undertakings as the innumerable multitude of small ones."[17] Now grandeur was to take the center of the stage.

It is neither my bent nor purpose to prolong this historical narrative, for the moment will shortly be upon me for a summing up, and there is more interpretive ground yet to be covered. Suffice it to say that our first century laid the basis for the second, still fresh in memory. We gradually moved toward a turning point similar to the one faced earlier in England. As Winston Churchill was to write at the turn of the twentieth century:

> The great victories had been won. All sorts of lumbering tyrannies had been toppled over. Authority was everywhere broken. Slaves were free. Conscience was free. Trade was free. But hunger and squalor and cold were also free and the people demanded something more than liberty. . . . And how to fill the void was the riddle that split the Liberal party.[18]

Changing opinion ultimately brought forth a second revolution, a revolution in social thought born of economic crisis some two-score years ago. In the formative years, we seemed determined to make up

[17] Alexis de Tocqueville, *Democracy in America* (New York: Vintage Books, 1954), vol. 2, p. 166.

[18] Winston S. Churchill, *Lord Randolph Churchill* (New York: Macmillan Co., 1906), vol. 1, p. 269.

for lost time in the realm of social philosophizing. The vanguard of social reformers comprised a multiplying band of intellectuals, spawned by affluence, emboldened by their own peculiar sense of superiority, motivated by the animus of the onlooking outsider, and hence, as Schumpeter perceived, inherently inclined to become angry social critics by profession. Learned economists, conspicuously absent during our first century, appeared in abundance and assumed a role of growing importance. To be sure, ardent defenders of the free society were to be found in the intellectual ranks, particularly among economists, but they were vastly overshadowed by the critics in due course. The way was prepared for the sharp inversion of social values that has taken place over the last generation, an inversion incarnate in the colossal government that has come into being as the share of the nation's net product passing through the hands of government has risen from less than a sixth to more than two-fifths. Security, protection, comfort, equality—all seem to have advanced in the scale of importance above self-reliance and freedom.

Fundamentally, what has been transformed is the prevailing conception of the good society. In the nineteenth century, it was the way of life that was idealized—the process whereby the achievable was to be achieved. Today, it is the achievement itself, the outcome of the process, that is prized. We value the way of life less and the content more.

Why has this happened? The easy answer is that freedom did not live up to promise. The evolution of legal principles during our first century suggests that freedom was valued in the economic sphere for what it was expected to yield, that its worth was deemed to be instrumental rather than intrinsic, that economic progress was the goal and freedom merely the means.

There are two things to be said about this interpretation. First, by the test of progress, freedom can hardly have been judged a failure. Production, despite periodic bad times, moved upward in a trend that was the envy of the world, while population multiplied fifteenfold.[19] This was, after all, the "land of opportunity."

Second, freedom was surely desired for itself as much as for its consequences. To interpret the moving spirit of our founding years as nothing more than a craving for greater material comfort would be a travesty of history. Not even the sustained paralysis on the slavery issue can lead us to a similar conclusion about the succeeding period. Nor do

---

[19] See Lance E. Davis et al., *American Economic Growth: An Economist's History of the United States* (New York: Harper & Row, 1972), pp. 21–26, 33–50.

we need to become mired in the metaphysical to define liberty as it was then conceived. The documents of our Revolution protested against too much government, against the dead hand of paternalism and arbitrary power. Liberty to our Founders meant freedom from government.

Perhaps, then, Marx was right in proclaiming that the benefits of capitalism would be far outweighed by its evils: increasing monopoly, misery, inequality, and insecurity. Here, too, the evidence argues otherwise in the main.

Of course, poverty did not vanish amidst plenty, but in a broader sense there was no discernible worsening of material inequality during our first century. A recent study shows, for example, that slaveholding, then unfortunately an important aspect of wealth, was no more concentrated in 1860 than in 1790: in both years, the top 1 percent of slaveholders owned about an eighth of the slaves. Better and more direct evidence indicates a small but perceptible reduction in the inequality of incomes during the last four decades of the nineteenth century.[20]

Changing circumstances and lack of records make it impossible to assess the trend of monopoly in the nineteenth century. Seemingly obvious appearances can be deceptive: the era of trusts toward the end of the century accompanied the emergence of a national market and hence did not necessarily signify a decline of competition. Those who envisage an earlier age of more pervasive competition in isolated localities are likely to be indulging in myth. In any case, the evidence for the twentieth century has been carefully sifted, and it shows no upward drift in the extent of monopoly.[21]

To give Marx his due, one must acknowledge that, over most of our history, we were plagued by cycles of boom and bust with intensifying social impact, so that the attendant insecurity and periodic unemployment constituted a major source of discontent and ultimately of social crisis. But recurrent depressions are not enough to account for the profound change in social outlook.

Instead, I would argue, success has had more to do with our changing mentality than failure. It was Mark Twain who said: "If you pick up a starving dog and make him prosperous, he will not bite you. This is the principal difference between a dog and a man." Progress did not,

---

[20] See ibid., pp. 29–32, 50–54; and Lee Soltow, "Economic Inequality in the United States in the Period from 1790 to 1860," *Journal of Economic History* 31 (December 1971): 822–39.

[21] See G. Warren Nutter and Henry Adler Einhorn, *Enterprise Monopoly in the United States: 1899–1958* (New York: Columbia University Press, 1969).

by and large, aggravate inequities, but it made us more aware and less tolerant of them. Sharpening contrasts in circumstance aroused our humane sentiments, sentiments that could be better afforded by virtue of augmenting affluence. Progress shook loose the age-old endurance that man had customarily displayed for his lot and bred in its place an attitude of insatiable discontent with the pace at which remaining problems were being met. And so we find ourselves in a society in which progress and discontent are engaged in an almost desperate race with each other.

This is perhaps as it should be as long as there is poverty and injustice in the midst of plenty. If social change is to move in the right direction, in accord with the standards of the civilized world, there must be those who stir and prod, who keep the public alert to inequities, who find fault with the established ways of maintaining social order. It is natural to point the finger of blame at the existing system and to seek salvation in its opposite, but therein also lies the great danger of our day.

Those who protest against failures of the market, real and imagined, too often see their remedy in turning affairs over to government, in expanding the political order and diminishing the economic—in relying more on coercion and less on mutual consent. The danger we run in looking first to government to solve problems is that progress will grind to a halt—that discontent will vanquish progress, and the race will be over. Over the ages, the bane of progress has been too much government, not too little.

IV

The time has therefore come, as we approach our bicentenary, to look back to the origins of our economy and to reflect on where we go from here. The revolutionary content of ideas popularized by Adam Smith and implemented by our Founders is to be found in the vision of a complex social order organized not by custom and command, the methods of the ages, but by voluntary exchange and association. Economics arose as a scientific discipline when the economy became a social order distinct from the polity. Those who, inspired by the spirit of freedom, sought to broaden the individual's control over his own destiny were naturally inclined to enlarge the scope of markets and to reduce that of the body politic. The economy became an area of social activity coordinated through voluntary agreement, and economic activity became in the main synonymous with liberty.

Progress came with the loosening of political bonds, but the resulting freedom could be translated into action only through power. The individual acquires power through ownership of private property, the other side of the coin to liberty. In the absolute state, subjects enjoy neither freedom nor power: the despot reigns over slaves. By becoming concentrated in his hands, private property ceases to exist in any meaningful sense. Put the other way around, private property is the means whereby power may be dispersed within a society. It is no wonder that our legal system devoted so much attention to strengthening and vitalizing this institution.

The opposite of the absolute state is anarchy, where everything is privately owned. Just as there can be no freedom in the absolute state, so there can be no order in anarchy—and hence no freedom either. On this earth, there must always be collective property embodied in the power of even the freest state and accumulated through the instrument of taxation, itself an inherent property right of every state. It is equally clear that a society becomes free and democratic only as property becomes broadly dispersed and predominantly private.

Over most of our history, the question of what middle ground was to be occupied by our society between the poles of anarchy and despotism was resolved by the presumption that matters are best left to individual choice and mutual consent unless the contrary is proved beyond reasonable doubt. The burden of proof was upon him who maintained that a task entrusted to the market could be better performed by transferring it to the government.

The state had much to do, but classical liberalism implied a certain ordering of tasks to guide the emphasis of governmental activity. First, the state had to provide the necessary political and legal framework for the market by maintaining order, defining property, preventing fraud, enforcing contracts, and assigning responsibility. Second, it should disperse power by diminishing inequality of income and opportunity and by inhibiting monopolization. Third, it was to perform desirable functions too costly for individuals or voluntary associations, such as establishment of a sound monetary system, maintenance of public health, and promotion of safety. Fourth, it should help the poor and unfortunate and act as guardian for the incompetent, protecting those who could not cope with the normal responsibilities of life. Fifth, it should stabilize general economic conditions. Sixth and finally, it should provide welfare services to the public in the form of social security, unemployment assistance, and various other desired collective goods.

2

Economic Aspects
of Freedom

The history of mankind is in the main a dreary story of hunger, disease, despotism, and warfare—a constant struggle of man against the elements and against himself. The blessings of democratic rule, liberty, tranquillity, and material comfort have been enjoyed by only a tiny fraction of mankind over a tinier fraction of time and space.

Today on this continent one may move from a country where the life expectancy is seventy years to another where it is close to forty, and in the age of medical miracles this is one of the lesser signs of poverty. The contrast is, of course, greater in relation to more remote parts of the world, where the masses are normally one small step away from starvation.

Yet, poor or rich, men have never seemed to lack ambition to conquer, dominate, and oppress their fellow men. Any excuse will do, whether salvation, acculturation, or liberation. No lust is more obsessive or compulsive than that for power, and even the most humble of men may succumb to its seduction when he finds power thrust upon himself.

This essay, which served as the basis for a discussion at a conference, is reprinted, with minor omissions, from *Liberty under Law, Anarchy, Totalitarianism —This Is the Choice,* American Bar Association Standing Committee on Education about Communism and Its Contrast with Liberty under Law, 1969, pp. 45– 59.

Where progress has emerged from man's struggle through history, it has done so by virtue of a unique combination of circumstances that have, at once, dispersed power and channeled competitive drives into productive activity. That unique combination of circumstances has come to be known as capitalism, though this single word is hardly an adequate description of the complex nature of Western civilization.

Our civilization can hardly be considered the product of inexorable workings of history. There is no grand design in history, no predetermined course. Nor is history a mere jumble of accidents, a succession of "just one damned thing after another." Chance and choice are both its ingredients, together with no small amount of sheer momentum. History is made up of opportunities and constraints, and neither flow mechanically from the nature of man, conscious actions, ideology, custom, institutions, or any other easily identifiable source. History is instead the product of all these interacting forces mutually influencing each other.

It would seem to be no historical accident that democracy, individual freedom, and capitalism have gone hand in hand. In saying this, one need not launch an unmitigated panegyric on capitalism with a capital *C*. No system is absolutely good under any and all circumstances or in any and all respects, just as no system is immutably fixed in any mind, scripture, or set of institutions. Many features of the capitalistic system, in both philosophical and institutional forms, are bound to be repugnant to those with sensitive and humane instincts. I, for one, would surely support some other order if I could only have power at the same time to remake the world and the peoples inhabiting it. I have at least as many complaints against capitalism as I do against the weather.

But we must choose between feasible alternatives in this world and not between utopias. The capitalistic order, as it has evolved, is the least bad one I know, and it is the order most susceptible and amenable to reform and improvement.

The paramount virtue of capitalism is that it fosters progress through diversity and freedom without sacrificing efficiency, justice, and charity. One can be even stronger: it is also more efficient, more just, more charitable, and more egalitarian than any other viable system. Provided only that there is effective dispersal of power, the capitalistic order is driven by competition in manifold ways, in the field of ideas as well as commodities. The competitive marketplace, in its broadest sense, is the most potent guardian we have against authoritarianism and all that it implies. In a truly competitive society, there cannot be a single gospel, a single scripture, or a single priesthood to interpret them.

Power is embodied in property rights, and it is dispersed through the institution of private property, properly defined and circumscribed. In its most absolute sense, a property right conveys to the individual possessing it a license to use some thing, concept, or idea in any way he pleases within the context of social activity. But property rights are never absolute, for one right can scarcely be absolute without infringing on another. It is ultimately the body politic that must define, circumscribe, and enforce property rights through whatever legislative and coercive powers are at its disposal.

It is an important tenet of Marxism that, under capitalism, property must become progressively more concentrated, business progressively more monopolistic, and the working class progressively more miserable. One can flatly state that none of these predictions has come true in any major capitalistic country. As our own national income has risen above the imagination of an earlier age, it has become more, not less, evenly distributed. The worker's standard of living has risen more than apace. And there has been no evidence of a decline in competition. On the contrary, the evidence points strongly toward an increase. On this matter, I speak with conviction, since I have studied the evidence carefully.

Yet we must give Marx his due. Surely there is nothing in capitalism in and of itself that guarantees a dispersed and just distribution of property or a generally competitive environment, and those who try to argue otherwise harm their cause. This historical record is, in part, the result of conscious political policies designed to alter the economic environment. These policies are quite consistent in the main with a predominantly capitalistic system. One may note here such things as antitrust legislation, subsidized education, income and inheritance taxation, and so on and on.

Other forces have also been important. Of course, luck plays a major role in how well a person is endowed with those qualities valued by his society: brains, cunning, beauty, at times ugliness, material wealth— in sum, anything rare relative to the demand for it. Effort also plays a role. And from one generation to another, the distribution of luck and effort varies, so that some fortunes may vanish and others accumulate. Simultaneously, the competitive process generates perpetual innovation, destroying old property values and creating new ones. Within the ecological equilibrium of the economy as it moves over time, many things are being born, many maturing, many decaying, and many dying. Everything considered, the record of American society in the dispersal of power has been outstanding in the history of the world. But, as is so often the case, it has apparently not been satisfactory to a growing body of the citizenry.

The traditional American way of life rests on the twin foundations of freedom of choice and equality of opportunity, never fully achieved but always striven for in greater perfection. We have believed that every individual, given his natural endowments and the objective social conditions surrounding him, should decide for himself how to make his way through life. As long as he is mature and normally competent to make decisions, he has been considered the best judge of his own welfare, free to do as he pleases provided that he does not injure others or ignore his familial responsibilities. In brief, each individual is supposed to have the right to make his own choices, and by the same token he must stand ready to accept responsibility for their results. If there are to be mistakes, let each person make them for himself.

Choice cannot, of course, extend beyond the range of open opportunities. There is no such thing as ideal weather, but only the best available. And so a person cannot control where he is born, but, subject to his material means, he may move to any other place in the United States or to any other country that will accept him. As a child, he must depend on the wisdom of his parents for many vital decisions shaping his life, while government stands by to protect him against parental abuse.

He is free to choose his own trade and job and to shift from one to another as he wishes. If he is willing to bear the consequences and imposes no harm on others dependent on him, he may devote his life to loafing in one degree or another. Only the society that tolerates the hobo is truly free.

As a worker, he may belong to a union, as about one out of every five does. To enter some occupations or to work for some firms, he has no option under existing legislation but to join a union, although some nineteen states now have laws protecting the right not to join. Through unions and similar organizations, workers are permitted to bargain collectively with their employers on wages and other conditions of work, to set up grievance procedures to protect themselves against arbitrary and capricious behavior by their bosses, and ultimately to strike. These rights of organized labor are all subject to restriction in order to limit damage to other affected parties and the general public, and we are constantly trying to achieve the proper balance between the rights of individuals and those of voluntary associations, here as elsewhere. Meanwhile, our labor unions have been relieved from most normal legal restraints against concentration of economic power while being granted many special immunities and privileges.

Just as an individual may decide how to divide his time between leisure and work, so also may he choose how to dispose of most fruits of his labor. After paying his taxes, by no means an insignificant sum these days, he may divide his income and accumulated wealth as he sees fit among consumption, saving, and investment. As he spends his dollars, he casts his votes in the marketplace, where they wield their proportionate influence over the kinds of activities undertaken by the economy. In response to these relative demands, resources are allocated among literally millions of uses through the basic mechanism of competitive enterprise operating within a regime of private property.

Within the gigantic market organized by free enterprise, which still dominates our economy, the consumer is sovereign. The intense forces of competition that continue to rule over at least four-fifths of market activity ensure that the consumer is confronted, when he makes decisions on how to spend his income, with prices that reflect costs of production. Hence, when he spends five dollars on a shirt, he can be reasonably certain that he could not get better value for that amount by spending the same sum on something else. By and large, each price represents the value of the other things he must give up in order to purchase the item in question. Once he has adjusted his purchases so that each thing is worth to him what he must pay to get it, he can be reasonably sure that there is no way by which he can be provided with more material comforts out of the resources available to him.

In the face of the growing role played by government in our society, it would be foolish to suggest that each individual is as free to shape his own life as this picture may suggest. Almost two-fifths of the total net product of our country now passes through the hands of government at all levels, as compared with less than a sixth a generation ago. There are many reasons why this development has taken place, and we cannot survey all of them here or pass judgment on the accompanying effects. But we may note a few areas in which freedom of choice has been curtailed.

For one thing, laws prescribe the lowest wage for which one may work, a minimum that currently exceeds the average wage in such countries as England. Those who seek jobs but are not sufficiently productive to command that wage are effectively banned from gainful employment. Maximum hours of work at regular rates of pay are also set by law. Many farmers are, for all practical purposes, told what they may produce and how much.

Almost all Americans are required to purchase old-age insurance, and they must do so through the social security program of the federal government; they are not allowed to substitute equivalent private insurance even though it may be cheaper. American business and financial institutions are, by virtue of a simple executive order issued by the president, forbidden to enter into certain types of financial transactions in foreign countries, and there have been proposals to impose similar restrictions on the travel of Americans abroad. No individual or private concern is allowed to run a postal service or to engage in a host of other activities reserved for legally protected monopolies, governmental and private. The list could easily be extended, but these few examples are sufficient here.

One important impetus to growth in government has been the desire to improve opportunities for all Americans, though there is considerable disagreement over whether this goal has been best served by the specific programs that have been enacted. Together with freedom and justice, equality of opportunity is one of the basic pillars of the democratic creed. Yet it is not easy to give a precise definition of what it means.

In one sense, it means that people with equal endowments should all have the chance to make the same use of them in the pursuit of happiness. There should be no privilege accorded to one person or burden placed on another because of such irrelevant considerations as ethnic customs, religious beliefs, color of eyes or skin, and so on. In other words, a person should not be discriminated against for trivial and inconsequent reasons.

In a quite different sense, to make opportunities more equal means to redistribute resources from the more fortunate to the less. Some inequities of endowment can be overcome by effort, but others cannot. Some may be countervailed by education, and some by redistribution of income and wealth. But a world of absolute equals is, of course, a will-o'-the-wisp.

We have surely not been as vigorous as we should have been in combating unfair discrimination in American society. Everyone who believes in a civilized and humane society must condemn the coercive segregation of Negroes enforced by law over so many years in various parts of the United States. Fortunately, these barriers are being rapidly removed. We should continue to deplore unfair discrimination in private affairs and attempt to reduce it through persuasion, while recognizing that it will weaken only with the passage of time.

We must also recognize the importance of the market as an escape route from discrimination. This point is vividly illustrated by Milton Friedman, the eminent economist, in his book *Capitalism and Freedom*.

> It is a striking historical fact that the development of capitalism has been accompanied by a major reduction in the extent to which particular religious, racial, or social groups have operated under special handicaps in respect of their economic activities; have, as the saying goes, been discriminated against. The substitution of contract arrangements for status arrangements was the first step toward the freeing of the serfs in the Middle Ages. The preservation of Jews through the Middle Ages was possible because of the existence of a market sector in which they could operate and maintain themselves despite official persecution. Puritans and Quakers were able to migrate to the New World because they could accumulate the funds to do so in the market despite disabilities imposed on them in other aspects of their life. The Southern states after the Civil War took many measures to impose legal restrictions on Negroes. One measure which was never taken on any scale was the establishment of barriers to the ownership of either real or personal property. The failure to impose such barriers clearly did not reflect any special concern to avoid restrictions on Negroes. It reflected, rather, a basic belief in private property which was so strong that it overrode the desire to discriminate against Negroes. The maintenance of the general rules of private property and of capitalism have been a major source of opportunity for Negroes and have permitted them to make greater progress than they otherwise could have made. To take a more general example, the preserves of discrimination in any society are the areas that are most monopolistic in character, whereas discrimination against groups of particular color or religion is least in those areas where there is the greatest freedom of competition.[1]

In other words, the marketplace is colorblind. When the family head shops for a new television set, he asks about its quality and price, but not about what color the hands were that assembled it. When a person applies for a loan at the bank, he wants to know the interest rate, but not the religion or ethnic background of the lender.

This is not to say that unfair discrimination is absent in the choice of customers or employees—on the part of fellow shoppers and workers

---

[1] Milton Friedman, *Capitalism and Freedom* (Chicago: University of Chicago Press, 1962), pp. 108–9.

as well as bosses. But competition means that there will be many alternative places to work and shop, and the search for profits will lead some entrepreneurs to employ and cater to those who suffer unfair discrimination elsewhere. Moreover, the opportunity is always open to go into business for oneself in an economy based on private property and free enterprise.

Our economy is most accurately characterized as a free enterprise system in which a vast multitude of firms undertake an enormous variety of business ventures. Those who bear the risks of these ventures are the entrepreneurs, and they are the ones who capture the profits or suffer the losses corresponding to success or failure.

In a complex market economy such as ours, enterprises play the central role of undertaking activities in response to consumer demands within an atmosphere of constantly altering tastes, technology, and resources. Decisions on what to pay for resources and how to use them must be made now on the basis of guesses about the availability of resources, the state of industrial arts, and the marketability of products at some future time. The affluence, progress, and diversity of our economy are living tributes to the efficiency of the free enterprise system in making these speculative judgments.

The prospect of rich rewards stimulates private initiative and encourages venturesome behavior. At the same time, the discipline of losses serves to restrain recklessness and to enforce efficiency. Creative drives are mobilized for the benefit of the individual consumer. Even the smallest potential markets do not escape the watchful eye of entrepreneurs in search of profits. The hallmark of our economy is creative diversity.

We should be clear about one thing. Free enterprise means the right of anybody to engage in a business, not the right of an existing firm to do anything it pleases. To promote freedom of entry, policies against monopolization and restraint of trade have long occupied an important place in the American tradition. It would be foolhardy to expect all traces of monopoly to be eliminated from a market economy, and studies indicate that perhaps a fifth of total production in this country occurs under varying degrees of monopolistic control. But despite assertions to the contrary, particularly on the part of Marxists, the evidence shows no discernible growth in the extent of monopoly since at least the turn of the century. Our economy is and has been predominantly competitive.

While the intense competitive spirit driving our economy may bring with it conduct that seems undesirable in some respects, it provides at the same time a mighty engine of progress and innovation consonant with individual liberty. As the great English economist Alfred Marshall once observed, our system has the virtue of harnessing the strongest, if not the highest, motives of mankind for benefit rather than harm. It has surely been better to channel the competitive spirit into productive activity within a regime of free enterprise and dispersed power than to let it assert itself in a political struggle for dominance over fellow men, such as we observe in totalitarian societies.

Our system makes it possible for the ordinary man to serve the welfare of others by pursuing his own interests. By responding to the incentive to improve his own lot, he will be drawn generally to seek out those employments of his labor and property that are worth most to others. The system will not work unless some disparities in income and wealth are tolerated, but this does not mean that any degree of inequality in material well-being is justifiable. On the contrary, we have deliberately chosen to make the shares in our economic pie more equal even though that has made the pie smaller than it otherwise would have been.

We have probably gone too far in some respects. For example, the steeply graduated rates of taxation on higher levels of personal income sharply reduce incentives without yielding much revenue or providing a significant redistribution of income. The heavy and progressive taxes on corporate income are even more in point, for they inhibit venturesome and productive activity while bringing about quite mixed effects on income distribution. We must remember that there are more stockholders in our country, drawn from a wide range of income classes, than there are members of labor unions.

In this rather discursive essay, I have wandered back and forth between the discussion of general principles and illustrations of how they have and have not become embodied within the institutions of our own society. It may be well to conclude with some reflections on the economic aspects of freedom and how they derive from classical liberalism.

We should perhaps note, first of all, that economics as a scientific discipline arose from the emergence of an economy distinct from the political order. As markets based on private property and enterprise came to play an important role in the organization of various Western societies, a new form of social organization was created in which voluntary exchange and association displaced command and custom as a means of ordering a significant domain of social activity. The economy became by definition an area of human conduct coordinated through voluntary agreement. Economic activity was in the main synonymous with liberty. Since the basic objective of classical liberalism was to introduce more freedom and less force in the affairs of men, there was a natural desire to expand the scope of the market and diminish that of the body politic.

Consequently, the traditional liberal presumed that matters are best left to individual choice and mutual consent unless the contrary is proved beyond reasonable doubt. The burden of proof was upon him who maintained that government could accomplish a task better than the market. This presumption was, of course, closely related to the philosophical proposition that truth is to be gradually revealed through discussion and consensus, not through authority.

If there has been any discernible trend in public attitudes in the West, it has been toward a complete inversion of the basic presumption of state versus market action. The modern-day liberal—the advocate of the so-called welfare state—places the burden of proof on whoever would argue that the market can outperform government in a particular task. As this philosophy increasingly prevails, we shall have less and less reason to speak of the economic aspects of freedom.

3

For a Free Economy:
The Need of Our Time

We live in an age of inversions. A liberal used to be somebody who believed in individualism, in a society of free men organized as far as possible through mutual consent. Now a liberal is somebody who believes in the opposite, in paternalism, in a society organized primarily through coercion where the individual is looked after by his state. Those who used to be called liberals with respect are now called reactionaries with disdain.

Democracy used to mean a social order based on mutual respect for the individual. It now means little more than decisions by majority vote—or simply choice of a leader by majority vote.

We are being asked to place the state above ourselves in importance, growth above consumption, science above humane studies. We are asked to do all these things in the name of liberalism: this is the new liberal order. Only the word remains. All else has been turned upside down.

There are deep roots to this curious inversion of ideas, not unknown at other times over the course of man's history. They go back a long way, but they were undoubtedly strengthened most during the Great Depression.

This piece is one of a set of speeches on capitalism dated November 1963, probably given at the Freedom School in Aspen, Colo.

That was a period not many of you in this room will distinctly recall. We students of that era were told by our professors: "Look around you in this classroom at your neighbors beside and in front of you. When you leave here, one of you four will be out of work." The question arose whether there was not a fatal flaw somewhere in an economic system based on private enterprise. An answer was provided and avidly proclaimed: as a country grows wealthy, people deciding to save are not matched by people deciding to invest unless some resources are left idle—unless there is permanent unemployment. The unemployed can be put to work only if the state permanently makes good the deficient investment. In brief, private enterprise must be supplemented by political direction of resources if permanent unemployment is to be avoided. We now know this analysis to be fallacious, but few saw the fallacy then. They didn't want to see it. Unemployment was real. There was starving and suffering amidst great wealth. Injustice abounded. Something serious was wrong, and it was perhaps natural to expect to find that something in the foundations of our system.

It was natural to be a radical, as I was a large part of this period—to call for a remaking of society. Freedom, it was said, is after all empty without power. So why not give up some freedom to achieve some power? This is easy in any case: just take from the rich and give to the poor. The rich don't deserve what they have anyhow. They are rich and others poor solely because of the blind, haphazard forces of the market. Let us supplant the whims of the market with the careful planning of our most brilliant leaders. Then we'll straighten out the mess.

So the argument ran. It naturally had great appeal to those who fancied themselves part of that brilliant leadership. For few are more confident of their superiority than professional intellectuals. It has been a rare event in history when persons favored by intellectual endowments have recognized the limits of either their intelligence or their capabilities to manage other people's affairs. One such event was the founding of our country. The normal condition is for professional intellectuals to consider it their obligation to order the lives of those presumed less fortunate.

Hence there is little wonder that intellectuals in this country have come to worship government as the means to solve all problems, real and imagined. To them government means nothing more than themselves. They ask only to be given the power and they promise to set things right. The prescription for all ills is simple: have the right people do the right thing at the right time in the right measure. In other words, put your trust in the natural elite of intelligence and all will be fine. Error is synonymous with decisions by ordinary men.

Yet all this is offered in the name of democracy, liberalism, equality, and welfare. Democracy means voting for the proper leaders. Liberalism means liberality with confiscated resources. Equality means equal subservience by the governed. Welfare means what the leaders say is good for you.

We are living to see this philosophy ascend among those with political power. In fact, we are being ruled by an intellectual elite. The Greeks had a word for this, the ultimate sin—hubris, the sin of pride.

This is not to say that these people have bad intentions, but there is a big difference between meaning well and doing well, which I would like to illustrate with a favorite story.

There were a couple of friends who wanted to go for a trip one day and they had only a motorcycle at their disposal and it was a very bad day. It was cold and rainy and they didn't know how to protect themselves. They finally decided that the best thing to do was to take their overcoats and put them on backward and button them down the back so that at least they'd be protected from the wind. So, they set off, the two of them on the motorcycle. They had gone along a short distance when the driver thought there was something wrong. He looked around and his partner was gone. He turned around in a hurry and went back down the road looking for his partner and saw off to the side of the road a group of people huddling over a form. He saw immediately that it was his friend. Pulling off to the side of the road, he stopped and jumped off the motorcycle and rushed over to the group. As he was approaching them, he said, "Gee! I hope he's all right." One of the men looked up very slowly from the group and said, "Well, I guess he was until we turned his head back the right way around."

Well, we are getting our heads set the right way around. But what has emerged has little relation to its origins. We are seldom told today that our economic system cannot provide wealth, that we face stagnation and permanent unemployment on a large scale, that there are fatal flaws in our economic system, or that wealth is on the whole badly distributed. We are told, instead, that we are not growing fast enough; that we face a challenge from Communist countries not being met; that collective needs are being neglected for private greed; that we ask something of our country instead of offering to do something for it. In each case we are told the solution lies in giving government more power to handle the situation. Economists have a saying that questions never change, only the answers. The modern liberal might well say: answers never change, only the questions. Their answer is always the same: turn the problem over to a special group who can force others to behave right. We are told, in effect, to adopt an organic view of society, not an individualistic one.

The changed ground of the modern liberal should not surprise us. The one power a facile mind holds over others is its unlimited ability to rationalize. Having decided in advance what to do—generally on emotional or ideological grounds—the intellectual can always prove, to himself as well as to others, that it is the right thing to do.

But the universal prescription now being placed before us is wrong both morally and pragmatically. It is morally wrong to concentrate power in the hands of a few, and it is disastrous as well. The foundation of our humane civilization is the belief that society is a collection of individuals, that the state is the servant not the master of the citizen. Nothing is more symptomatic of the sickness of our society than that we should have to remind ourselves of this. Men should be free to decide for themselves what is good for them and how to achieve it. This means they should be free to make their own mistakes as well—and be obliged to bear the consequences.

The trouble is that, if we are to be honest, we must immediately add that none of these principles is absolute. What about the child? Somebody has to serve as parent. The child is incompetent to make his own decisions. And there are other incompetents as well. Where do we draw lines? Or, more importantly, *who* draws the lines? Every society must define who are to be its citizens—which is to say, the citizens must define themselves. Stated so boldly, this is a paradox without a solution. But it does get solved, and the important matter is the procedure by which it gets solved. At base, there is no difference between what a society does and how it does it. The means are what count, not the ends, if indeed ends have any meaning independent of means. But more of this later. For the moment let us merely recognize that there is a wide gulf between the traditional and the modern liberal views of society, even if that gulf cannot be summed up in the simple difference between anarchy and collectivism. The difference lies rather in presumptions. The traditional liberal presumes that matters are best left to individual choice and mutual consent unless the contrary is proved beyond reasonable doubt. The modern liberal presumes the opposite: affairs should be run by government unless the contrary is proved. The division of opinion is not between so-called conservatives and so-called liberals, but between meddlers and nonmeddlers. It is clear that the more the meddling view becomes entrenched in the minds of the citizenry, the more difficult it will be to reestablish a truly liberal climate.

One great problem is that people are responding to an atmosphere of crisis. They are being told that our survival is at stake. Doubts are constantly being put in their minds about the ability of a free society, as we have known it, to guarantee its own survival. The tasks before us are said to demand greater efficiency than a free economy can provide. In brief, faith in our traditional system is being undermined.

What are the facts about the courses of action we are being asked to take? First of all, economic growth. What do we have to be ashamed of on this score? The greatest economic progress in man's history has taken place in the free market economy. In the space of scarcely two centuries, a mere dot in the scale of history, the common man has been raised from the level of a starving, grubbing, disease-ridden animal to that of a dignified, civilized, prosperous human being.

Let us look at the record over periods in which we can measure growth. From 1875 to 1920, American industrial production multiplied *nine* times, transportation output *fourteen* times, and agricultural output *two* times. Now, our industrial production in 1875 was about as large as that in Russia around 1913. What has happened there in the succeeding forty-five years? Industrial output multiplied no more than *seven and a half* times, freight traffic *thirteen* times, and agricultural output less than *two* times. In each of these three fields, our performance excelled Soviet performance.

Now, this growth of ours took place under conditions in which no government was trying to do anything about it. Certainly no efforts were made to achieve any particular growth rate. In fact, statistics were such that nobody knew how fast we were growing. What happened came out of millions of individual decisions intermeshing in a market economy. These were individual decisions to save and invest and innovate motivated by desires for individual improvement.

It is well to remember this when we ponder on what to do now. Our pace of growth has faltered within the last decade. Perhaps this is the result of government and privileged groups doing too much rather than too little. It does not hurt to go back and read Adam Smith once again. Remember that he was arguing against the mercantile system, against the endless regulations and restrictions impeding operation of the market. Remove the encumbrances, he said, and you will achieve wealth beyond imagination. Attend to consumer interest and you will seldom go wrong; attend to producer interests and the economy is put in a straitjacket.

There are enormous energies waiting to be released in our private economy. Simple but fundamental tax reforms would without doubt unleash powerful forces of growth. Of course, there would be other costs. We would have to accept greater disparity of income among individuals. But that is the lesson of economics: you cannot have your cake and eat it too. Earlier socialists were willing to sacrifice growth for egalitarian aims, recognizing that the two conflicted. Present-day socialists—outside the Communist world—want both. They can't have both. Russia learned this long ago and gave up all pretense of egalitarianism. In fact, typically, they labeled this goal as "bourgeois equalitarianism" to indicate it was odious.

There are other brakes on growth. With the foreign aid planned for this year, we shall have spent $90 billion of tax revenues abroad in this gigantic program since 1945. Ponder on the magnitude of this sum. It exceeds private gross investment in this country last year, which was only $70 billion. Again, the point is that we cannot do everything simultaneously.

What is the aim of economic growth? Certainly not growth for its own sake. This has no meaning. If the object is greater welfare, free choice is implied on the part of each individual as to how much he will consume now and how much he will save. If the object is to meet our needs in national security, the problem is more complex but not really different. We cannot pay heed to cries that government is the proper guardian of future generations. Who is government? Why should individuals make better decisions through elected representatives, ultimately reflecting—imperfectly, at that—only majority vote, rather than through the marketplace where each has a voice? Most persons who want government to plan for future generations really mean: I can do better for your children than you can or will.

Let us look at the second popular argument for more government direction of the economy: collective needs are being neglected. Little needs to be said about this other than to cite the facts. In every decade since 1900 there has been a rise in the share of employment in the economy accounted for by government and government enterprises. In 1900 that share was 4 percent. Now it is about 15 percent. Since 1929, government purchases of goods and services have risen from 8 percent of national income to 20 percent. Reflect on that. At present one-fifth of the resources in our economy are put to uses determined by the state. With our progressive income taxes, we have an automatic revenue machine, constantly raising the fraction of income going to government. Are collective needs being neglected? How much of our production should be decided by government? Proponents of greater government participation have the same answer Gompers gave when asked what his labor union wanted: More.

And, finally, is the American public shirking its duty to the country? Last year the gross product of private enterprise amounted to $470 billion. Taxes paid to government amounted to $144 billion. Thirty percent of private production is turned over to government use. We now have almost three million men under arms, more than at any time in our history except major wars. What additional sacrifices are required?

The task of policy is to improve on what we have, little by little. We must always start from where we are with what we have. We improve by nibbling away at the undesired. There is little point in constructing ideal states of society that bear little resemblance to the institutions and people here and now. If there is to be improvement, it must be brought about by people as they now exist, through institutions now at their disposal. There will, of course, be times when progress is impossible without revolution, but fortunately this is not now so in our country.

Fortunately we need little more than a change in emphasis. We need only recognize once again that power corrupts as well as corrects; that government can do wrong as well as right; that the individual is competent as well as incompetent. The great need in this country is for a sensible middle to displace radicals of the left and the right. It must call for intelligence and reason in the conduct of affairs, for subjecting all proposals to the test of good sense. In our present environment, this calls for emphasizing the benefits of individualism and mutual consent, as opposed to collectivism and coercion. In the economic sphere, it calls for renewed faith in the market and greater skepticism of political direction. The burden of proof needs to be shifted to those who claim that government can do the job better.

The problem of our time is to preserve liberty in the face of the overwhelming growth of our social creatures. We are creating giants everywhere—economic blocs, large nations, and international blocs. The individual and his family are bound to lose stature in the face of these developments. The danger is that we shall be organized to death. The challenge is to adapt to changing circumstances—for we can scarcely do otherwise—without losing our freedom. The answer lies in old-fashioned faith in free, competitive markets, with sober acceptance of unavoidable compromise.

4

I Choose Capitalism

Let us compare the environment in societies that embody communism in its institutional form. Without exception, Communist societies have been monistic and authoritarian, while capitalist societies are typically, though not always, pluralistic and liberal. There is *one* truth and *one* truth alone in a Communist country, and its source is the Communist scriptures as interpreted by the leaders of the self-appointed elite. What is the fate of the dissenter or the member of a minority—of minorities themselves? Where are the forces of diverse experimentation and innovation? Where is freedom, equality, or justice?

There is the apocryphal story of the Soviet political commentator who, on being asked to describe the difference between capitalism and communism, replied: "As you know, capitalism is the exploitation of man by man. Well, communism is the precise opposite."

In the Soviet Union tyranny and conquest are justified in the name of the scientific laws of communism, just as they were in old Russia in the name of the divine right of the tsars. In many respects but with important qualifications, communism has become throughout the world little more than the modern rationalization for arbitrary power, and this is precisely why would-be dictators everywhere have been so

This piece is excerpted from a debate with Herbert Aptheker held in London, Ontario, in February 1967.

37

easily brought into the Communist camp. The major Communist powers constitute themselves the grand protectors of lesser dictatorial regimes in exchange for feudal allegiance in much the ancient way.

If I may digress for a moment, I would say that I view the Russian Communist Revolution, now approaching its fiftieth year, as one of the great reactionary events of history. As I read the history of tsarist Russia, it is the story of a slow and tortuous movement over the centuries away from oriental despotism toward a liberal order in the Western tradition. Reform of the system accelerated in the last half of the nineteenth century and first decades of the twentieth, reaching a climax with the constitutional revolution of February 1917. But the Bolshevik coup of October and its ultimate aftermath threw the country back to conditions of despotism, terror, and serfdom unsurpassed under the worst of the tsars—all in the name of "construction of socialism." The slow and tortuous movement toward liberalism continues to assert itself beneath all the turmoil, and we may perhaps expect the reaction to be overcome eventually. But I venture that this will not happen unless capitalistic institutions gradually infiltrate the society.

Let me briefly explore the plight of minority groups under communism. I speak here with some authority and experience, since I seem to have been in some minority or other as long as I can remember—religiously, ethnically, academically, politically, or what have you.

Minorities suffer in every society simply because they differ from the dominant group in some way considered significant and undesirable. They are, in the current phrase, discriminated against, and the roots of such discrimination lie in the concrete personal attitudes of members of the dominant group, not in some abstract mentality of some abstract collectivity. Discrimination may be practiced privately or collectively, and the latter is always more effective and harmful than the former. In any event, it is vain to expect private manifestations of prejudice to vanish until we enter a golden age of angels on earth. In the world of practical alternatives, the important question to raise in judging a society is whether there are means whereby minorities may escape the rigors of collective discrimination, coercively enforced.

How do minorities fare in a Communist country with its authoritarian rule? The answer is found in the treatment of such groups in the Soviet Union: the Jews, Jehovah's Witnesses, the gypsies, the Kazakhs, the Crimean Tatars, the Volga Germans—in brief, every nonconformist group. Where can these groups turn to escape persecution by the all-powerful state? Only to the weak and generally illicit marketplace.

Without exception, Communist countries have gone as far as possible in eliminating the market from their economies, substituting instead a system of administrative planning, control, and management. The price they have paid is gross inefficiency as well as loss of freedom.

Communist countries are now trying to find more and more ways of using the market in place of centralized administrative planning. Here I will let a prominent Soviet economist, Professor Abel Aganbegian, speak for himself.

> The seven-year plan has failed. Not only that, but with the end of the first ten-year part of our twenty-year plan none of the quotas have been attained. . . .
>
> There has not . . . been any rise in the standard of living during recent years. Ten million people have suffered a decrease in their living standards. . . .
>
> Our systems of planning, establishing incentives, and managing industry were developed in the 1930's. Ever since then nothing has changed except the names given things, but in fact everything remained based on the administrative methods of planning and management. The extreme centralization and the absence of economic democracy have a very serious effect on our economy. . . .
>
> As a matter of fact our prices and our monetary value relationships serve no purpose at all. The thing most important is centralized distribution. . . .
>
> The national plan is in no sense equilibrated, and it would be impossible to equilibrate it because that would require balancing 4000 different items against one another. Nor is the plan equilibrated in even its essential elements because, if it were, then one could not achieve some goals without achieving others. To attempt such an integrated program would cause a breakdown of the whole economy. And so it is not done. . . .[1]

Let me conclude on this note: the Communist world is in a state of flux, ideologically, economically, and politically. The Soviet empire seems to be disintegrating, the Communist economies are passing through a crisis of decision, and great upheavals are under way in countries like China. With typical irony, the Poles have developed the saying: "Under communism, only the future is certain; the past is always changing."

---

[1] *ASTE Bulletin,* summer 1965, pp. 1-4. Needless to say, this speech was not published in the Soviet Union. The purported text was first published in Italian in the July 1965 issue of *Bandiera Rossa,* a Trotskyite journal printed in Rome. There are persuasive reasons for believing the text to be genuine.

Given this state of flux, what one has to say today about the two great systems, capitalism and communism, may not hold tomorrow. And surely one must focus on far more than differences in material achievements.

The greatness of a society does not come from its monuments but from the kind of people it produces. Justice, responsibility, and humanity—these are the qualities of greatness in a people. Only the humane can remain free, and only the free can remain humane.

It is for this reason that I choose capitalism.

5

Economic Welfare and
Welfare Economics

Economics, a child of the Enlightenment, was born as moral philosophy or the science concerned with how to build the good society. In that age of optimism and enthusiasm, leaders of thought in the West looked forward to unimagined progress through reason and liberty. The Enlightenment marked a fundamental revolution in outlook, in which hope for the future and faith in freedom displaced endurance of the present and worship of authority. It was an exciting age of great expectations.

Adam Smith gave concrete form to the vision of his age in *The Wealth of Nations,* one of the most influential works in man's history and the foundation of economics or, more properly, political economy. Yet, as a necessary product of its time, Smith's treatise—as its title proclaimed—was concerned overwhelmingly with the problem of improving material well-being. A rising standard of life in its narrow sense was viewed as the first order of business if mankind was to progress, and this rising standard was to be brought about by greater efficiency in the use of resources and by accumulation of wealth.

This essay, which is based on a lecture given at Bethany College in November 1965 in a series on Some Unsettled Questions of Political Economy supported by the Relm Foundation, is reprinted from *Journal of Economic Issues* 2 (July 1968): 166–72, by special permission of the copyright holder, the Association for Evolutionary Economics.

Over the years, those who call themselves economists have studied a widening circle of problems, but in the main they have kept material welfare as the central issue of their discipline. Although there have been notable exceptions, these have not pointed the direction of study for the profession as a whole.

One is perhaps justified in characterizing economics today as the study of how to create the comfortable life, not how to build the good society. By and large, the word "progress" has disappeared from the economist's vocabulary to be replaced by "growth," which means "more of the same." Curiously, many economists seem to believe that, by thus restricting their range of interests, they have become more scientific, that they avoid value judgments by being concerned with the comfortable life rather than the good society. There is even recurrent talk of establishing a purely objective, value-free theory of economic welfare, which would tell us how to make society better off while maintaining ethical neutrality.

It is sufficient to say that all such thinking is wrong. Economics cannot be purged of moral content if it is to be concerned with the question of welfare; and economists must be concerned with this question, at least implicitly and indirectly, if economics is to be anything more than an intellectual game. This is not to say that economists are obliged to advocate their own versions of the good life, or that they should confuse matters of fact and normative assertions, or that every aspect of economic study must be tied directly and explicitly to a specific issue of social welfare. Rather, it is to say that the subject as a whole takes on meaning only as it keeps in contact with real social problems, which by the nature of man and society have ethical content. Economics can escape moralizing, but it cannot escape morals.

To avoid misunderstanding, let me be clear: this is not an essay on what economists should or should not do. They should do whatever they want to do and can find a market for. I am leading up to a different point, namely, that the narrowed vision of economists is largely responsible for the poor state of welfare economics.

Let me be more specific. According to modern welfare economics, an economy is in an ideal state if no one can be made better off without making someone else worse off. This state is often referred to as the Pareto optimum. Conversely, the state of society is said to be improved if someone can be made better off without making anyone worse off, even though some may have to be compensated by others for this to be so.

The trouble with this approach is clear: the optimum state is never achievable. Society is not only never there; it can never get there. In the first place, the optimum state is constantly changing as wants, resources, and technology undergo change. In the second place, and more importantly, such a state cannot be defined independently of the path through which it is to be approached. Hence such theorizing is utopian and sterile. For example, suppose analysis of an economy leads one to conclude without a doubt that, by the "Paretian" welfare standard, to tax one industry and subsidize another would be desirable. Let this be done. An immediate consequence is that the structure of durable assets in the economy is altered, thereby changing the structure of costs relevant for any practical purpose. The Pareto optimum corresponding to this revised state of affairs will be different from the one corresponding to the earlier state. In the course of trying to move toward the optimum, the economy moves the optimum itself.

In addition, of course, the optimum moves of its own accord, in response to any significant change in the "givens" of the economic system. It is literally impossible to keep up with these changes analytically. What makes sense as a policy today, viewed in terms of the Paretian standard, will make no sense tomorrow.

Why, then, do economists persist in this utopian analysis? Although some have obviously grown uneasy, they seek a curious way out. They have created a theory of the "second best" which seems to say that the "best" policy in the optimum state of affairs is not necessarily the best policy for moving toward the optimum. Hence some other, or second-best, policy should be followed.

But if the best is not the best, why call it the best? Or, more to the point, if the second best is really the best, why call it the second best? The answer seems to be that these economists, too, are victims of utopian theorizing. They are judging the "betterness" of a policy on the basis of how far it advances a society toward an unattainable, inconstant goal. If we were to think this way about nature, what would we deem to be the best weather and what the second-best?

Let me emphasize that I am not taking economists to task here for dealing with normative issues. Nor is the question that of whose norms are the right norms. Instead, I am challenging the vision of the problem, the mode of analysis, the outlook of economists.

To rephrase the question raised earlier, how did economists fall into this habit of thinking, and why do they find the habit so hard to shake off? One important reason is that economists have been preoccupied with the notions of efficiency, optimality, and growth, conceived in the context of an unchanging world. Too little attention has been given to change itself, in large part because there is no simple and easy way to analyze and assess the effects of change. But the economy changes at least as much as it grows, and an appraisal of performance that takes no account of this fact is bound to be misleading if not irrelevant.

Economic change in the main is the product of expanding knowledge, and neither change nor knowledge can be optimized. Future knowledge is unknown and unknowable now, and that is that. It is utter nonsense to speak of optimum knowledge or optimum change. Both come from a process of exploration, chance, and discovery. What sense does it make, then, to think of improvement in economic welfare as movement toward an optimum state of affairs?

More concretely, a society is surely made better off, in any ordinary sense of the term, as much by discovery and introduction of new products as by growth in the volume of old ones. The automobile, airplane, radio, television, computer, medicine, and countless other innovations are what make our standard of living today incomparably higher than it was a century ago. These innovations enter our lives continuously and unpredictably. They work out their effects pervasively and unpredictably in the economy. Theories of welfare economics that abstract from the very nature of modern economies are bound to give the wrong answers.

In short, we need a fresh approach. I do not pretend to know what it is, but I will try to suggest some of the ways in which our thinking needs to change.

Economists must, first of all, grasp the fact that where an economy goes depends on how it gets there. There are no practical alternative policies that will lead to the same state of affairs. Once any significant economic decision is made, it leaves its imprint on society, and conditions can never be restored to their original configuration. Any given imprint can be erased only by leaving other imprints. We must therefore give up any notions we may have of casting the economy as a whole into a preconceived structure.

We must think, instead, of changing a little bit here and a little bit there while taking the rest for granted and as beyond our immediate control. Similarly, we must be content to appraise the changes in terms of their primary effects and not their total impact on social welfare, which we can never know. Perfectionists may wish to argue that piecemeal improvements in welfare, however defined, are likely to lead to less total improvement than a policy that takes all interactions into account; but they must face the fact that the course they advocate is simply impossible. Society is condemned to a certain amount of drift, no matter how much conscious control is exercised over its activities. Too much control, in fact, merely magnifies the drift, because the task of directing social behavior grows disproportionately faster than the extent of control.

In any case, the problem of welfare economics is essentially the problem of choosing and implementing social policies. The first task is to decide who is to make the decisions. Put more broadly, it is to choose the economic system. I would argue that this is the foremost task, to which all others are quite subservient. Viewed in this context, the fundamental problem is not one of making the rules to guide social activities, but rather one of making rules for making rules. The Constitution comes first, and then specific laws and policies.

There is much to be said for encouraging economists to abandon altogether the field of welfare economics as it has developed and to substitute more sophisticated study of alternative economic systems. Let economists raise the question of what system works best, all relevant considerations being taken into account, and not what specific policies are desirable regardless of the system.

At least two difficulties must be expected with regard to this approach. First, utopian theorizing is even more tempting when an entire system is to be chosen than when only specific policies are at issue. Analysis may degenerate into search for the perfect system instead of choice among attainable alternatives. The second difficulty is closely related to the first. In choosing a system, the bad features must be accepted along with the good, and remedy must come through evolutionary change in the social structure if it is to come at all. But one is likely to be impatient and try to have his cake and eat it too. Before long, economists will begin to advocate monkeying with the operation of the system, no matter what it is, to try to give it characteristics which it cannot have; and we are back where we started, approaching the problem from the point of view of specific issues and specific solutions.

Once again, a fundamental change in outlook and attitude is required. If welfare economics is to be something more than bickering about day-to-day actions on the part of government in carrying out its role in the economy, it must focus on constitutional issues. It must be supplanted, in other words, by political economy in the classical sense: a science for building the good society. The first step, it seems to me, is to revive the notion of progress as the test of a good society. Leaving aside the ethical content to be given progress as a goal, we may illustrate how much difference it makes to broaden our vision of the economic process.

Consider the large volume of loose talk these days about the "optimum path of growth" for an economy. We are told that there is some best way of achieving a given expansion of productive capacity in the shortest time with a given rate of investment. Once that way is discovered, policies should be enacted to bring it about.

I find it difficult to take this line of reasoning seriously. How, in the first place, are we to determine the goal toward which society is supposed to move as quickly as possible? Is it to be a particular state of affairs, specified in advance? If so, why? Or is the objective simply to be to move as far as possible in a given period? If so, what does that mean? Furthermore, if we know in advance where we are trying to head, how are we to find the quickest way to get there? And even if we were sufficiently omniscient to mark out the path, what happens when we try to control growth to conform to it? Deliberate social control can be achieved only by creating political instruments for that purpose, and those instruments have other effects on society, inhibitory as well as stimulative to "growth." The institutional framework must change in the course of implementing policies formulated on the assumption that it would not change. The nature of the problem is altered in the process of solving it.

Most important of all, to predetermine "growth" is to forestall it in the most meaningful sense. As already noted, the economy changes at least as much as it grows, and the prospects of the future can never be foreseen. The best path of growth is the one that unfolds as the economy cuts its way through a jungle of ignorance, coming here and there and now and then onto places where the cutting is easier. These discoveries enable the economy to move more swiftly through the jungle if it is adventurous enough to explore for them in the first place and supple enough to exploit them when they are found. All the while, we remain in the jungle, seeing only a few feet ahead. We cannot know in advance the "optimum" way out or what lies on the other side. We grope our way forward.

Is this not what the philosophers of the Enlightenment meant by progress? Somehow, little by little, conditions were to get better because we would know more. We would approach closer to the truth even though it would continue to elude us. The problem was to construct the social order most conducive to progress. That order was to be judged not by its efficiency in achieving predetermined concrete objectives but rather by the kind of people it created.

Turning to a different but related matter, we may observe that progress is not the only thing we cannot predict. Every economy is subject to unforeseen disturbances and stresses requiring response and readjustment. Often the problem, at least temporarily, is to keep things from getting worse, not to make them better. Here, too, the design of the economic system is critical. Constitutionally, a system may be more or less flexible and responsive to unforeseen demands placed on it, and economists should give more attention to this matter and less to working out specific remedies for specific crises. On the whole, it would seem better to have a system that corrects disturbances slowly without allowing them to degenerate into crises than to have one that lets crises develop but deals with them swiftly. In any event, the system is at least as much at issue as the details of specific corrective policies.

So much for these discursive comments on the desirable nature of welfare economics. Now let me consider briefly whether there is much hope that economists will move in this direction. I am not optimistic. We live in an age of fragmentation and estrangement. Specialization, the fetish of scientism and ethical neutrality, and the contradictory utopian spirit have moved most economists out of contact with reality. Although many economists are quick to label the considered opinions of others among them as mere prejudice (when they disagree), they cannot recognize ethical bias in themselves. They have convinced themselves that ethical bias is not there—because it "ought not" to be there: scientists "ought not" to allow ethical judgments of any kind to enter their work in any way, but instead "ought" to be objective and scientific.

The situation has become so bizarre that output and growth in output are often viewed as if they were ends in themselves, without regard to the uses to which they are put. What other meaning can be attached to the recent fashion of judging economies solely on the basis of how much they produce or how fast they grow? It is, of course, ethically neutral to count broken crockery or empty pyramids produced in one economy as equivalent to food and housing consumed in another. But such ethical neutrality removes all meaning from the question of how the two economies compare. The simple fact is that all such questions have implicit ethical content. We are asking whether one state of affairs is better than another, and the judgment of better or worse has to be made with reference to some normative standard.

Unless economists quit hiding their heads in the sand of pseudo-scientism, economics will disintegrate altogether. Such practitioners as remain will be little more than social engineers or rationalizers, serving whoever will pay for their services. Perhaps that is just as well, but we should not delude ourselves that welfare economics will come to an end. It will merely pass into the hands of others with different training and qualifications, as we witnessed in the rise of the economic priesthood in the Soviet Union under Stalin.

Such a development would be unfortunate, for there is much to be gained by having persons who are thoroughly and expertly versed in economic analysis specialize in studying ways of achieving the good society. Of course, their views should not be treated as authoritative pronouncements from on high, but they should be welcomed into the arena of discussion as informed opinions deserving serious attention. In a market of ideas, competing ethical judgments have as important a place as competing interpretations of fact, provided care is taken to keep the two separated as much as possible.

I would conclude by urging the economics profession to wander back to the path laid out for it by the Enlightenment. Perhaps my condemnation of the profession has been too sweeping, consisting as it has of a blanket indictment of economists in general, without any accompanying bill of particulars. However, my aim has not been to indict or to condemn. It has been to stimulate economists to think about the state of their profession, which could stand improvement.

The essential step, it seems to me, is a bold confrontation of the real issues of social policy. Let economists seek more after policies which will make conditions better and less after policies which will make them best. Let economists think more about progress and less about growth. Let them look for ways of improving the economic system rather than for gimmicks and schemes that will "solve" narrow problems. In short, let them try to build a good society instead of trying to do good for society.

None of these tasks is easy. No simple standards are close at hand on which the necessary judgments can be made. They never have been and never will be. The problems will, however, always be with us, and they must be handled one way or another. We must simple apply reason and intelligence and do our best. At least we would be doing something important and fruitful.

6

A Comment on Okun

There seems to be an implicit pairing of speakers and discussants so that the same arguments will not be made twice. I will therefore merely acknowledge that I agree, by and large, with Irving Kristol's remarks, and turn to Arthur Okun's paper.[1]

As I understand it, Okun's basic argument runs as follows. There ought to be a more equal distribution of income in the United States because people like equality. We know they like equality because our political institutions over the years have come to provide for equal freedoms, equal rights, and equal obligations for all. Yet, he says, our society accepts far more inequality in the distribution of its economic assets than in the distribution of its sociopolitical assets. It accepts this inequality because equalizing incomes diminishes efficiency. But, Okun argues, the trade-off is almost certain to be small as long as the market is not destroyed in the process of redistributing income, and the market need not be destroyed. That the leakage from the redistributive bucket is low would be demonstrated if social scientists would spend more time measuring it. The American society, in deference to its

This piece, which was originally given as a comment at a conference in May 1976, is reprinted from Colin D. Campbell, ed., *Income Redistribution* (Washington, D. C.: American Enterprise Institute, 1977), pp. 43–46, where it appeared under the heading "Commentaries."

[1] Irving Kristol, "Thoughts on Equality and Egalitarianism," in ibid., pp. 35–42; and Arthur Okun, "Further Thoughts on Equality and Efficiency," in ibid., pp. 13–34.

preferences, would then strive for and achieve far greater equality in the distribution of incomes through government action, once it knew that the leakage was low.

Value judgments are obviously entangled with empirical propositions in the case Okun makes. I will not try to disentangle them because the whole line of reasoning is so much at odds with my own that I do not know where to begin discussing it or how to find a common universe of discourse. To Okun, the good society is one that maximizes equality of circumstance. To me, it is one that maximizes use of voluntary agreement in organizing social activity. Neither ideal accords, I suppose, with popular sentiment today, but mine surely is closer to the historical aspirations of the American people than is his. It is for this reason, I believe, that Okun so seriously misinterprets the rationale of so-called equal rights.

In our political and social arrangements, he says, society diligently pursues equality. Witness that the right to vote, speak, and worship is the same for all, as is the judicial process and every public service and obligation. Surely these institutions reveal a social preference for equality. And what difference is there between equal freedom of speech and equal health care?

In deducing equal treatment as the common essence of these diverse aspects of our political order, Okun misreads history and confuses fundamental issues. Let me note first the rather obvious fact that our social and political arrangements are replete with unequal treatment. We treat children differently from adults, ordinary citizens differently from convicted felons, public figures differently from private citizens, challengers for elective office differently from incumbents, robbers differently from those they rob, and so on. Why not, then, infer a social preference for inequality?

The point, of course, is that our social institutions embody a host of social values and principles of equity that cannot be reduced to a single norm of equality without depriving them of meaning. There is no doubt, for example, that the adoption of the Bill of Rights was motivated by a desire to minimize coercion in the affairs of man. Our Founders were certainly preoccupied with this issue, as anyone can reaffirm by taking another look at the discussions of that time. They did not concern equality but freedom, meaning freedom from government. Freedom was to be embodied in individual rights, through self-denying ordinances of government. Classical liberalism came to rest on what might be called the minimum principle: government should exercise the minimum of coercion required to minimize coercion.

Freedom of speech was not designed to give everybody equal time on a soapbox but to make sure that nobody who wanted to speak was prevented from doing so by being hit over the head, locked up, tortured, or shot. In its use of coercion, government was not to prevent speech while it was preventing others from preventing it. In contrast with this concern, Okun's treatment of the problem of coercion seems rather cavalier. What difference does it make, he asks, whether government coerces to provide for defense or to reshuffle wealth and income? Or for any other reason? Coercion is coercion is coercion. It is nothing more or less, he says, than the necessary political definition of property rights, which always involves taking from some and giving to others.

At this point I must confess that Okun loses me. He argues that, whenever government creates a property right—"out of thin air," as he puts it—everybody who does not receive that right is automatically coerced. In my opinion, this way of looking at the issue invites unbounded confusion. Okun gets off the track, I think, when he makes the very mistake he accuses his critics of making—the mistake of confusing liberty with private property. As far as I can see, he makes the same mistake in the passages of his lectures that he cites as describing the importance he attaches to liberty.

Needless to say, I do not have time here to straighten all this out. But I would say that, in a nutshell, freedom is one thing, power another, and equality something else again. The problem is to find an optimal mix of the three. Property is an aspect of power, and private property, widely dispersed, complements freedom, but the only private property implied by freedom itself is ownership of one's self. *Coercion* means use of physical force, explicitly or implicitly, by one person or agent for the purpose of altering what someone else wishes to do voluntarily with his property, including himself.

The paradox here concerns the way *property* is to be defined in the first place. Okun finds it difficult, as I do, to assign the origin of private property to natural law or natural rights. But that does not mean that one must move to the opposite extreme, as Okun does, and say that *property* should be subject to instant definition and redefinition by majoritarian will, in its crudest sense. This position is advantageous if one wants government to have unlimited power to redistribute property because it begs the question of liberty.

Our Founders recognized the paradox of property and resolved it by imposing severe constitutional limits on the power of government to tax and to take. For all practical purposes, time has swept away those restraints and, with the barest popular support, government may now take and give whatever, whenever, and wherever it wishes. The fact that I favor restoring restraints hardly means, as Okun's line of reasoning seems to imply, that I do not care what happens to the poor, or that I am opposed to any form of coercive redistribution of income. I favor redistribution but subject to strong restraints on the taking power of government. The great question of our time is this: what is to prevent a government already taking more than 40 percent of national income for one purpose or another from becoming a leviathan that ultimately devours freedom, probably in the name of greater equality of circumstance? Might it not be better to impose some limits on the taking power of government?

Okun does not find that question interesting, but he should, because any government of a large nation with the power to provide the greater equality he considers desirable would impose greater inequality instead. At least that is the lesson of recorded history as I read it. If the American people really want more equality, not much coercion is needed to achieve substantial redistribution of income. Much will occur voluntarily and charitably. Unfortunately, what Okun sees as a revealed preference for equality is something quite different. What most people want is more than they have, and, in a majoritarian democracy, majorities will often coalesce for the purpose of getting more by taking from others. The transfer need not be from the rich to the poor and, in fact, usually is not. As an empirical proposition, Aaron Director's law asserts that it is the middle class that benefits by taking from the poor as well as from the rich. Director's explanation is, I believe, closer to the truth than Okun's. Moreover, the more that government takes, the less likely that democracy will survive.

So much for the broader issues. Let me now conclude with a few brief remarks on some specific points.

The trade-off of equality and efficiency heralded by Okun becomes almost trivial once he has plugged most of the leaks in his bucket. Progressive taxes, he says, have no discernible effect on effort and very little on investment. The latter effect does not matter anyhow because government can make investment whatever it likes simply by twirling a few fine-tuning dials. No failures, no trade-offs, no anything. Whatever investment we want, government will conjure it up with dials (or perhaps with mirrors). I find this faith in fine-turning astounding in the face of stagflation and all that.

While endorsing Henry Simons's principle that redistribution of income should be superimposed on a free market, Okun offers a strange proposal for subsidizing borrowing by lower-income groups. It is not clear how one learns how much of the interest premium charged to low-income borrowers is due to inability to repay and how much to relatively unproductive use of loans. But why try? The remedy is to raise income, not to subsidize the interest rate.

In passing, Okun cannot resist praising recent legislation on campaign spending as a welcome curb to the "counterfeiting" of votes and hence a boost to a more "democratic" political process. Here is another example of miscomprehension of the complex issues underlying the First Amendment, with which this legislation is wholly inconsistent, to say the least. Let me merely observe that, as far as the democratic process is concerned, there is likely to be more to fear from a silver tongue than from a gold finger.

7

Business Role
and Responsibility
Today

I have no good answer to the question of what to do about the trend of affairs. The only advice I can give to businessmen is that they, acting singly or together, should keep cool, take the long view, and help to build and preserve the foundation of a free society. In these few minutes, I shall try to elaborate on what I have in mind with this advice.

Let me start by observing that the veneer of civilization is more fragile than we sometimes want to believe. You may know the story of the missionary who devoted his life to converting the heathen on a remote island in the South Seas. On his retirement, he was given a testimonial dinner at which he spoke about his experiences. When he had finished, questions were invited from the floor. A member of the audience raised his hand and posed this question: "Reverend, what can you tell us about cannibalism? I understand this wicked custom used to be practiced everywhere on your island. Did you manage to stamp it out?"

The missionary shook his head sadly and replied: "No, I'm sorry to say that I did not. When I arrived on the island the natives were eating each other, and when I left they were still eating each other. But," he said, his face lighting up, "now they use knives and forks."

These remarks were given at a meeting of the Business Council in May 1975 at the Homestead, W. Va.

There is some confusion of manners and morals in this story, but the point is well made that little things can make a big difference. Civilization is distinguished from barbarism by a host of beliefs, attitudes, and morals, no one of which need have great significance by itself.

At the university where I teach, there is an honor code enforced by the students on themselves. It prescribes that an honorable person does not lie, cheat, or steal and that any student who does is to be cast out of the community of students. The purpose of the code is, of course, to build character, not to purge the student body of undesirables. The broader implication is that society cannot be free, prosperous, and self-governing unless the honorable somehow outnumber the dishonorable.

This simple point can be easily illustrated in the world of business. Everybody expects to be cheated a little once in a while, but things have gone too far when one is shortchanged by a bank, as I once was in a foreign country I will not name. No market can work if everybody always has to count his change.

A good example is the mail-order business. A telegrapher named Sears had the better idea of selling pocket watches by mail. If you order from me, he advertised, I'll send you a watch. Take a look at it and decide whether it's worth a dollar. If so, send me back a dollar. If not, send me back the watch. It takes no imagination to see that success in this kind of enterprise depends on the elemental honesty of buyers.

Sears did succeed, and his success did not go unnoticed by merchants in imperial Russia, where such merchandising seemed ideal for a market scattered over a vast territory. A mail-order house was established there around the turn of the century. Orders rolled in and goods rolled out. The only hitch was that nothing came back, and thus ended the venture.

Put in a broader context, what I am talking about is the need for republican virtues, which Irving Kristol has described with typical facility in these words:

> Just a few weeks ago, one of our most prominent statesmen remarked to an informal group of political scientists that he had been reading *The Federalist* papers and he was astonished to see how candidly our Founding Fathers could talk about the frailties of human nature and the necessity for a political system to take such frailties into account. It was not possible, he went on to observe, for anyone active in American politics today to speak publicly in this way: he would be accused of an imperfect democratic faith in the common man. Well, the Founding Fathers for the most

part, and most of the time, subscribed to such an "imperfect" faith. They understood that republican self-government could not exist if humanity did not possess—at some moments, and to a fair degree—the traditional "republican virtues" of self-control, self-reliance, and a disinterested concern for the public good. They also understood that these virtues did not exist everywhere, at all times, and that there was no guarantee of their "natural" preponderance. James Madison put it this way: "As there is a degree of depravity in mankind which requires a certain degree of circumspection and distrust; so there are other qualities in human nature which justify a certain portion of esteem and confidence. Republican government presupposes the existence of these qualities in a higher degree than any other form."[1]

In other words, a free society requires a form of representative government capable of surviving in an atmosphere in which some people are corrupt all the time and all the people are corrupt some of the time. But no self-governing society can be preserved by any form of government if most of the people are corrupt most of the time.

There must be more than a curbing of passions. There must also be a cultivation of beliefs, principles, and precepts to guide civilized conduct. In Kristol's words, there must be "self-control, self-reliance, and a disinterested concern for the public good."

The weakness of republican virtues is most evident today in the ascendant attitude toward personal responsibility. Western thought is drifting rapidly in the direction of romanticism, the conception that every experience is unique—that everything in the world is different from everything else. This antiscientific outlook implies that everything depends on everything else, which is to say that nothing depends on anything, since looking at the world in this light leaves no way of assessing cause-and-effect relations between particular events. Hence there is no way to assign responsibility for a particular state of affairs.

Concretely, the individual ceases to be held accountable for his actions. If the outcome is bad, "society" or "the system" or "the establishment" is blamed, not the individual. If the outcome is good, one or the other gets the credit, not the individual. And so the criminal should not be punished, the poor student should not be failed, and the errant official should not be judged. It is in this vein that the outcry is raised for "no recriminations" over Vietnam. Nobody is to be held responsible.

[1] Irving Kristol, "The American Revolution as a Successful Revolution," in *America's Continuing Revolution* (Washington, D.C.: American Enterprise Institute, 1975), pp. 6–7.

The weaker the belief in personal responsibility, the stronger the attraction of collectivism as a political philosophy, for the essence of collectivism is a conception of society as an organic entity, not as a composite of individuals.

The question at issue is not whether Americans should believe in either individualism or collectivism. Neither is adequate to serve by itself as the philosophic foundation of a viable democratic republic. The underlying philosophy must be a mixture of both. But it is critically important which outlook dominates.

Well, what has all this to do with the role and responsibility of businessmen today? Essentially, my message is that the philosophic and moral underpinnings of the free society are being rapidly eroded away and that time is short to halt a deadly drift toward collectivism. But, unfortunately, the process whereby a civilizing ethic gets worn into society is that of water dripping on a stone. Equally unfortunately, that ethic can be lost much more quickly.

Historically, family and church have been the institutions most effective in instilling civilized moral sentiments. But as society has become secularized, the podium has replaced the pulpit. Intellectual brokers of ideas have become the primary molders of social thought. Therefore, if you businessmen, as concerned citizens, want to be effective in combating the deadly drift of our society toward collectivism, you must do so by amplifying the voices of those responsible members of the intellectual community who speak with professional authority and integrity and who believe in individualism. The task requires effort: you must seek out the proper voices and focus support on them.

In my lifetime, the believer in our traditional free society has found it increasingly difficult to thrive through intellectual pursuits, no matter how able he might be. The intellectual heights are commanded by critics of the market and advocates of big government. Their voices are strong in classrooms and public forums. Their institutes and centers are richly endowed with funds. Advocates of the market and limited government are the ones whose voices are weak and weakening. Their institutes and centers are frugally financed.

The one set of voices is drowning out the other. It is not a question of turning things around, because neither should drown out the other. What is lacking is that healthy competition of ideas needed if opinion is to be formed through reason. Unless subjected to intelligent challenge and modified accordingly, the beliefs now in ascendancy threaten destruction of our system of government.

The task before us is to avert the fate of another time, described so graphically in these words:

> And thus the frame of the democracy was dissolved; and gave place to the rule of violence and force. For when once the people are accustomed to be fed without any cost or labour, and to derive all the means of their subsistence from the wealth of other citizens; if at this time some bold and enterprising leader should arise, whose poverty has shut him out from all the honours of the state, then commences the government of the multitude: who run together in tumultuous assemblies, and are hurried into every kind of violence; assassinations, banishments, and divisions of lands; till, being reduced at last to a state of savage anarchy, they once more find a master and a monarch, and submit themselves to arbitrary sway.

Thus spoke Polybius, Greek historian of the second century B.C. The history he recounted could easily be repeated unless those concerned about present trends act to change them. The most effective course you businessmen can follow is, I believe, to apply your considerable weight where it will help most in restoring the moral sentiments requisite to a free society based on limited government and a market economy.

8

Union Power in a
Free Society

Dispersion of power is the natural complement of individual freedom. A free society has little content when power is heavily concentrated, nor can it long survive. Our free society has flourished because such a large area of social activity has been organized by competitive markets. Nothing disperses power as effectively as a competitive market, but it must be kept competitive. One of the hardest problems we face is to disperse power that arises from normal exercise of free choice in the marketplace.

The fact is that power can, and does, originate in voluntary association, in groups formed by individuals joining together in a common pursuit. When such a group exercises its power, it infringes on the liberty not only of others but also of its members. It can never be that every action of a group is approved by every member. Every individual who joins a group recognizes that he is necessarily sacrificing freedom of action in order to gain augmented power. We therefore continually face the question of how strictly freedom of association should be regulated by the political order and whether this regulation should take the form of limiting the objectives, practices, or constitutions of voluntary associations.

You members of the business community assembled here today hardly need to be reminded of the host of restraints imposed by law on

Although undated, these remarks were probably given at a meeting of the Machine and Allied Products Institute in 1963 or 1965.

your activities. I will not say that all are wisely imposed, for many are not. But some are essential if a free, competitive economy is to be maintained. You are forbidden to get together with your competitors to fix prices and output. You are forbidden to monopolize or attempt to monopolize a particular line of trade. You are forbidden to engage in certain practices that would be harmful to the reputation or property of your competitors. You are forbidden to discriminate in the terms you set for different customers, except where the discrimination is justified by differences in costs. You are forbidden to merge with other firms where the effect might be to lessen competition.

At the same time, you are required to protect the rights of those who invest in your companies, or extend credit to them, and to assume responsibility for the harmful effects of your activities on others. You must make public your financial condition. You must let all stockholders have a voice in the selection of governing bodies. Your corporate bodies and their officers must accept responsibility for civil and criminal wrongs of agents. And so on at great length.

Voluntary associations engaged in private enterprise are, in a word, forced to incorporate themselves into special legal entities. The powers, or property rights, of these entities are prescribed and circumscribed in detail, because our society has recognized the need to prevent undue concentrations of power. The body of law is more vigorously enforced at some times than at others, but its basic content is always with us and has been for decades.

A sane and reasonable observer must therefore wonder about his sanity and reason when he views the body of law governing behavior in the largest and most important market for economic services—the labor market. Here individual sellers are permitted and even encouraged to collude in fixing prices and output. They are permitted to monopolize trades, to defame competitors, to discriminate among customers, and to merge together.

Until very recently, they were not required to make their financial condition known to anybody, including members. They are still not required to give members a voice in selecting officers. They are not required to accept responsibility for the acts of agents that lead to collective action. In fact, in matters involving collective action, they are called before the bar as associations of individuals acting individually. They are, for all practical purposes, treated as private clubs.

In many respects they are clubs, and they perform many functions beneficial to members without harming the legitimate rights of others.

In this respect they are no different from the many other associations organized on occupational, industrial, fraternal, or similar lines.

Moreover, unions can perform a valuable service in protecting the lone worker from capricious and arbitrary treatment by his immediate supervisors. There is no reason why a foreman should be permitted to deprive a worker of his job because he does not like the color of the worker's hair or because their wives do not get along socially. To the extent that management becomes careless in allowing such practices—and this is not unknown—workers have every right to collective processing of grievances.

But under our laws a union is much more than a club. It is a business organization whose primary function is to market labor services. It is a cartel, an association of workers legally entitled to act in concert in selling their services. The power to collude has its basis in the right to strike, reinforced in cases of legalized and compulsory collective bargaining by the right of striking workers to retain their jobs during the strike. Armed with the right to strike and other extralegal powers, a union can, under appropriate circumstances, turn its power to collude into a power to exclude as well. It can become a monopoly as well as a cartel.

Let me make it clear, before there can be any misunderstanding, that I am not at this point advocating any policies, explicitly or implicitly. In particular, I am not passing judgment on the right to strike. I am merely trying to deal with the facts as they are, trying to analyze the bases of the economic power that some unions possess. The right to strike may be, and indeed has been, justified on grounds quite independent of the matters I am discussing. However that may be, certain consequences in terms of economic power and its exercise are derivative from the right to strike, and they cannot be wished away.

Nor am I trying to say that all unions are powerful monopolies. Many unions have little or no monopolistic power. To have this power, the union must first control the bulk of the supply of a particular kind of labor. It must, second, command the strict loyalty of a large enough group of workers to enforce it in the remainder, through one pressure or another, depending on what the public condones. Loyalty depends ultimately on the economic gains that can be gotten through collusive action, and the gains depend in turn on the kind of market being faced.

The power of a union is organic in nature. There is a very real sense in which success breeds success and strength begets strength. It takes time and skill and aid from the law and public mores to build massive structures of power such as we see in the teamsters' union. It takes time and skill and aid from the law and community mores to undo the doing.

Now the critical factor in union power is, in my opinion, the ability to discriminate among buyers of labor. Monopolistic control over any kind of labor service immediately implies the power to sell labor on different terms to different buyers. The buyer must purchase his labor services directly from the monopolistic source or he cannot get it at all, since the services of a worker cannot be separated from the worker himself. It is this legalized discriminatory power that enables a monopolistic union to enforce its demands through coercion.

To make this clear, let us consider the ordinary monopoly that produces a readily storable commodity. This monopolist has the power to set a price and produce an output that will bring him the most profit, but the price will be essentially uniform for the entire market, and each purchaser will be free to choose how much or how little of the product to consume. If the monopolist tried to charge each consumer a different price or to dictate the amount each consumer could purchase, his efforts would soon be defeated by a secondary market that would arise to promote desired exchanges. Those buying at a low price would offer to sell to those being charged a high price.

This cannot happen in a market for services. They must pass directly from producer to consumer; they cannot be easily purchased by intermediaries for sale to others. The monopolist selling a service can, if allowed by law to do so, set different terms for each buyer, and the buyer must accept the terms or get nothing at all.

We may, for instance, imagine the electric company striking a different bargain with each of us, depending on our demands for electricity, specifying how much electricity each of us can buy each day and how much each of us must pay for it. The company would, of course, politely inform us that nobody was being compelled to do anything he didn't want to do. If anybody didn't like the terms being offered, he needn't accept them. The company would be glad to cut off its service. If the law allowed electric utilities to do this, we can be reasonably sure that they would not be lax in collecting the toll each of us would be willing to pay rather than go without electricity altogether. This is so obvious that laws have long prohibited discriminatory pricing of this type. This is not to say that discriminatory pricing is unknown in the business world, for it isn't. But, as practiced, it is mild compared with this example.

On the other hand, that is exactly the way an efficient monopolistic union deals with its customers. It assesses how much each firm would be willing to pay rather than go without the particular labor services altogether, and it charges accordingly. This is done by figuring how much damage could be done to the firm by a strike. This damage, put in monetary terms, marks the maximum sum of money that the union can extract from the firm by being good enough not to strike. It can collect this sum in a variety of ways: by merely setting a wage rate and letting the firm hire however many workers it wishes; or by setting both the wage and the number to be employed, along with conditions of employment, work rules, and the like; or by collecting a lump-sum payment.

It is helpful to think of the powerful union as a state within the state. The powerful and efficient union acts as a government levying "taxes" on the firms subject to its power, enforcing the levies with the coercive power at its disposal. It then distributes the proceeds to its members, in such a way as to get the most loyalty to union policy. The "taxes" may be levied on wages, output, or profits. For example, Reuther's misnamed "profit-sharing" scheme is actually a form of profit tax without a loss offset. The distributed benefits of this and similar "taxes" may be in the form of wages, pensions, unemployment compensation, seniority rights, graft, and so on.

Strong unions develop their own enforcement agencies. Extralegal police forces are established to make sure that the loyalty of members does not weaken, to persuade firms that the wisest course is to be friendly with the unions, to prevent nonunion competitors for jobs from causing trouble, and so on. These police forces are generally staffed by the kinds of people most efficient in this type of work: hoodlums and racketeers. They practice their trade at the pleasure of the public at large, which has typically condoned violence on the part of labor unions that would not be condoned on the part of others. So far, the public has become outraged only at an incidental mark of all corrupt governments: wholesale graft by the officers of some powerful unions. It is puzzling that the public has apparently not yet realized an obvious fact: officers can flourish as racketeers only if their unions possess strong monopoly power.

I do not have time today to elaborate on the conditions most favorable for exercise of the discriminatory powers of a monopolistic union. Briefly put, the damages of a work stoppage will be greatest in firms producing services or custom products. In the case of storable products, damages can be anticipated and at least partly offset by accumulated inventories, as in the recent steel strike. But in the case of services, nothing of this sort can be done. Production halts, and that is that.

Moreover, the damage may immediately spread far beyond the area being struck. This is one important reason why we see such economic power in the hands of the teamsters, for instance.

The effect of a monopolistic union is to raise the production costs of the enterprises it sells to, and this leads to an allocation of resources away from the dictates of a competitive market. Monopoly of labor has the same effect as monopoly of enterprise. The value of the social product is made lower than it would be in the absence of monopoly. If this holds true generally for the one type of monopoly, it holds true for the other.

Too often we tend to think of the primary effect of monopolistic unions as raising wage rates. This is only partly the case. Monopolistic unions can raise production costs without doing anything to wage rates—by, for instance, dictating employment, conditions of work, so-called work rules, and so on. Hence we should not judge their effects solely in terms of success in raising wages.

This leads me to the final point I want to consider in this brief talk. We are becoming increasingly aware of the relation between monopolistic unions and inflation. It is clear that full employment can be maintained in the face of an increase in production costs in excess of productivity gains only with a rise in the general price level. Every time unions exercise newly gained monopolistic power in a significant sector of the economy, the stage is set for a rise in the general price level, or for a rise in unemployment. If the monopoly power of unions shows a continuing growth, the price level must continually rise if growing unemployment is to be avoided.

There are grounds for believing that the monopoly power of unions has grown over the last two decades. This is not to say that unions have been the sole or even primary cause for all the inflation we have experienced in the postwar period. Other important causes have been at work. But the influence of growing monopoly power in unions cannot be ignored.

There are signs that the power of unions may have reached a turning point, that laws will be gradually enacted imposing on unions at least some of the restraints now imposed on enterprise. If so, there will have to be a continuing change in public opinion. We need look no farther than the general public and its attitudes toward labor unions to find the reason for the power of unions. The public has condoned and even encouraged the development of union power. It remains to be seen how fast and how far opinion will change.

9

The Energy Question

The myth has been spread, with the aid of politicians and energy tsars, that there is something unique about the energy problem requiring abnormal sacrifice by the public and curbing of greed by the oil companies. The moral has been proclaimed: without centralized government planning of energy production, we will run out of energy.

This myth has no basis in fact. The energy "crisis" is a classic example of an economic problem: how to make the best use of scarce resources. There is nothing about the energy problem that cannot be resolved by the market economy if it is not hampered by the wrong kind of political controls.

The myth is based on five fallacies. Fallacy (1), we are running out of energy. This is obviously wrong in its literal sense, as the law of conservation of energy shows. What is actually meant is that there is a limited supply of the cheapest known and producible energy agents. It is not certain that supply from undiscovered oil fields will be less than from already discovered ones, but merely more likely, because explorers move from least costly to more costly to produce. Cheaper oil might be struck. There are constant improvements in technology that reduce costs of production of known products and introduce new products, such as nuclear energy.

This piece is taken from notes for a class lecture at the University of Virginia, Charlottesville, Va., spring 1978.

Fallacy (2), energy is an essential product—a necessity—different from other products. Demand for energy does have a low elasticity, but particular forms are no more essential to life than many other products. There is always human energy to fall back on.

Fallacy (3), we have a duty to conserve energy for future generations. This apparently means we should consume less than the equilibrium market quantity to save exhaustible resources for generations to come. But how much less? Why? Why should we pay more for energy and consume less so that some future generation can pay less and consume more? Future generations extend to eternity. Surely, there will be at least one along the way that will squander what we have "saved" for it, at cost to ourselves. The *only* way to make sure that the future is not deprived of oil, or any other exhaustible resource, is to consume *none* of it *ever*.

As a matter of fact, all predictions of impending catastrophe in the exhaustion of particular resources have proven wrong. What would we now have gained if our ancestors had used less wood so that we would have had "enough" fuel? Or peat or coal or oil?

The only course that makes sense is for each generation to economize in terms of the conditions facing it. Each generation should consume the cheapest fuel and let progress take care of the future. Since gradual exhaustion of resources will lead to rising prices over time, producers will take account of that and hold increasing inventories relative to output since it pays them to do so. That is, the rate of exhaustion diminishes. In a reasonably functioning market economy, no "irreplaceable" resource would ever disappear entirely; its relative price would simply rise higher and higher.

Fallacy (4), we cannot adjust to artificial manipulations in supply (such as the Arab cartel imposes) except through extraordinary political measures. On the contrary, the adjustments can easily be made in the marketplace. There is no need for arbitrary political measures.

Fallacy (5), letting the market regulate production and consumption harms the poor. Every price above zero harms the poor, who suffer not because of prices but because of lack of purchasing power. The solution to the poverty problem is instant money, not regulation of prices.

The energy question does, however, have important implications for foreign policy.

10

Is Competition Decreasing
in Our Economy?

It is always useful in a paper of this nature to settle as quickly as possible what is going to be talked about. It would take little ingenuity on my part to turn the assigned topic into a springboard for virtually any theme I might want to expound, since the notion of competition has come to mean so many things. If we may judge from recent literature, this seems indeed to be a case where it is quite legitimate to make a word "mean just what I choose it to mean—neither more nor less."

I choose competition to mean what it used to mean in economics: a configuration of forces in a market economy that causes goods to be priced, in the "normal" run of events, at their costs of production, at least in the marginal sense. There are many possible configurations that can lead to competition, the only requisite being that they must operate within a market framework where economic choices are made by individuals, each acting either by himself or in voluntary association with others. Competition performs its work by making it impossible for a seller to gain anything by varying the price he charges: when he acts in his own pecuniary interests, he is forced to accept the price set by market forces.

One of the unfortunate things in the development of economic theory has been the tendency to prescribe a very rigid set of conditions that

This essay is reprinted from *Journal of Farm Economics* 36 (December 1954): 751–58.

must be met if the demand facing a seller is to be completely elastic. These conditions are familiar to us all: the product must be homogeneous, the sellers must be many (to the purist, infinite in number), and every seller must be an unyielding economic man. If these conditions were taken literally, they would have no application at all in the world we live in, for we could never even get so far as to find a truly homogeneous product: "nature makes no leap." No two grains of wheat are identical in terms of all physical criteria that might be applied. Homogeneity exists only in the imaginary world of electrons, or perhaps now even farther away in the world of quanta of energy.

The point is, of course, that we do not take the concept of homogeneity literally, and we do not have to in order to find competition in action. This raises the whole question of where we need to draw the line in identifying products, counting sellers, and specifying economic motivation. The answer is that no hard and fast rules can be laid down. In very loose terms, we can say that a seller operates in a competitive regime if his customers have access to a wide continuum of substitute products that are or could be produced by a sizable number of firms, and if an active minority of his customers and rival sellers are cagey.

This leads us to the obvious point that competition itself is a continuum: there is more or less competition as prices tend more or less toward cost of production. Where we draw the line between competition and "noncompetition" must be somewhat arbitrary, just as it is arbitrary where we draw the line between night and day.

Conceptually, it should be easier to know whether competition has increased or decreased than to know how much there is at any time. As a practical matter, however, both jobs are about equally awkward. In an economy characterized by pervasive change, there are all manner of crosscurrents and few unchanging landmarks: some developments promote competition, and others impede it; the mixture of developments differs in different sectors of the economy; and the sectors themselves may change so much that all sound bases of comparison seem to disappear. For these reasons, there are some economists who would counsel that the best way to answer the question whether competition is decreasing is to call it a silly question, that is, a question incapable of being answered. But it seems to me that this question is no sillier than many others that are raised and answered in one way or another, such as how fast our economy is growing. We certainly have not hesitated to devise, by bold and ingenious methods, answers to these other "unanswerable" questions, and I see no compelling reason why we should hesitate here, unless the underlying issue is considered to be unimportant, which I take it is not the case.

There are two general ways of attacking our problem. We can investigate the forces tending to affect the degree of competition throughout our economy; and we can investigate whether the regions that pass muster as competitive, on some set of criteria, are tending to occupy more or less of the economy. We want to rely as much as possible on quantitative information, but we must realize in advance that much must be qualitative. Moreover, the final answer to be found to the question at hand will necessarily rely on judgment and opinion more than on numerical quantities.

Factors Changing the Degree of Competition

Changes in the degree of competition depend on a great many things— in fact, in a purist sense, on everything; any selection of the most important involves the danger that significant factors will be overlooked and that factors with diverse effects will be improperly grouped together. We cannot avoid such selection and classification, however, if we are to bring order into our thinking. I find it useful to concentrate on three factors: changes in the scope of markets, in the array of products, and in technology.

As we look back over the last fifty years, one of the most striking developments in our economy has been the revolution in transportation and communication. There is scarcely any sector of the economy that has escaped the impact of this revolution. Markets have been expanded in all dimensions: sellers have gained easier access to buyers, buyers have gained easier access to sellers, knowledge of market conditions has been made more easily available to everyone, and so on. The result has been an intensification of competitive conditions in virtually every sector of the economy. Moreover, there seems to be no end in sight to the improvement in means of communication and transportation. Some significant adverse effects for competition might have come because of the channels opened up for massive advertising, but I cannot believe that these adverse effects come anywhere close to balancing the favorable ones.

The array of products and alternative sources of supply has grown independently of the expansion of market areas. It is difficult to find a single major industry in which there has been a secular increase in concentration of production, calculated on a national basis, over the last fifty years or so. The nearly universal pattern seems to be a decline in the share of output accounted for by the largest firm and by the three, four, or five largest firms taken as a group. In addition, the variety of products in the economy as a whole incessantly grows. Thus every buyer, whether a consumer or a firm, faces a spectrum of substitute products that is becoming increasingly continuous and deals with industries whose firms do not, at worst, seem to diminish in number or to usurp larger shares of output.

The effects of changing technology on competition have already been revealed in large measure, and they will be further revealed later on. It seems justifiable to single this factor out, however, because of the special interest economists have shown in the phenomenon of mass production, and the tendency in some quarters to assume that this development must make for a decline in competition. The two need not go hand in hand, of course, if the expansion of markets grows at least apace with the economies of mass production. I submit that this is precisely what has generally happened in our economy; the exceptions are few and usually temporary. The recent increase in concentration in the automobile industry suggest that this may be an important exception. But where is another? It seems to me that, on balance, technological change has worked overwhelmingly in favor of competition.

This superficial and sweeping survey of historical forces at work in our economy reveals no tendency for the foundations of competition to weaken. On the contrary, the signs seem to point to increasing vigor of competitive forces throughout the economy. This is not to say that these forces have been allowed to express themselves unimpaired, but this is a point I cannot go into in this brief paper. I should like to move now to a somewhat more quantitative examination of the trends in competition.

Estimating the Degree of Competition

The question to be explored is whether industries that can be called competitive have tended to account for a decreasing share of total output. As a practical matter, the only feasible method for classifying industries as competitive is on the basis of concentration of output. The shortcomings of this procedure are well known and do not have to be repeated here. It may be noted, however, that the procedure is probably less objectionable when it is used for the purpose of observing changes in the extent of competition than when it is used for the purpose of measuring the extent at any particular time.

Studies have been made of the changing fractions of production accounted for by industries with relatively low concentration of output. In presenting the results here in summary form, I am perhaps violating the precepts of good scholarship, for these results should be surrounded by qualifications and caveats that cannot be detailed here. In fact, the import of those qualifications can be fully grasped only by being familiar with all the steps followed in such a study. I take it, however, that the invitation for me to speak here implies that I am expected to give the results of these studies in abbreviated form. The only way I can discharge my scholarly obligations, therefore, is to suggest that those who are interested should look into the studies themselves for all the necessary qualifications.[1]

Comprehensive data have been compiled by the Census Bureau showing the degree of output concentration in manufacturing in 1935, 1937, and 1947. I have brought together a body of data, much less complete and much less reliable, for the period around the turn of the century. If we count as "monopolistic" all census industries in which the four largest producers accounted for at least half the value of products,[2] we find that such industries as a group accounted for 32 percent of income originating in manufacturing around 1900, for 28 percent in 1937, and for 24 percent in 1947. In other words, the industries that show up as "competitive" on this criterion of output concentration accounted for 68 percent of income originating in manufacturing in 1900, for 72 percent in 1937, and for 76 percent in 1947. These figures, even with considerable allowance for error, give no indication of a decrease in the extent of competition in manufacturing.

A similar comparison can be made for mining between 1900 and 1937. "Competitive" industries accounted for 60 percent of income originating in 1900 and for 73 percent in 1937. Again, there is no indication of a decrease in competition.

When we move outside these two sectors, we are on extremely shaky ground in making any quantitative estimates. The minumum requirements for data are simply not met, and the best we can do is to make intelligent guesses. If we leave aside for the moment governmental

[1] Morris A. Adelman, "The Measurement of Industrial Concentration," *Review of Economics and Statistics* 33 (November 1951): 269–96; Solomon Fabricant, "Is Monopoly Increasing?" *Journal of Economic History* 13 (winter 1953): 89–94; G. Warren Nutter, *The Extent of Enterprise Monopoly in the United States, 1899–1939* (Chicago: University of Chicago Press, 1951); George J. Stigler, *Five Lectures on Economic Problems* (London: Longmans, Green & Co., 1949). The data in the present paper are taken from these sources.

[2] This is an oversimplified description of the criteria used. See the above studies for more detail.

intervention in the marketplace, it scarcely seems plausible that the extent of competition, defined in any relevant sense, has diminished in agriculture, trade, and services. If pressed for a judgment, I should argue that it has increased in these sectors because of the expansion of market areas. In the field of finance, the extent of competition may have decreased with the growth of the insurance industry, which probably cannot be admitted to the competitive group. In transportation, a decision on what has happened depends on how one classifies railroad transportation now as compared with fifty years ago. There is no question that railroads have become increasingly subject to competitive forces and that they have only a small fraction of the monopoly power they possessed thirty, forty, or fifty years ago. I am inclined to believe that, if governmental regulation were largely removed, railroad transportation would now behave in general like a competitive industry. But opinions will differ on this matter.

Everything considered and variations one way or the other in estimates allowed for, there are in my opinion no grounds for concluding that competitive industries now account for a smaller fraction of the income originating in the private sphere of the economy than they did some fifty years ago.[3]

At the same time, the private sphere has been shrinking. The fraction of workers employed in governmental activities has risen from about 4 percent in 1900 to around 12 percent in 1949.[4] Moreover, this does not take account of the growing sector of the economy that falls under close governmental supervision. Because of this shrinkage of the private sphere, it is quite possible that, in the sense we have been discussing, competition is decreasing in the economy as a whole even though it is not decreasing in the private sphere.

Another point needs to be made: industries have been called competitive on the grounds that they will behave competitively if allowed to. As you all know, perhaps too well, there is a significant amount of governmental restriction of competitive behavior in certain sectors of the economy. If this intervention is taken into account, it becomes more and more likely that competition is decreasing. But in this case governmental action is the cause, not the result, of less competition, and this is an important distinction to keep in mind.

[3] For some specific figures on changes in estimated fractions of national income originating in competitive industries, see my study cited in ft. 1 above.

[4] Solomon Fabricant, *The Trend of Governmental Activity in the United States since 1900* (New York: National Bureau of Economic Research, 1952), p. 14.

Arguments Pointing toward a Decrease in Competition

If I am right in my argument that there is no evidence to show a diminution in either the vigor or extent of competition, how is it possible that so many economists have embraced, at one time or another, the decline-of-competition thesis? There are several plausible explanations.

In the first place, there was the Great Depression. The thirties were a time ripe for acceptance of any simple explanation of what seemed then to be a catastrophe of indefinite duration. A severe distrust of monopoly was then, if not now, deeply ingrained in the mind of the typical economist. If he believed that the Great Depression was the result of forces cumulating over a long period, it was natural for him to look to monopoly, among other things, as the villain of the piece. Superficial evidence pointing to growth of monopoly in a few isolated areas was rather recklessly blown up into a case proving general growth of monopoly and concomitant decline of competition. There is little doubt that the decline-of-competition thesis reached its peak of acceptance in the late thirties, as anyone can readily see from a rapid survey of the TNEC [Temporary National Economic Committee] documents.

Curiously enough, the temper of the times has so completely reversed itself that nowadays one could expect to find emotional support for the thesis arising from the belief that a decline of competition is good, rather than bad, for the economy. This change of viewpoint is perhaps not unconnected with the shift from bad to good times, which has caused us to shift our attention toward problems of economic growth and away from problems of economic efficiency.

A deeper reason for acceptance of the thesis lies in the empirical nearsightedness of economists. Most of the generalizations about monopolistic conditions come from observations in the field of manufacturing and mining, and these observations in turn involve an incredibly small number of industries. It is easy to overlook the fact that manufacturing and mining, taken together, account for only slightly more than a quarter of our national income; that services and trade, taken together, match them in importance. I doubt that most economists would seriously challenge the statement that competition is, in any relevant sense one might choose, much more extensive in services and trade than it is in manufacturing and mining. This is to say nothing of the differences in conditions among the remaining sectors of the economy.

Economists may also incline toward a belief that competition is decreasing because they see that fundamental changes have been occurring in the organization of business. The most important has probably been the rise to supremacy of the corporate form, which has accompanied a general increase in the average size of firms. Most importantly, the giants seem to get increasingly gigantic, and it becomes more and more difficult to believe that they can behave in the manner called for under competition. Whatever we may think about the matter when we look at it from this point of view, there does not seem to be any evidence that the rise of bigger and bigger business, in absolute terms, has materially affected the structure of markets. The explanation lies in part in the fact that firms have gotten bigger by moving out into new lines of business and that they have granted virtual autonomy to the various branches in conducting affairs in their own industries. The explanation lies also in the fact that markets have grown along with firms.

Finally, the role of competition may seem to have declined in the world about us because it has declined in the theories we use. The appearance of the theories of monopolistic and imperfect competition marked an abrupt break in the traditions of theorizing. The point was driven home, much too strongly, that absolutely pure competitive behavior is comparatively rare, that the typical behavior involves a subtle mixture of monopolistic and competitive elements. This was certainly not the first time the point had been made by outstanding theorists, but it had never been made before with such analytical elegance and refinement. It is easy to imagine that many economists assumed that the belated appearance of the theories implied the belated appearance of the phenomena they described. This is, of course, far from the truth: there never has been a golden age of all-pervasive competition; the notions of monopolistic competition are just as applicable to the ''good old days'' as they are to the present.

As a closing note, I find it appropriate to read from Marshall, who on this matter, as on so many others, had something wise to say.

> It will in fact presently be seen that, though monopoly and free competition are ideally wide apart, yet in practice they shade into one another by imperceptible degrees: that there is an element of monopoly in nearly all competitive business: and that nearly all the monopolies, that are of any practical importance in the present age, hold much of their power by an uncertain tenure; so that they would lose it ere long, if they ignored the possibilities of competition, direct and indirect.

This interlacing of monopoly price policy and of competitive price policy has indeed always existed. But it needs more careful study now than formerly: and this for several reasons. The temper of the age is increasingly analytical; while the contrast between the influences of cost of production on competitive and on monopoly values is more complex than it was when the foundations of modern economic science were laid. Again, though the progress of analysis has taken nothing of importance from the foundations which were then laid, it has built much upon them; while the progress of events has brought into prominence many considerations, which might reasonably be neglected for the practical purposes of business at that time, but which the modern student is bound to examine with some care.[5]

[5]Alfred Marshall, *Industry and Trade*, 4th ed. (London: Macmillan & Co., 1923), p. 397.

11

Monopoly, Bigness, and Progress[1]

Within the last decade there has been a strong revival of interest in an old topic: the role of monopoly and big business in promoting economic progress. This revival has stemmed in large part, of course, from the stimulating reflections of the late Professor Schumpeter on what he called the process of "creative destruction."[2] His basic theme, with minor variations, has since recurred many times in economic literature, both professional and popular. It will not be repeated here, except incidentally, nor will it be subjected to close scrutiny. The main purpose of this essay is to clarify some of the fundamental issues that have become obscured in recent discussion. This calls for covering ground that, upon being revealed, is recognized as painfully familiar. But no apologies need to be offered for this, for it is precisely the familiar things that are most readily overlooked.

Some Basic Concepts

We may start with the notions of competition and monopoly, and we immediately encounter difficulties of language. There is little sense in

This essay is reprinted from *Journal of Political Economy* 64 (December 1956): 520 – 27 by permission of The University of Chicago Press. Copyright 1956 by The University.

[1] I am grateful to Milton Friedman for his useful suggestions on an earlier draft of this essay.
[2] Joseph A. Schumpeter, *Capitalism, Socialism, and Democracy,* 2d ed. (New York: Harper & Bros., 1947), pp. 72 – 106.

quarreling over words when the important things to distinguish are concepts—that is, concepts relevant to the issues in controversy. "Competition" and "monopoly" unfortunately mean many different things to many different people and in many different contexts. There is no point in trying to settle what they "really" mean, for they "really" mean everything that they are used to mean. Nor is there much point in inventing a unique word for each usage, for this could go on endlessly. Perhaps a good case could be made for throwing out both terms and starting over again, on the grounds that they have become distorted by moral overtones, one set suggesting good and the other evil, and hence have lost the dispassionate neutrality appropriate for scientific inquiry. Aside from being impossible, this could take only temporary effect in the face of an inevitable tendency to attach moral qualities to factual states of things, usually in accord with the fashion of the time. It is instructive to compare Schumpeter's concern over the word "monopoly," because of the opprobrium attached to it, with Marshall's like concern over "competition."[3] In any event, it makes little difference what terms are used in a discussion of specific issues, as long as they represent concepts relevant to the issues and as long as they are used unambiguously.

The big issue underlying the discussion regenerated by Schumpeter is whether economic efficiency, as traditionally defined by economists, conflicts strongly with economic progress. At the present level of discussion one is justified in avoiding the complexities of welfare economics and asserting straight away that economic efficiency is generally understood by economists to be achieved by marginal-cost pricing. Having said this, one must hasten to add that this does not necessarily apply to those cases in which productive services could be paid the values of their respective marginal products only with the aid of subsidies—that is, to firms with decreasing costs. But such intricacies need not concern us for the problem at hand. The important thing is to separate those cases in which marginal-cost pricing occurs in the normal run of events from those in which it does not.

Competition, as we ordinarily conceive of it, does normally lead to marginal-cost pricing. Short definitions are always faulty, but perhaps I can get by here with saying that competition is a set of conditions in the marketplace that causes demand curves for firms to be horizontal, over the normal course of events. It then follows from the most elemen-

[3] Ibid., pp. 99–100; Alfred Marshall, *Principles of Economics*, 8th ed. (London: Macmillan & Co., 1936), pp. 6–10.

tary propositions in economics that competitive firms will tend to produce up to the point where marginal cost equals price.

There is even less cause to labor over the meaning of "big business." A big business is simply a firm that is large in terms of assets controlled, persons employed, or income generated. There is no obvious boundary between big and small business; but we usually speak of the one or two hundred largest corporations in this country as big business, and that definition, widely understood, is satisfactory for most purposes. A big business can be either competitive or monopolistic, or both.

We come finally in these introductory remarks to the question of economic progress. No amount of refinement can get rid of the basic ambiguity in the meaning of "economic progress." In a phrase we are faced with an "index number problem," in its broad as well as its technical sense. If economic progress is to refer solely to growth of output, the problem is seemingly reduced to a technical one—but not really. For the process of growth is also one of change; and products change along with the product-mix. In an abstract sense economic progress may be defined as an increase in the range of alternatives. That is, there has been progress if the community can have more of some things without having less of anything, irrespective of how it chooses to make use of the alternatives facing it. This definition, however, contains few hints on how to tell whether there has in fact been progress, for a community never chooses to have more of some things without taking less of others. Hence progress can be measured only through indexes and through qualititative observations. For instance, increased variety of goods, taken together with a significant rise in a "reliable" index of output, clearly indicates economic progress.

There is usually little doubt whether there has been general economic progress, taken in this sense; but there is always question whether a specific change somewhere in the economy has made a net contribution to progress or a contribution as large as would have been made under alternative conditions. To put the matter concretely, an innovation introduced by a monopolistic firm, even though accepted in the marketplace, may not add so much to output as the existence of the monopoly subtracts; or, even if it does, the net contribution may be smaller than it would have been under competitive conditions. Questions such as this are crucial to the discussion of the problem at hand; yet there is no apparent way to get direct answers to them. The following discussion certainly does not provide the answers. In fact, the questions themselves are approached no more than obliquely.

There seems to be no better way to get at the basic issues than to consider individually the relations between economic progress, on the one hand, and monopoly, competition, and bigness, on the other. After such an exercise, we are still left with the problem of weighing the net contributions of each under varying circumstances and with the broader problem of relating all this to the general social welfare. At this stage we must move entirely into the realm of practical judgment, where neither theory nor empirical fact can give us the answers.

The Theoretical Argument

The basic issue is really twofold. There is first the question whether competition can survive in the wake of economic progress—that is, whether economic progress, origins disregarded, implies pervasive monopoly. There is second, and more importantly, the question whether significant economic progress can arise in an atmosphere saturated with competitive and small business; that is, to what extent monopoly and bigness are necessary stimulants of economic progress.

It can be flatly stated that economic progress need not lead to monopoly. In the first place, competition is quite compatible with the growth of output that follows from growth of resources through investment, the kind of progress typically envisioned by classical economists. Little more needs to be said about this case, other than to point out that it is growth without innovation. Though continuous innovation is an important characteristic of our economic development, this does not mean that all growth stems from it. On the contrary, to the extent that any joint effects can be segregated, a large measure of our economic growth can be attributed simply to expansion of our stock of resources. There is no reason to suppose that competitive industries cannot thrive in an economy growing in this way.

In the second place, innovation[4] need not destroy competition. This is most obvious in the case of technological improvements. The competitive nature of an industry is not automatically destroyed when some firm finds a way to reduce its costs, even if the innovation cannot be effectively imitated. For the fall in costs to the innovating firm must be large relative to costs in other firms and to the extent of the market before that firm can gain significant control over the market. Otherwise it will simply earn economic rent for superior performance, just as it

---

[4] "Innovation" is used here and in the rest of this essay to mean inventions that are introduced into the marketplace, a usage different from Schumpeter's but probably closer to the common meaning.

would if it owned a specific resource with high productivity in this industry. Competition does not preclude the existence of economic rents, and conversely. Put another way, a firm can monopolize a technological innovation without realizing monopolistic control over the product, which is to say that internal economies of scale may not be significant, or that certain diseconomies may operate internally but not externally. A similar line of reasoning applies less obviously to innovation in the form of product differentiation; for a "physical" change in a product, possibly accompanied by lowered costs, need not represent an "economic" change, that is, a change in economic value in the eyes of the marketplace. Or, if it does, the demand facing the innovating firm may still be completely elastic or close to it over a relevantly wide range of output, though at a different price.

In the third place, where innovation does bring about monopoly, that condition may be very short-lived; and the degree to which the monopolistic postion can be profitably exploited while it persists may be severely limited by competitive forces, latent as well as active. Once a lucrative innovation has become established in the marketplace, the higher the rate of profit of the innovating firm, the more strongly are potential imitators impelled to take immediate action. For the adventurous entrepreneurs will scramble hardest after the largest plums, and the more cautious recognize this. Hence the latter must move quickly if they move at all; and, whether they do or not, the adventurous will. Since the innovating firm is probably interested in maximizing its (discounted) stream of future profits rather than its current rate of profit, it will take account of the nature of this reaction. There must be cases, whose frequency is at present anyone's guess, in which the wisest course for the innovating firm is to act competitively from the start, or shortly thereafter, if only to reduce the rapidity with which its market is eaten away, the price of its product reduced, and the elasticity of demand raised. There must be more cases in which, no matter what the intermediate behavior of the innovating firm, the final result is development of a competitive industry.[5]

This is not to argue that monopoly is a less frequent consequence of innovation than competition; that is a complex question of fact, whose

[5] It might seem that this is simply a paraphrase of one of Schumpeter's basic arguments. But, as I read him, he says something else, namely, that the typical time sequence is a succession of temporary partial monopolies, none ever developing into a competitive industry before it is destroyed by some newly arising monopoly. He states at some points and implies at others that this process leads to behavior more competitive than behavior under pure competition (see, for example, Schumpeter, *Capitalism, Socialism, and Democracy*, pp. 84–85). It is here that I lose touch with him, for I do not understand what meaning he is trying to attach to "competition."

answer nobody knows. The important point is that monopoly is neither the universal nor an inevitable consequence, a point regularly overlooked or belittled in much recent literature.

Similarly, monopoly is not a unique stimulant of economic progress. Desire and necessity drive competitive and monopolistic producers alike to innovate: desire for better-than-average profits motivates the venturesome and industrious to introduce new products and techniques; loss of profits forces the cautious and passive to imitate or perish. Just as monopoly does not ensure extraordinary profits, so competition does not preclude them. To the extent that expansion of old firms and entry of new ones cannot be prompt, all members of a competitive industry— and outsiders as well—stand a chance at rewards for innovations, though the rewards may have to be shared. The important element for the competitor, just as for the monopolist, is friction: delay in effective response by others to the lure of high profits. The risk and cost involved in innovating determine the friction needed to induce it. In many industries a modest research program, in part quite informal, can yield significant technological improvements and new products; they often arise spontaneously from the ordinary course of business or from creative impulse. For many of these the chances of being accepted in the marketplace are very good. They will spring forth as long as there is a reasonable prospect of moderate rewards, that is, of moderate friction. They can and do flourish in the typical competitive setting.

On the other hand, some products and processes can be discovered and introduced only at great risk and expense; they will be called forth in volume only if there are favorable prospects for spectacular prizes, such as are provided by exceptional friction. It is easy to get an exaggerated notion of the prevalence and importance of such innovations: they are the most advertised and frequently the most striking, and they are generally introduced by the industrial giants toward which our attention is constantly turned. There is no doubt, on the other hand, that the course of progress would have been significantly different without them; their contribution should not be belittled. But to recognize the contribution of large firms is not to give blanket approval to all monopolistic conditions, some of which make no discernible contribution to economic progress, either directly or indirectly. This is particularly true of the well-insulated monopoly, which may indeed become quite backward. Those that do contribute to progress also have bad effects, against which benefits must be balanced. Finally, as with all economic problems, the question is one of "more or less," not of "all or nothing." The problem is to decide how much difference it makes to have various degrees, extents, and locations of monopoly—a problem neither new nor easy, as shown so well by the long-standing debate over the role of the patent.

Where does the question of bigness fit in? As pointed out at the beginning of this essay, bigness, in the sense in which the term is ordinarily used, cannot be uniquely associated with either competitive or monopolistic conditions. A firm is big or small in terms of something other than the market facing it, possibly persons employed or assets owned or income generated. The big firm is typically a hybrid, producing some products in competitive and others in monopolistic markets, although one set frequently predominates. Just as the prospect of monopolistic position raises the odds in favor of the most risky innovations, so bigness makes possible the most expensive; the combination of the two conditions increases the likelihood that innovations involving both high risk and high cost will be made. Nevertheless, some industrial giants cannot be justified on any relevant grounds. What social benefits are derived from Du Pont's owning a large share of General Motors? From complex holding companies? From monstrous insurance companies exempted from antitrust laws? Others have undesirable along with desirable effects. The problem is again to determine the proper mixture, in this case of bigness and smallness.

The Empirical Picture

Up to this point the discussion has concerned what can be, rather than what is. The unimpressed will say: "It is all very well to argue that innovation need not destroy competition where it prevails, or that competition can promote economic progress; it remains true, nonetheless, that competition, in the sense you mean, does not survive where innovations are profuse, and that significant innovations do not occur where competition persists." They may go on to say that big business has, in the nature of things, taken on the role of the "engine of progress" and that we must look to it for the economic progress of the future. This is the common thread of argument to be found in writings of Schumpeter, Galbraith, and Lilienthal, for instance.[6] I believe that this argument is either wrong or misstated, depending on the interpretation given it.

[6] John K. Galbraith, *American Capitalism: The Concept of Countervailing Power* (Boston: Houghton Mifflin Co., 1952); and David E. Lilienthal, *Big Business: A New Era* (New York: Harper & Bros., 1953).

In the face of rapid and almost continuous progress throughout the American economy, competition has not diminished in vigor or extent; if anything, it has increased. Its locus has shifted from time to time, in some instances as a direct result of innovation. But it has remained a powerful force—indeed the dominant force—in our economy. There is of course no evidence that conclusively proves this contention; and there never could be such evidence. However, the evidence in any way relevant certainly points more in this direction than in any other. The fraction of private income generated by industries with low concentration of output exceeds by a considerable margin the fraction generated by industries with high concentration; and those fractions, insofar as they can be determined, probably have not changed significantly since the turn of the century.[7] This is as true for manufacturing as for the economy as a whole.[8] The validity of inferring competition from low concentration seems to be well recognized; for, while many economists doubt that monopolistic behavior always results from high concentration as typically measured, most seem to believe that low concentration is sufficient for generally competitive behavior. To my knowledge, there have been no studies, covering a large number of specific cases, that shed light on the relationship between innovation and survival of competition. But this issue would seem to lose importance if, as the evidence indicates, loss of competition in some areas is usually matched by equivalent gain in others.

There is probably no satisfactory way of measuring the importance of competition as a stimulant of innovation—or, for that matter, the importance of any specific innovation. It seems inevitable, however, that thinking on this question will be strongly colored by an unconscious bias in favor of the spectacular products of extensive research and development. Yet there are few persuasive reasons for supposing that the complexity of an innovation, or the innovating process, is a sound measure of the importance of an innovation. One may reasonably question, for instance, whether the electronic computer has as yet been worth more than the pushcart of the self-service market.

Furthermore, there is little justification for taking the amount spent on research and development as an index of innovational activity. This

---

[7] See my book, *The Extent of Enterprise Monopoly in the United States, 1899–1939* (Chicago: University of Chicago Press, 1951), pp. 44–45; and Solomon Fabricant, "Is Monopoly Increasing?" *Journal of Economic History* 13 (winter 1953): 89–94.

[8] See my *Extent of Enterprise Monopoly*, pp. 41–42, and Morris A. Adelman, "The Measurement of Industrial Concentration," *Review of Economics and Statistics* 33 (November 1951): 290–93.

practice is, nevertheless, quite common and is the basis for many sweeping generalizations to be found in the current literature. Galbraith, for example, attributes little progress to competitive industries on the grounds that they are "distinguished, one can almost say without exception, by a near absence of research and technical development."[9] He cites agriculture, coal mining, and the clothing industry as particularly backward. This assessment, even as it applies to technical developments, is much too harsh. The mechanization of coal mining, for instance, has been notably rapid and far-reaching. It is true that farmers, coal miners, and clothiers do not typically develop new equipment for their own use; but machinery industries develop it for them. Contrary to first thoughts, Galbraith's general contention is not supported by the fact that some machinery industries tend to be monopolistic; the point remains that farming, coal mining, and clothing manufacture themselves do not need to be monopolistic to induce innovation.

In a broader sense, there is surely little basis for contending that generally competitive areas of the economy—such as agriculture, services, and trade—have been relatively backward. At least, the list of innovations in those areas over the last two decades is impressive: hybrid corn, improved breeds of livestock, drive-in restaurants, self-service markets, frozen foods, decentralized shopping centers, discount houses, off-street parking, and so on. The same is true of many manufacturing industries—such as electrical appliances, clothing, and furniture—where, despite brand names, competition is very real and innovation very substantial. Finally, among new products with the greatest impact on modern living, many have had humble origins outside established monopolistic firms or big business: the automobile, the airplane, radio, and perhaps even televison are examples. Moreover, aside from patent protection for component parts, these products entered the market under highly competitive conditions.

This point is anticipated by some writers who claim that, while it may hold for the past, it holds no longer; for, they say, we have entered a new era—the era of the complex invention. As Galbraith puts it, "technical development has long since become the preserve of the scientist and the engineer. Most of the cheap and simple inventions have, to put it bluntly, been made."[10] It is difficult to know what to say about this except that it is wrong—unless the issue is to be begged by

---

[9] Galbraith, *American Capitalism,* p. 96.

[10] Ibid., p. 91.

defining "technical development" as expensive and complex invention. Moreover, insofar as inventing has become more expensive, as it clearly has in some industries, this calls for the big laboratory, not big business. Research and development can, in large part, be carried on in special institutes and research companies, which may need to be large but not gigantic. Research has come to be centered in industrial giants partly because the giants were there, ready to welcome the advances of science and the advantages of having scientists in their employ. Restricting the size of those giants by one means or another might merely shift the location of research without seriously hindering it.

It is perhaps more important to reiterate that a big firm can be a competitive firm. From the point of view of expense alone, complex research and development can thrive in the big competitive firm. Of course, the more risky the projects, the less likely it is that they will be undertaken. However, I venture the opinion that the bulk of research and development is routine in the sense that, for a typical mix of projects, a marginal dollar expended can be expected to yield results that will bring at least a normal return. As Schumpeter customarily emphasized, invention is the least risky aspect of innovation; the big risks are assumed by those whose job it is to introduce the invention into the marketplace. The innovational process in the big competitive and monopolistic firms will thus differ not so much in amount of research undertaken as in the nature of research and of the results that eventually flow into the marketplace. The real issue is whether, by restraining monopoly, more would be lost in this respect than would be gained in others.

Some Concluding Remarks

The question of the relation between monopoly and economic progress seems to be one of those critical issues in economics that never get resolved by study of "the facts," in part because of a failure to examine the facts as carefully as they might be examined and in part because of the formidable difficulties in interpreting what the facts actually say. As a result, economists engage in a running debate, which gets won only in the sense of gaining adherents to one side or the other. There was a time when most economists seemed to believe that competition was the "engine of progress"; the time has come when an ever-growing number seem to believe that this role is assumed by monopoly. This essay has been designed to raise doubts about the latter position, without at the same time unconditionally supporting the former. The method of doing this has been to lay bare the fundamental issues that need to be resolved and to suggest, by implication, how little has been accomplished toward resolving them.

The greatest present danger is that we shall be blinded to our ignorance in becoming enamored of the monopolistic giants. In this period of serious threat to the survival of our country and our social system, we call upon big and powerful government to protect us; it is natural that we should also incline toward big and powerful business. For one thing, we find that the leaders of big business are frequently the most capable and the best-prepared persons to direct the massive defense effort, as we should expect. More than this, we tend to feel that if centralized direction of the defense effort is good, then so is centralized direction of business. This is a serious error in judgment. But even more serious is the tendency to look only to the immediate future and to neglect the long view. Difficult as it may be, we should continue to view social problems in the light of long-run aspirations and developments, subject, of course, to modifications imposed by the contingencies of the moment.

The problem of our time is to preserve democratic freedom in the face of overwhelming growth of the social creature. We are raising giants of all sorts: populations, national blocs, nations, governments, economic blocs, and enterprises. The individual and his family, while growing in economic and possibly in political strength, must gradually lose stature relative to these organizations. The danger is that we shall be organized to death. The challenge is to adapt to the world—for we can scarcely do otherwise—while dispersing organization. Old-fashioned faith in competitive markets, tempered by sober acceptance of unavoidable compromise, points the way.

12

Strangulation by Regulation

"**P**erhaps, in general, it would be better if government meddled no farther with trade, than to protect it, and let it take its course. Most of the statutes, or acts, edicts, *arrêts,* and placarts of parliaments, princes, and states, for regulating, directing, or restraining of trade, have . . . been either political blunders, or jobs obtained by artful men for private advantage, under pretense of public good."

These are the sentiments of two revolutionaries, Benjamin Franklin and George Whately, expressed some two hundred years ago in protest against the mercantile system then dominating Europe and its colonies. Mercantilism was, of course, nothing more than the economic side of the authoritarian state. It was common for government to regulate all kinds of economic activity: to fix prices, wages, and interest rates; to prohibit speculative trading; to specify the quality of goods; to license labor; to prescribe what people should and could consume; to create monopoly rights for favored proprietors; to control chartering of corporations; to foster state enterprises; to control foreign trade; and so on. The American colonies revolted against this excessive governmental meddling in economic life as much as anything else.

These remarks were given before the American Advertising Federation in Washington, D.C., in June 1976.

Mercantilist controls were justified by economic doctrines of the day, which proclaimed—among other things—that one party to a transaction in the marketplace could gain only at the expense of the other. In other words, if a seller made a profit, the buyer must have been ripped off. It occurred only to a few radical minds that both buyer and seller must gain from trade because it is a voluntary act of exchange. If both do not gain, the exchange obviously won't take place.

The single most important source of enlightened economic thought was Adam Smith's *Wealth of Nations,* which appeared in print just three months before our Declaration of Independence. Both documents were revolutionary in the full sense of the word, the one proclaiming a new economy and the other a new polity. Smith revealed an entirely novel concept of order when he showed that, in the right kind of competitive environment, an individual pursuing his own interests will be "led by an invisible hand to promote an end which was no part of his intention." He went on to point out something even less obvious.

> By pursuing his own interest [an individual] frequently promotes that of the society more effectually than when he really intends to promote it. I have never known much good done by those who affected to trade for the public good. It is an affectation, indeed, not very common among merchants, and very few words need be employed in dissuading them from it.
>
> What is the species of domestic industry which his capital can employ, and of which the produce is likely to be of the greatest value, every individual, it is evident, can, in his local situation, judge much better than any statesman or lawgiver can do for him. The statesman, who should attempt to direct private people in what manner they ought to employ their capitals, would not only load himself with a most unnecessary attention, but assume an authority which could safely be trusted, not only to no single person, but to no council or senate whatever, and which would nowhere be so dangerous as in the hands of a man who had folly and presumption enough to fancy himself fit to exercise it.[1]

There is much wisdom in those words, which have been so badly misinterpreted and misrepresented in recent years. But I am not here to praise Adam Smith, praiseworthy as he is, particularly in this bicentennial year. Let me merely say that it was the spirit of liberty and free enterprise that motivated the making of our revolution, our Constitution, and our first century of development.

[1] Adam Smith, *The Wealth of Nations* (New York: Modern Library, 1937), p. 423.

In the late nineteenth century, a new ingredient was added: intervention by the federal government in the workings of domestic markets. Establishment of the Interstate Commerce Commission (ICC) in 1887 marked the beginning of the era of government regulation. One can hardly argue with the good intention: to curb monopolistic practices of the gigantic railway corporations. But outcome doesn't always accord with intention, and in this case it certainly didn't. What happened has since become a familiar pattern: an agency designed to protect consumers from an imperfect industrial structure was quickly taken captive by the industry and made into its protector instead. The ICC was guided into constructing a maze of fares and standards of service that swept away such competitive elements as there were in railroading. In the earlier days when rapid technological advance was building pressure for declining fares, the cumbersome rate-making process kept them from falling and made life easier for the railroads.

As competing forms of transportation grew in importance, the rationale for regulation shifted 180 degrees. The purpose became to protect all parties, but particularly small trucking firms, from the ravages of "unrestrained" competition. The tentacles of the ICC were spread by legislation to regulate rates, routes, and practices of trucking, bus lines, oil pipelines, domestic water carriers, and freight forwarders. To make sure nobody was missed in regulation, Congress added the Civil Aeronautics Board (CAB) for airlines, the Federal Maritime Commission (FMC) for ocean-going carriers, and the Federal Power Commission (FPC) for natural gas lines. The resulting transportation has certainly become effectively regulated and sick. Private railroads have ended up, by and large, in bankruptcy and virtual nationalization. Needless to say, Amtrak and its various relatives have not been subject to ICC regulation.

The dismal history of the ICC and its cousins did not dampen enthusiasm for regulatory commissions, and one has followed another, particularly after a sharp spurt of creation in the 1930s. Their alphabetic notations have become part of the American language: SEC, FCC, FPC, FTC, FDA, FDIC, CCC, and so on and on. These are fixtures of what we now call the old regulation: regulation of specific industries to correct presumed structural defects. The overwhelming verdict of economists of all persuasions is that this form of regulation has done more harm than good, and this attitude is spilling over into the political arena where momentum seems to be gathering behind a movement to reform and reduce the old regulation.

Yet Congress continues to grind out regulatory commissions of this type. The latest and in many ways the most menacing is the FEC, the Federal Election Commission. It was quickly taken captive by the incumbents who, sitting in Congress, can fix the regulatory powers. In its haste to prevent new Watergates, Congress may well have created a monster far more dangerous to cherished American institutions, not the least being freedom of speech.

But suppose the tide is turning against the old regulation. What about the new, the creature of the 1960s and 1970s? I speak, of course, of the spate of new agencies and commissions whose mission is not to remedy structural defects of industries but to control various harmful side effects of economic activity. The new regulations are created for the purpose of improving the health, safety, and moral attitudes of the public by controlling pollution, perilous circumstances, and discrimination. Beginning in 1962, Congress went on a spree of legislation over the next eleven years that resulted in acts establishing government regulation for the following stated purposes: strict pretesting of safety for medical drugs, equal pay by sex, equal employment opportunity by race and ethnic origin, warning on labels of the hazards of cigarette smoking, fair packaging and labeling, prohibition of hazardous toys, promotion of traffic and automobile safety, fixing standards of flammability in fabrics, better inspection of meat, prohibition of job discrimination by age, truth in lending, truth in land sales, better protection against impure poultry, control of radiation for health and safety, requirement of environmental impact statements for projects by federal agencies, control of credit cards, protection of investors in securities, child-resistant packaging of hazardous products, clean air, occupational safety and health, elimination of lead-based paint, national program for boating safety, safety standards for consumer products, elimination of discharge of pollutants into navigable waters, control of noise pollution, and affirmative action in hiring the handicapped.[2]

Many of the problems attacked by this legislative spree are important ones that won't be solved by the market. Arrangements on the part of consumers and producers acting privately can't be relied upon to clean up the air in our cities. The pollution that spills over from private activity is so diffuse in origin and impact that it is prohibitively

[2] See Murray L. Weidenbaum, *Government-Mandated Price Increases* (Washington, D.C.: American Enterprise Institute, 1975), pp. 4–6.

expensive for a calculation of social costs to enter into private market transactions. If something is to be done about some of these problems, it must be done politically.

But that does not mean that any government action is better than none. In some cases there are better and worse ways for government to intervene. In others there may be nothing government can do to make things better. In still others the discipline of the market may be far superior to any government intervention. What Congress has done all too frequently is to throw a regulatory commission at a problem without bothering to think it through. Solve the problem, the commission is told, by doing the right thing at the right time in the right measure.

The greatest danger in this approach is that the regulatory commission will act arbitrarily and irresponsibly, creating more problems than it solves. Consider the problem of cleaning up the air. I can get you clean air in Washington in a very simple way: just let me ban all economic activity within some convenient radius of Washington, and make everybody walk everywhere or ride a bicycle. What about the cost? Well, you told me to clean the air. What has cost to do with it?

Why should a regulatory commission take account of the cost of fulfilling its mandate? Or any other complications? Murray Weidenbaum calls attention to the case of the unfair toilet.

> The Labor Department, carrying out its weighty responsibilities under the Occupational Safety and Health Act (OSHA), has provided industry with detailed instructions concerning the size, shape, dimensions, and number of toilet seats. For well-known biological reasons, it also requires some type of lounge area to be adjacent to women's rest rooms.
>
> However, the EEOC (Equal Employment Opportunity Commission) has entered this vital area of government-business relations and requires that male toilet and lounge facilities must be equal to the women's. Hence, either equivalent lounges must be built adjacent to the men's toilets or the women's lounges must be dismantled, OSHA and state laws to the contrary notwithstanding. To those who may insist that nature did not create men and women with exactly identical physical characteristics and needs, we can only reply that regulation, like justice, must be blind.[3]

One wonders why the invisible hand of market competition cannot be entrusted to work out this ordinary dilemma. Where has it failed

---

[3] Murray L. Weidenbaum, *The New Wave of Government Regulation of Business* (Washington, D.C.: American Enterprise Institute, 1976), p.7.

and with what consequences so horrendous as to call for intervention by the mighty visible hand of the federal government?

One thing is sure: regulation begets more regulation. A recent count of federal regulatory organizations made by the Center for the Study of Government Regulation at the American Enterprise Institute reveals eighty-five agencies and offices employing almost 175 thousand people with a budget of some $9 billion for fiscal 1976. These figures might be larger or smaller depending on the definition of regulation, but in any case they indicate only the dead-weight administrative cost of regulation, not the full economic cost. What regulation does to impair the efficiency of the market and its ability to bring about adjustments to economic shocks is a far larger element of cost, but unfortunately one that cannot be summarized in a simple set of numbers. Regulation is gradually strangling the pricing mechanism of the market without creating anything to take its place in organizing the incredibly complex economic activity of our nation. Why should we be surprised when we experience inflation in the midst of rising unemployment? Regulation has been very effective in worsening downward rigidity in the structure of prices.

But never fear, the regulators have a cure for the ills of regulation. It is more regulation—not the old type or the new, but something even better: central economic planning. The schemes going by that name may vary in this or that detail, but all have the common characteristic of turning over to a government bureau the task of controlling which specific products are to be produced in what quantities and how the great multitude of economic activities is to be put together into a coherent whole. In other words, a collection of public officials is to take over the allocative function of the market economy based on private enterprise, the best system of democratic planning there is.

I have revealed my thoughts elsewhere on the movement for central economic planning that is gathering force in our country today, and I don't have time to go into them in any detail here. [4] And so I will merely assert that such efforts have never led to economic improvement anywhere else and can be expected to cause great harm here if put into effect.

If I may now conclude on the note with which I started, I would say that we have come full circle and then some these last two hundred

---

[4] For my views, see G. Warren Nutter, *Central Economic Planning: The Visible Hand* (Washington, D. C.: American Enterprise Institute, 1976). Reprinted in this volume as Essay 15, pp. 107–29.

years, as far as the economic role of government is concerned. We are faced once again with a mercantile system of governmental controls over the economy, and we are being urged to plunge into the world of central economic planning. Public spending by all levels of government in the United States has already crossed the boundary line of 40 percent of national income, and we seem to be catching up with countries like the United Kingdom, which has crossed the 60 percent boundary. Perhaps the time has come to resist this dangerous trend as strongly as our forefathers did two centuries ago.

13

Markets Without Property:
A Grand Illusion

It is now thirty years since Oskar Lange wrote his famous essay on how a socialist economy might rationally allocate resources without a capital market.[1] His objective was to refute the contention, which he attributed to Ludwig von Mises, that economic calculation is impossible unless markets are organized on the basis of private ownership of property. While granting the case for competitive pricing, Lange argued that it could be simulated within a regime of collectivized property by setting prices centrally and instructing productive units to behave in accord with a simple set of rules. A socialist economy could, in his view, thereby gain all the allocative benefits of competition without suffering the distributive evils of capitalism.

Experience has cast many doubts on the feasibility of Lange's simulated market socialism, but his theoretical case would seem to remain entrenched as economic orthodoxy. It is widely viewed in Eastern

This essay is reprinted from Nicholas A. Beadles and L. Aubrey Drewry, Jr., eds., *Money, the Market, and the State: Economic Essays in Honor of James Muir Waller* (Athens: University of Georgia Press, 1968), pp. 137–45. It was also published in Eirik G. Furubotn and Svetozar Pejovich, eds., *The Economics of Property Rights* (Cambridge, Mass.: Ballinger, 1974), pp. 217–24.

[1] Oskar Lange, "On the Economic Theory of Socialism," *Review of Economic Studies* 4 (October 1936): 53–71, and 4 (February 1937): 123–42. A revised version was published in Benjamin E. Lippincott, ed., *On the Economic Theory of Socialism* (Minneapolis: University of Minnesota Press, 1938), pp. 55–142.

Europe today as pointing the way toward economic efficiency in a collectivized society. The time has perhaps come to question the soundness of Lange's theoretical case.

I

Let us start with Lange's basic premise.

> The economic problem is a problem of *choice* between alternatives. To solve the problem three data are needed: (1) a preference scale which guides the acts of choice; (2) knowledge of the "terms on which alternatives are offered"; and (3) knowledge of the amount of resources available. Those three data being given, the problem of choice is soluble.
>
> Now it is obvious that a socialist economy may regard the data under 1 and 3 as given, at least in as great a degree as they are given in a capitalist economy. The data under 1 may either be given by the demand schedules of the individuals or be established by the judgment of the authorities administering the economic system. The question remains whether the data under 2 are accessible to the administrators of a socialist economy. Professor Mises denies this. However, a careful study of price theory and of the theory of production convinces us that, the data under 1 and under 3 being given, the "terms on which alternatives are offered" are determined ultimately by the technical possibilities of transformation of one commodity into another, i.e., by the production functions. The administrators of a socialist economy will have exactly the same knowledge, or lack of knowledge, of the production functions as the capitalist entrepreneurs have.[2]

Thus posed, the problem of economic organization becomes purely technical; it is merely one of coordinating given wants and resources through given technology. Lange would solve the problem essentially by instructing plant managers to minimize costs and to equate marginal cost with price, and officials in charge of whole industries to set prices so that markets are cleared and to determine investment so that marginal cost for the industry equals price. He would allow competitive selling of labor and competitive buying of consumer goods, both motivated by self-interest, but neither is required in his system.

Lange recognized that formal rules alone will not make a system work. His mechanism for establishing an equilibrium state is the process of trial and error, the *tâtonnement* of Walras. The central planning board is to set a pattern of prices and observe what happens as plant

[2] Lippincott, *Economic Theory*, pp. 60–61.

managers, consumers, and workers adjust to it. As surpluses arise here and shortages there, the board is to revise the pattern of prices and observe once again the effects. Through successive repetition of this procedure, an equilibrium pattern of prices is ultimately to emerge. The resulting state of affairs will presumably be indistinguishable from competitive equilibrium: costs will be everywhere minimized and output optimized.

There are many grounds on which Lange's theoretical apparatus can be attacked, but I want to take his basic premise as my point of departure. In what sense is it true that "the 'terms on which alternatives are offered' are determined ultimately by the technical possibilities of transformation of one commodity into another''? In what sense is technology a "given" in the economic system and in what sense a consequence? Is the employed technology independent of the process of *tâtonnement?*

Since an economy must always start from where it is, let us imagine one in being with an established system of prices, however it may have been determined. The question arises among the decision makers, whoever they might be, whether it is desirable to set up a new productive unit in a particular industry. The engineers are called in to sketch out the production function based on the current state of the arts, and the accountants to detail the terms on which resources can be hired or purchased. This information will enable the decision makers to chart out minimum costs for alternative scales of plant on the basis of present and anticipated costs of resources.

Even at this stage of decision, the choice of employable alternative technologies, narrowly defined, cannot be disentangled from the existing price structure. Many possible arrangements of resources are ruled out because, under prevailing prices, they are relatively uneconomical. For each significantly different price structure that might exist, the array of optimal employable technologies will differ. There is no such thing as "the best set of techniques" independent of economic valuations.

Hence the choice of technology becomes an economic problem even in the planning stage, before resources have been committed into specific forms, plants, and facilities. Commitment requires appraisal of still another economic variable: the anticipated price of the commodity to be produced. And once resources are committed—plants are built— the range of technological-economic alternatives is altered from what it was before commitment. What is done cannot be undone without cost.

Consider the case of a mistake that has been made by building too large a plant. Even in a completely stationary economy there would be no costless way of remedying this error. The cheapest way to disinvest would be to let the plant depreciate. If the resources released through depreciation were employed elsewhere to yield a normal return, those still embodied in the plant would be bound to yield less than they would have if the correct plant had been erected in the first place. The original production function would become relevant only after the plant had been fully depreciated, a process that might require a century or more of time.

Needless to say, correcting of errors and misjudgments in investment is much more costly in a changing and growing economy. Within any relevant economic environment, the rational policy to follow over some period of time is a mixture of depreciating and altering committed investments, and the best policy in any instance depends in a complex manner on a host of expectations about costs of resources, prices of products, and changes in technology.

These observations are commonplace in standard economic theory, and they have been thoroughly discussed in the literature.[3] The only point worth stressing is that every equilibrium state of an economy depends on the dynamic path through which it is reached. The economic outcome at any moment—or, to revive a neglected term, the economic conjuncture—may or may not represent an equilibrium state in a meaningful sense, but whether it does or not, it is the result of the process of adjustment as well as the so-called "givens" of the economy. For every significantly different dynamic path, there will be a different equilibrium state even if the basic "givens" were to start out the same in every case.

In other words, the Walrasian principle of *tâtonnement* is valid only in the formal sense that a competitive economy can reach *some* equilibrium state through a process of trial and error. It is invalid in the strict sense that there is a unique equilibrium regardless of how it is reached, except possibly for the most primitive market economies.

We are surely led to conclude that economies must be judged at least as much on their mechanisms for adjusting to changed circumstances as on their formal apparatus of pricing. The important question to raise about a Lange-type socialist economy, from the point of view of "static efficiency," is whether its adjustment mechanism would be as sensitive

---

[3] See, for instance, George J. Stigler, "Production and Distribution in the Short Run," *Journal of Political Economy* 47 (June 1939): 305–27.

and responsive as that of a private enterprise market, whether its process of trial and error would dampen to an equilibrium solution as quickly and effectively—whether, in fact, it would ever reach an outcome with characteristics of efficiency commonly attributed to a competitive market.

II

We may approach this issue by observing how a private enterprise economy runs. Consider the classical firm cast in the role of an enterprise within a market economy and a regime of private property. The entrepreneur—the owner of the enterprise itself but not necessarily of the capital invested in it—is interested in earning as much as he can. This simple motive combined with the entrepreneur's skill determines the size of the firm or how many activities are organized within it and how many through the marketplace. It also determines the methods of organization used and the costing and pricing policies followed. Whatever increases the entrepreneur's earnings for a given effort will be done; whatever decreases them will not be. Private property and freedom of enterprise fix simultaneously the firm's role in the economy, costs incurred, prices charged, and output produced.

There is nothing automatic about this process, of course. The firm must be managed in accord with the owner's interests, and this task grows geometrically with the size of the firm. Proper orders must be both given and obeyed, and hired managers and workers as such normally have no direct interest in either giving or obeying orders that benefit the entrepreneur alone. The entrepreneur must therefore link the manager's interests to his own through surveillance or partnership, in varying degrees and mixtures. Managers must do the same with respect to workers.

Badly supervised management must be expected to press forward its own advantages to the detriment of the entrepreneur. If salaries are fixed, other means will be found to raise incomes at company expense. Secretaries will be hired for beauty as well as and instead of efficiency; offices will be comfortably furnished with plush carpets and original paintings; richly appointed executive dining facilities will be arranged on the premises; a park of limousines and aircraft will be set up and staffed with courteous and personable chauffeurs and pilots; ample allowances for business entertainment will be provided; and so on. Ways will also be found to reduce the workload: banker's hours, lengthy business lunches, conferences on the golf links, and so on.

Lesser workers and employees will have more limited opportunities for on-the-job leisure and perquisites, but they will not lack ingenuity in exploiting them.

Mismanagement may go undetected as long as it merely keeps the entrepreneur's earnings lower than they might otherwise be, but it is immediately brought to light when it results in actual losses. Private property sets a limit to divergence of interest between manager and owner. Lack of success in one or the other—management or entrepreneurship—will eventually be eliminated by the ultimate disciplinarian: bankruptcy.

Private property rights are, of course, never absolute, being always restricted by the political order of any society. Property rights in fact measure the degree of the holder's liberty; the amount of property together with the rights, the degree of his power. As Armen Alchian has so clearly argued in much of his recent work, the pricing behavior of a firm will depend directly on the nature of property rights held by its effective owner.

For example, let the owner's earnings be taxed at a flat percentage rate. It is now in his interest to consume some of his income in perquisites enjoyed through his business. Like the badly supervised manager, he will try to set up a well-appointed office staffed with attractive personnel and to add other well-known side benefits. Business affairs will be discussed at expensive restaurants and nightclubs, or in conferences scheduled at pleasing localities. In hiring managerial personnel, it will become worth while to pay less attention to managerial talents and more to conversational skills, golfing or bridge-playing abilities, and the charm of wives. Tax authorities will naturally frown on such practices, but they can control them only to a limited extent, short of taking over actual management of the firm. And then similar practices would arise to the benefit of the tax office.

In other words, costs of doing business will rise as the entrepreneur takes advantage of his firm as a place for consuming services at a bargain rate in terms of net earnings forgone. The changed cost conditions will probably also lead to higher prices and lower output as well as smaller take-home earnings.

Let us take one further step and fix a progressive schedule of tax rates beginning with the flat rate already supposed. Presumably even more income will be consumed through the firm, raising costs and prices and lowering output and earnings further. If the tax rate becomes confiscatory at some point, the entrepreneur loses all personal incentive to realize higher earnings. He will try to gear his business so as never to generate more than that maximum net revenue before taxes, eating up any excess in perquisites if necessary, unless motivated by patriotism or concern for the public good as attended to by government out of tax revenues. As Alfred Marshall once suggested, such motives may be high, but they are not always strong or abundant.

III

How do these situations differ from behavior of a state-owned enterprise? The first thing to do is to identify the effective owner. If an abstract entity such as the state is to be called the owner, then government must be the concrete agency charged with trusteeship. Government will be of some definite form, ultimately responsible to some group of persons for whom it is acting as agent, and it will presumably be responsive at least indirectly to their interests. Ultimately, then, the persons controlling government are the effective owners of state-owned enterprises, while government or some part of it serves as manager.

The interests of owner and manager will diverge here just as surely as within a regime of private property, and the means of bringing accord are the same: surveillance and partnership. But the political order raises new problems. In the first place, it is seldom easy or sensible to change a government because a single enterprise has been mismanaged. In the second place, mismanagement is not readily recognized by interested parties and communicated among them.

Government is, after all, a unified institution, capable of only a limited degree of divisibility. In the market for private property, on the other hand, ownership can be subdivided almost indefinitely, and each owner can divest himself of his property at any time and transfer it elsewhere. Hence management of a single enterprise can be turned over at any moment without materially affecting the rest of the economy, and awareness that something is wrong in an enterprise is quickly transmitted from owner to owner through transactions in capital markets.

An even graver drawback for state-owned enterprises is virtual absence of the ultimate discipline of bankruptcy. In principle, there may be no reason why each enterprise cannot be endowed with its own limited capital and be forced to make its own way on those fixed resources, being put into bankruptcy when it becomes insolvent. But in practice every government is reluctant to follow this course: an enterprise serves political as well as economic ends; bankruptcy reflects on the credit of the government itself; receivership for collective property can hardly be transferred from the political arena; the managers and workers in an enterprise, having no transferable property rights, have more to gain from preserving a losing venture than from dissolving it; and so on. It is generally more expedient to subsidize a floundering state-owned firm than to put it into receivership or out of business.

In the face of all these difficulties, how can those to whom government is responsible keep a close eye on the efficiency of governmental enterprise, in the first place, and remedy divergence of interest, in the second? Few examples of institutions successful in promoting these objectives come to mind.

The sheer technical problems of costing and pricing in state enterprises are minimized when they operate within a general environment of private enterprise, since the marketplace resolves most difficulties. An ocean of private enterprise will determine the level of a bay of governmental enterprise. It is only when the roles are reversed—when governmental enterprises become the ocean and private ones the bay—that the problem becomes serious. Are prices and activities to be set by some central political organ or by some kind of market or quasi market?

One hardly needs to catalog the shortcomings of a centralized command economy. They are well known and acknowledged, perhaps most forcefully at the moment by commentators in the Soviet world itself. The virtues of decentralized decisions and mutual interaction are recognized throughout most of the civilized world today, and all Soviet economies except Communist China and its allies are seeking ways to decentralize economically while preserving an authoritarian political order.

These efforts are bound to be disappointed. Mutual interaction in an economy dominated by government enterprise can be accomplished only by subdivision of political authority, since collective ownership must be divisible into units subject to mutual competition if effective markets are to arise. The larger the economy, the more intensive the divisibility needed.

This is not to say that the extreme form of Stalinist economy cannot be improved upon without sacrificing an authoritarian political system. Yugoslavia is a case in point. Quasi markets were created by establishing semiautonomous collectivized enterprises with the right, although limited and controlled, of competing with each other. Obvious improvements in efficiency have been experienced without an immediate threat to the political system, but serious problems have also accumulated that may have no easy solution without political changes as well. The most pressing is the one already emphasized: how to deal with firms that are suffering persistent losses. So far, the system has provided no answer, no effective surrogate for bankruptcy proceedings.

IV

If we now come full circle and return to Lange's model of socialism, we see how empty his theoretical apparatus is. Markets without divisible and transferable property rights are a sheer illusion. There can be no competitive behavior, real or simulated, without dispersed power and responsibility. And it will not do to disperse the one without the other. If all property is to be literally collectivized and all pricing literally centralized, there is no scope left for a mechanism that can reproduce in any significant respect the functioning of competitive private enterprise.

We could go further and dwell on the problems of generating innovation and progress in a Lange-type system, but something should be left for others to discuss. We may be content here with criticism cast in a static context.

Lange's error began with his basic premise. It is not true that administration of an economy is simply a technical problem devolving from the basic "given" conditions. Nor is it true that "the administrators of a socialist economy will have exactly the same knowledge, or lack of knowledge, of the production functions as the capitalist entrepreneurs have." Nor could simulated markets work in the same way as real ones if those administrators did have the same knowledge.

If capitalism has faults, so has socialism. At the top of the list is absence of competitive markets, simulated or otherwise.

14

Liberty and Growth
of Government

The greatest present danger to liberty is posed by the seemingly unhindered growth of government in societies that have considered themselves free. There is no important country in which growth of government has not become the rule. Examination of the records accumulated over the last quarter century for sixteen countries shows a virtually steady increase, year by year, in the percentage of national income accounted for by government spending.

The sixteen countries are Australia, Austria, Belgium, Canada, Denmark, France, West Germany, Italy, Japan, Luxembourg, the Netherlands, Norway, Sweden, Switzerland, the United Kingdom, and the United States. They were selected for study because they are all associated with the Organization for Economic Cooperation and Development (OECD), which has collected comparable and consistent data for them on national income and government spending for the years since the early 1950s.

In going back to the early 1950s, the median percentage of national income accounted for by government spending in these sixteen countries was around 30 percent. By the mid-1970s, that median had risen to over 50 percent. That is to say, for an average free country in 1950,

These remarks, which summarized findings in G. Warren Nutter, *Growth of Government in the West* (Washington, D.C.: American Enterprise Institute, 1978), were given at the ad hoc meeting of the Mont Pelerin Society in Taiwan in September 1978.

government was spending about a third of national income. For an average country today, government is spending more than half of national income.

This measure shows, of course, only a part of the growth of government because it does not encompass the expansion in governmental activities that require increased spending for various purposes in the private sphere through regulation and the like, nor does it encompass direct commands issued by government and not reflected directly in financial accounts. Two things are certain: first, government today is on the average larger than the size shown by government spending as a fraction of national income; second, government is growing more than is shown by the change in that fraction over time. Yet some numerical measure of size and growth must be used if any very useful analysis of what is happening is to be made and if we recognize that measures are biased downward.

The median fraction of national income accounted for by government spending rose from less than a third in 1950 to more than half in 1975. In both years, the fraction varied widely among countries, ranging from 22 to 39 percent in 1950 and from 29 to 64 percent in 1975.

Back in the early 1950s, West Germany, France, and the United Kingdom were the countries among the sixteen that had the largest governments, while Japan, Switzerland, and Denmark had the smallest ones. In the 1970s, on the other hand, Denmark had acquired one of the largest governments, following Sweden, Norway, and the Netherlands. Japan and Switzerland continued having the smallest governments.

The rate at which government spending relative to national income has risen varies from country to country, ranging from an average of 0.4 percentage points a year for France to 1.8 percentage points a year for Sweden. In the United States, government spending as a percentage of national income has been rising at an average of 0.5 percentage points a year.

Government has grown far more in the domestic arena than in the international one. The fraction of national income accounted for by external spending has been small for all countries concerned, running on the average—as shown by the median—around 6 percent in 1950 and around 5 percent in 1975. If anything, there has been a slight decrease in external government spending as a fraction of national income. On the other hand, the fraction of national income accounted for by domestic government spending has risen from a median of 28 percent in 1950 to 48 percent in 1975. And most of that rise has taken place in domestic transfer payments, the shifting of money from one set of pockets to another.

Having shown you the big picture, I will concentrate now on what has happened in the United States alone.

Growth of government seems to be universal among societies that call themselves free. An explanation of that growth requires going beyond the specific culture and institutional structure of any particular country. What is happening in the United States, for example, is not all that different in kind from what is happening in France or Japan or West Germany. A set of forces seems to be at work that transcends the more obvious cultural differences among countries.

Second, the growth trend is strong and persistent, and there are few signs of a stopping point. A very encouraging development in this regard is the possibility of a taxpayers' revolt. Any substantial retardation in growth of government remains to be seen.

The threat posed to liberty by big government seems plain enough, but the full ramifications are not always appreciated. There is, for one thing, the erosion of basic ideological values caused solely by growth of government, an erosion in particular of the principle of private property.

The question of what rights belong to the individual under the principle of private property is a complicated one, but those complications must not be allowed to becloud the most basic issue of ownership of property. A free society differs from a controlled one to the extent that the individual is protected against arbitrary seizure of his property by government. An individual owns property if he has acquired it legitimately, in accord with the principles of a free society. Taxes represent a claim that government asserts against private property, not a property *right* of government. Individuals alone have property *rights* in a free society. Government is permitted only to establish a claim to the proceeds of private property, and that claim must have the consent of the governed.

The most simple and fundamental of propositions regarding a free society has obviously eroded almost everywhere in the free world, one reason being that the tax claims of government have become so large that a government claim against property begins to be considered a government right to property. Thus, a government that collects income taxes amounting to, say, half of the income earned by private individuals quickly begins to argue that it must control what individuals do with their property because government has a high stake in the outcome. And so businessmen should not be allowed to travel first-class and so on, because that wastes property and income belonging to government. It has not taken long for the proponents of big government to turn the principle of private property on its head, maintaining that government is the ultimate owner of property against which the private individual may have a claim, instead of the other way around.

How the principle of private property is to be strengthened and reaffirmed is one of the great problems of the day as far as survival of a free society is concerned. The classical liberals clearly recognized the crucial role played by the principle of private property in ensuring liberty, and they accordingly justified that principle on essentially religious grounds. The divine right of kings gave way to the divine right to private property as property was proclaimed to be a natural right or natural law. Over time, this sanctified justification of private property has lost force and appeal, as various more utilitarian justifications have taken its place. The great danger now is that the attenuated ideological basis for private property may crumble altogether before the power of big government. It is therefore especially heartening to see growing signs of a taxpayers' revolt in countries like the United States. We may hope that the result will lead to a strengthening of the ideological force of the principle of private property.

How interesting it would be if the United States were to be the country to initiate a cutback in the size of government, repeating the role played by the American Revolution two centuries ago. What our forebears rebelled against in the way of taxation looks almost trivial compared with the burden of taxes today. In the United States, government spending exceeds 40 percent of national income. Back at the time of the American Revolution, government taxes and spending amounted no doubt to less than 10 percent of national income, probably even to less than 5 percent. The big surge in growth of government in the United States has taken place since 1929, or over about a half century, a surge to be viewed with trepidation, considering the political difficulty of reversing trends.

The West can learn from the free play given the marketplace in the Republic of China and, by taking heart, can turn the trend toward big government around.

I said at the start that growth of government is the greatest present danger to liberty. I would close on the same note.

15

Central Economic Planning: The Visible Hand

Planning is in fashion again as we experience an upswing in the Stein wave: the cycle of infatuation with economic planning.[1] While the inflation-recession dilemma has contributed to this revival of interest long dormant, deeper forces are at work, particularly the persistent Western trend toward ever bigger government. In the United States, a threshold has been crossed with the introduction in Congress of legislation to institute central economic planning. This essay addresses some of the fundamental issues raised by that historic event.

How Planning Started

Central economic planning is young in the time scale of history. After the briefest intellectual gestation, it came into being in the Soviet Union during the 1920s and acquired the characteristics of the unfolding totalitarian environment in which it matured. As both concept and system, planning is therefore scarcely more than fifty years old.

When the makers of the Bolshevik Revolution seized power, they were not prepared to run an economy. Neither Marx nor any other

This essay is reprinted from the monograph of the same title (Washington, D.C.: American Enterprise Institute, 1976).

[1] See Herbert Stein, "Better Planning of Less," *Wall Street Journal,* May 14, 1975.

Socialist ideologue had bothered to think through the problem of how economic activity was to be organized once capitalism was overthrown, and none of them had worked out a blueprint of the new order. Beyond prescribing destruction of private enterprise and nationalization of industry and finance, they had nothing to suggest, leaving it to men of action to fill in details.

Marxists in general and Lenin in particular viewed capitalism and the market as indivisible and hence insisted on eradicating money and markets as soon as it was feasible to do so. But they had no clear idea of what was to come next. "State capitalism," a vaguely conceived mixed system, was their way of getting from here to there, and Lenin took the German war economy as his model during the first months of the Communist regime. Once civil war had broken out, this ambiguous and transitional scheme of things rapidly degenerated into a crudely administered command economy based on confiscation, requisitioning, and rationing—a system that later came to be described as War Communism. It was clear from the start that some coordinative mechanism was needed, and various abortive efforts were undertaken to devise short-range plans linking actions in the different economic sectors together. Despite these efforts, central management consisted mainly in dealing incoherently with one crisis after another.

The economic consequences were disastrous: output plummeted and famine swept the land. Three years after the Bolshevik Revolution, Lenin took his famous step backward when he reinstated private trading and small-scale private enterprise under the New Economic Policy (NEP), the purpose being to gain time for building a new system while stimulating economic recovery. It was in this breathing period that economists and other technicians were put hard to work devising a mechanism to supplant the market.

Lenin, who once characterized the new Communist order as "Soviet power plus electrification," had paved the way in the last year of War Communism by commissioning a long-range electrification plan. The result, known as the Goelro Plan, was a thick technical document prepared by a staff of 200 specialists that set forth regional development plans for electric power ten to fifteen years ahead. To provide a rationale for the proposed electrification, the document presented goals for growth in key industries and in various economic sectors. An effort was made to set mutually consistent goals, but the overall plan was really no more than a forecast of what the authors considered to be a feasible pattern of economic development in the light of prevailing technology.

The question of how to implement the plan and coordinate economic activity in general was not addressed.

The next step, taken at the beginning of NEP, was to establish Gosplan, a state committee charged with preparing current and longer-range plans. Several years of coping with day-to-day problems passed before Gosplan was able to develop what would today be called an annual indicative plan. It consisted of control figures that, together with other data, were intended to serve as a basis for evaluating actual economic performance. One thing led to another, however, until the plan for 1927/28 became obligatory in the sense that administrative agencies were directed to implement it.

Drafting of middle-range plans was initiated in 1925, and the First Five-Year Plan was put in force as a directive in the spring of 1929. The combination of compulsory current and five-year plans issued at this point marked the origin of Soviet planning as we now know it.

How Soviet Planning Works

Over the succeeding four and a half decades, the Soviet planning system has evolved through trial and error into a set of institutions that has withstood the test of time. It did not result from any great debates over how an economy can be run most efficiently without markets, or from any other conscious process of search for an ideal economic system. It resulted from pragmatic judgments on ways to preserve and strengthen the Soviet political order.

Economic efficiency as such has never been the fundamental concern of Soviet rulers. They have sought instead to fashion an economic system that would promote their political goals without threatening the authoritarian and totalitarian nature of the state. The Soviet economy has, in other words, been shaped to serve political ends, not the other way around.

To understand the role of central economic planning, one must start with the question of how social activity is to be organized. There are three basic instruments of social organization: custom, contract, and command. Each will be used to some degree in any social order, but a particular society takes its character from the proportions in which they are mixed.

Even though it cannot exist, imagine for a moment a society run solely by authority. In this corporate order, everything is done in response to commands passed from superiors to subordinates. Everybody except the supreme commander has a boss whose orders he must obey. Such a society would simply be an army that ran everything.

At another extreme is an imaginary society organized entirely through contractual arrangements, a social order based on mutual interaction and voluntary association. The purest form is the ideal marketplace, where individuals freely exchange their wares for mutual benefit.

In a purely customary society, order would result from conformity to rules of status and conduct spontaneously accepted by all as part of culture. A caste system might be an example.

The Soviet Union is predominantly an authoritarian society, although there is scope for contractual and customary behavior—some authorized, some merely tolerated, and some strictly illicit. The economy is therefore fundamentally a command economy, and central economic planning is part and parcel of a command economy.

Central planning is simply a mechanism used by Soviet rulers to help them decide how the resources of the Soviet Union can best be employed to further their objectives. The plan itself, once adopted and sanctified, also serves as a means of rallying the public behind whatever course the rulers set out on. That is, it takes on a symbolic as well as practical value in the totalitarian Soviet system.

Taken literally, planning is merely a systematic way of looking ahead, of establishing a procedure for fulfilling purposes externally supplied. Once those purposes are spelled out in adequate detail, preparation of the plan can be assigned to a technical staff that proceeds by projecting a revision of the past into the future. Planners review the record of the past, attempt to correct perceived deficiencies, imagine what changes are likely or can be made to occur in basic economic conditions, and accordingly map out a program designed to serve the prescribed purposes in the best possible way. Since purposes are difficult to specify in the abstract and to disentangle from concrete goals, preliminary sketches are bound to go back and forth between those at the drawing board and those in power before a final plan is adopted. But the planning process is intended to generate means not ends. Ultimate ends, precise or imprecise, come from the minds of the rulers whom planners serve as hireling technicians. It is the rulers who make the plan in the sense of passing final judgment on what is the most effective way of achieving what they wish to achieve.

Just as to plan is not to decide, so to decide is not to do. Activities within the command economy of the Soviet Union are directed by a complex administrative bureaucracy that issues orders on what, where, and how things are to be produced.

There are, then, three mechanisms that together constitute the centrally planned economy of the Soviet Union: one for planning in the technical sense, one for making basic decisions, and one for operating the economy. All are authoritarian in structure and mutually suited to each other. They are predictable aspects of what we characterize as a collectivist and totalitarian society, in which a ruling elite tries to dictate the way of life for everybody.

Observers unfamiliar with how the Soviet system actually works can easily attribute an order and logic to central planning that does not exist. For example, one commonly held view portrays Soviet economic programs as a set of boxes within boxes. According to this view, the first box to be built is the one corresponding to the five-year plan, and even this one is said to have its general contours determined by a long-range plan, covering fifteen to twenty years. Once the five-year box is constructed, the next step is to fit successively smaller boxes inside it, each applying to a successively smaller time period. Thus, the schedules of day-to-day activity contained in quarterly and monthly plans are visualized as mere miniatures of the grandest scheme of all.

Whatever sense this image might make in the abstract, it has little resemblance to the way things really work. In the first place, the middle-range plan is at best a hazy vision of what it would be nice to have five years or so hence on the basis of projections from the past. In far less detail than current plans, it sets forth targets for a limited number of key activities, thereby providing something to shoot at and shout about in the form of selective concrete goals that the populace and bureaucracy can be exhorted to attain. It is not a blueprint for the economy in any other significant sense.

Since future goals grow out of past performance and since reports on accomplishments and prospects take time to prepare, a goodly portion of the period covered by a plan is used up in preparing it. It is therefore not unusual for a five-year plan to be issued as late as a year after the period has started. What, then, keeps things going in the meantime? Presumably current plans prepared on an annual, quarterly, and monthly basis. It follows that they must be drawn up before there is a five-year plan from which they are supposed to derive.

That is not the end of the story, for it also takes time to construct current plans. The first quarter may be over before the annual plan appears, the first month before the quarterly plan appears, and so on.

By that time, what has taken place in the economy is likely to be rather different from what emerges as the plan. So the plan is revised to correspond more closely with actual performance, and the process repeats itself endlessly.

Through this constant readjustment, current plan and performance converge in the course of time, and it is no wonder that the percentages of plan fulfillment published at the conclusion of each year are generally so high. The plan referred to is, of course, the final revision.

Plans can also be met in the short or long run, if fulfillment is an overriding objective, by simply letting things slide in those large areas where no precise goals are set or where goals have a low priority. There are plenty of built-in shock absorbers and residual claimants to dampen the blows of miscalculation. Finally, there remains the expedient of throwing the whole plan away and starting over, as was done in 1957 and 1958.

Foreign trade is one important shock absorber through which items in short supply may be acquired and those in surplus disposed of. And then there are the markets that pervade the Soviet economy. Some, like the so-called collective farm market, are open and legitimate. Others pass through the various shades of gray. Within the vast administrative bureaucracy itself, there are the "fixers" and "pushers" who trade outside the legitimate channels of procurement, and there is an elaborate system of influence peddling. Finally, there are the "speculators" and other illicit entrepreneurs who risk severe punishment, including execution, for their black-market activities.

The question naturally arises whether the plan is egg or chicken—whether performance derives from plan or plan from performance. The answer is that the relation goes both ways, though it is far stronger from performance to plan than is commonly appreciated. Beneath all the conscious efforts to impose central direction on what the economy does, the elemental force of momentum is at work, carrying the economy forward from one day to the next whether plans and all that have been properly attended to or not. And there are the many loose and flexible links that allow bending without breaking.

What Westerners Seek from Planning

Whether fully understood or not, Soviet planning has not proved seductive. No electorate has freely chosen a system like it, and none seems likely to do so in the near future. But in periods of bad times and social crisis, many Western eyes turn inquiringly toward the concept of central planning in hopes of finding in it a prescription for some kind of conscious coordination that might make the economy work better. The notion is that it should be possible to use central planning to supplement the market democratically without going so far as to supplant it. What is said to need improvement through planning varies with the times. And so planning has been advocated to increase economic efficiency, reduce unemployment, control inflation, moderate the business cycle, distribute income more justly, make the economy grow faster, make it grow slower, prevent discrimination, eliminate pollution, improve the quality of life, and so on. In other words, planning is frequently hailed as a cure for whatever seems to be the economic ailment of the moment.

It is hardly surprising that large segments of the public should get the idea that the way to solve a perceived problem is to turn it over to somebody and give him the power needed to get the job done. Nor is it surprising that many people should feel that such problems arise in the first place because nobody has been given the responsibility of preventing them. After all, the concept that, under the right kind of economic and political order, an individual pursuing his own interests would be "led by an invisible hand to promote an end which was no part of his intention" was articulated only 200 years ago. Understanding of this complex idea comes no more naturally at birth today than it did then. If it comes at all, it does so from learning, also not effortless as teachers of economics will wearily testify. Even less obvious is what Adam Smith went on to say.

> By pursuing his own interest [an individual] frequently promotes that of the society more effectually than when he really intends to promote it. I have never known much good done by those who affected to trade for the public good. It is an affectation, indeed, not very common among merchants, and very few words need be employed in dissuading them from it.
>
> What is the species of domestic industry which his capital can employ, and of which the produce is likely to be of the greatest value, every individual, it is evident, can, in his local situation, judge much better than any statesman or lawgiver can do for him. The statesman, who should attempt to direct private people in what manner they ought to employ their capitals, would not only load himself with a most unnecessary attention, but assume an authority which could safely be trusted, not only to no single person, but to no council or senate whatever, and which would nowhere be so dangerous as in the hands of a man who had folly and presumption enough to fancy himself fit to exercise it.[2]

[2] Adam Smith, *The Wealth of Nations* (New York: Modern Library, 1937) p. 423.

Adam Smith spent hundreds of pages explaining what these passages meant, but much of what he and other wise economists following him have said on this issue has come to be widely misunderstood and misrepresented, particularly in recent years. This is hardly the place to go into that matter, however, and it is not necessary to do so for the purpose at hand. It is sufficient to note that, since the end of World War II, more and more countries have experimented with some form or other of what, for lack of a better name, we shall call Western planning, to distinguish it from Soviet planning. The list of countries cited as practicing Western planning in one way and at one time or another has grown long. It includes France, Norway, the Netherlands, Sweden, Japan, the United Kingdom, Korea, Taiwan, and India.

French planning, in operation continuously since 1947, has received the most attention and come to be broadly accepted as the archetype for the general class. Because of the mixed nature of both objectives and characteristics, the system is variously described—depending on the feature being stressed—as indicative, flexible, soft, or voluntary planning.[3] Moreover, French experience with planning has varied so widely over the years in response to fluctuating political and economic fortunes that there has been no discernible evolutionary trend toward a system with stable characteristics. Many observers even scoff at the contention that planning has been practiced in France in any meaningful sense. However that might be, "French planning" is firmly established in our vocabulary, even though it has little to do with anything drawn from the history of France. It refers instead to an idealized model of French-style planning constructed out of a medley of historical experiences—rarely concurrent—and abstract philosophizing.

A French-style plan is a collection of middle-range targets for economic aggregates and specific economic activities, compiled in collaboration with the businesses involved and adjusted by the governmental planning staff for mutual consistency. The configuration of targets so constructed is supposed to represent a desirable and achievable state of the economy some four or five years down the road, and in that sense it is a forecast. It is designed to provide a preview of the national product, price level, employment, industrial production, agricultural production, and output of various products like oil, steel, coal, and automobiles. It shows what lies in store if participants in the market display the proper spirit of cooperation while exercising freedom of choice.

[3] For an authoritative analysis of the concepts behind French planning and the experience with it, see Vera Lutz, *Central Planning for the Market Economy* (London: Longmans, 1969).

Plan targets are said to be neither commands at the one extreme nor mere wishes at the other. They are instead viewed as objectives endorsed by government after an elaborate dialogue with the business community. The very existence of a coherent pattern of goals resulting from such a concerted effort is supposed to induce economic units to behave accordingly. But, to make sure, government will employ instruments of "persuasion" to facilitate achievement of key objectives.

"Persuasive controls" are said to be noncoercive because they merely convey special benefits to firms that conform to the plan. The instruments available for "persuasion" will vary with the powers exercised by the government in question, but it takes little imagination to realize that the distinction between persuasion and coercion is a fine one, and that it vanishes completely when a firm's survival comes to depend on accepting persuasive enticements. It is also clear that such a system of controls could be administered only by a discretionary authority with full power to decide, case by case, whether firms merit the privileges being dispensed. Just as the power to tax is the power to destroy, so the power to "persuade" is the power to coerce. Or, as Herbert Stein has put it, "if the government can make a private citizen an offer he cannot refuse, it can exercise coercion."[4]

What Central Planning Cannot Do

Suppose you have a sack of potatoes and want to make it as compact as possible. One conceivable way of doing so is to contemplate the general shape of the potato, devise some scheme for measuring its dimensions, measure every potato accordingly, put the measurements in a computer, and through some program or other try to find how to fit the potatoes together to take up the smallest space. Anyone familiar with advanced mathematics will recognize that this is a problem of such enormous complexity that it is silly to expect the computer to grind out an optimum solution, no matter how long it works.

Another way to resolve the problem is to give the sack a couple of shakes and let the potatoes settle in by themselves.

There are many lessons in this parable,[5] but one of the most important is that efficiency requires economizing in the use of knowledge, a costly resource. One great virtue of a market economy based on free

---

[4] Herbert Stein, *Economic Planning and the Improvement of Economic Policy* (Washington, D.C.: American Enterprise Institute, 1975), p. 25.

[5] Which comes from Michael Polanyi, the renowned English scientist and political economist.

enterprise is that it mobilizes knowledge for the benefit of society far more cheaply and effectively than any conscious effort can.

This point is clearly expressed in the words of Nobel laureate Friedrich Hayek.

> Fundamentally, in a system in which the knowledge of the relevant facts is dispersed among many people, prices can act to co-ordinate the separate actions of different people in the same way as subjective values help the individual to co-ordinate the parts of his plan. It is worth contemplating for a moment a very simple and commonplace instance of the action of the price system to see what precisely it accomplishes. Assume that somewhere in the world a new opportunity for the use of some raw material, say, tin, has arisen, or that one of the sources of supply of tin has been eliminated. It does not matter for our purpose—and it is significant that it does not matter—which of these two causes has made tin more scarce. All that the users of tin need to know is that some of the tin they used to consume is now more profitably employed elsewhere and that, in consequence, they must economize tin. There is no need for the great majority of them even to know where the more urgent need has arisen, or in favor of what other needs they ought to husband the supply. If only some of them know directly of the new demand, and switch resources over to it, and if the people who are aware of the new gap thus created in turn fill it from still other sources, the effect will rapidly spread throughout the whole economic system and influence not only all the users of tin but also those of its substitutes and the substitutes of these substitutes, the supply of all things made of tin, and their substitutes, and so on; and all this without the great majority of those instrumental in bringing about these substitutions knowing anything at all about the original cause of these changes. The whole acts as one market, not because any of its members survey the whole field, but because their limited individual fields of vision sufficiently overlap so that through many intermediaries the relevant information is communicated to all. The mere fact that there is one price for any commodity—or rather that local prices are connected in a manner determined by the cost of transport, etc.—brings about the solution which (it is just conceptually possible) might have been arrived at by one single mind possessing all the information which is in fact dispersed among all the people involved in the process.[6]

This view of the intelligence-gathering efficiency of markets has been challenged by some proponents of Western planning. Pierre Massé, the articulate French commissioner of planning from 1959

---

[6] Friedrich A. Hayek, *Individualism and Economic Order* (Chicago: University of Chicago Press, 1948), pp. 85–86.

through 1965, even formulated a theory of concerted forecasting that attributes to the resulting "logic of the Plan" a coordinative quality said to be missing in the market. As summarized by Vera Lutz, foremost authority on French-style planning, the theory runs as follows:

According to M. Massé and his followers the classical theory of the functioning of the decentralised market economy failed altogether to deal with the problem of differing expectations about the future. They point out that the usual description of the way in which market mechanisms guide economic operators in the making of their investment and output decisions runs in terms of "explicit price signals", consisting either of current prices or of the prices quoted on forward markets which, however, exist only for a few commodities and cover only a relatively short period ahead. Any number of examples can, indeed, be found in the literature of this conventional description; and it may be fairly commented that many exponents of the virtues of the market economy have been remarkably careless in their formulation of the way it works. Obviously the explicit price signals which exist are not a sufficient basis for making investment decisions of which the results depend on future prices, sometimes at dates many years ahead. In reality firms are generally obliged to rely, not on explicit price signals, but on forecasts of future demand and cost conditions compiled with the aid *inter alia* of market research studies. Over the past 30 years or more, economic theorists analysing the determinants of the investment decisions of the firm have given ample recognition to the fact that the "data" which have to be used are not known, but expected or estimated, prices (and costs). Without questioning the existence of this theoretical analysis and the fact that current business practice follows the same principles, M. Massé and other French planners contend that there remains a problem which the neo-classical theory has ignored. "The individual expectations of firms are", says M. Massé, "in serious danger of being inconsistent with one another." And since consistency of the forecasts is a necessary (though not, of course, a sufficient) condition for their accuracy, they must be harmonised. . . .

Collective forecasting, or "market research on a national scale", is supposed to make a twofold contribution to the solution of this problem. The first is that of rendering the economy "transparent", by gathering together and making generally available the knowledge, beliefs and intentions (often referred to for short as "information") of the individual economic agents regarding future developments in their respective sectors. The second is that of making economic activity "coherent", by welding the individual forecasts and plans into a consistent whole, corresponding to a "common view of future economic development".[7]

7 Lutz, *Central Planning*, pp. 56–58.

It is worth noting that in France, as in the Soviet Union, a plan typically acquires legal status only some time after the start of the period to which it applies, so that the "common view of future economic development" comes into play rather late in the game. For example, the second plan was ratified by the French parliament twenty-seven months after its starting date. The third plan was legally promulgated fifteen months late, and the fourth plan six months late.[8]

After careful analysis, Vera Lutz concludes that the "logic of the Plan," far from improving performance of the market economy, actually makes it worse. The reason is that

> the "logic of the market economy" pre-supposes that different operators, having different expectations, different judgements and access to partly different information, make their forecasts and take their decisions independently of one another. It implies that competition in prediction is an integral part of competition in the wider sense and a part which cannot be eliminated without eliminating the whole. It also implies that the many different views of the future held by independent operators cannot, for various reasons discussed at length in the preceding chapters, be aggregated into a "common view". We have observed that the "liberal philosophy" regards this decentralisation of the forecasting function as one of the advantages of the market economy over the centrally-directed economy, so long as the future is uncertain. In other words, the "liberal philosophy" regards it as natural and desirable that the economy should work to a plurality of views, rather than to a single view of such a future. . . .
>
> Our analysis has confirmed the opinion, held by many planners, that there can be no such thing as central planning (or *ex ante* co-ordination) of all economic activities which is purely "indicative". In other words, there is no such thing as "liberal" or non-interventionist planning. We are therefore obliged to regard as undeserved the place given in recent literature on comparative economic systems to "indicative" planning, conceived as a new kind of integral central planning of the economy.[9]

The effort to impose conformity on the market's multitude of forecasts has many adverse consequences, a serious one being the compounding of probable error. To concoct a so-called collective forecast of the quantity of petroleum that will be demanded and supplied five years down the road, the planning authority must pick some one figure

---

[8] Ibid., pp. 15–16.
[9] Ibid., pp. 149–50.

from the host imagined by buyers and sellers of petroleum. The single forecast arbitrarily chosen is just as likely to be wrong by a given margin as virtually any forecast rejected. If every decision-making unit in the economy adopts this particular petroleum forecast instead of the one it made on the basis of its own experience and foresight, the economy will follow a more wasteful course than it otherwise would while adjusting expectations to outcome over time. That is, the likely mistake inherent in a centralized forecast will have a more harmful impact on the economy than the variety of mistakes distributed among individual forecasts, since the very spread in the latter, involving overlapping margins of error, generates differential market adjustments that diminish average forecasting error over time.

In any case, the highly competitive firm pays attention to expected *prices* and *costs* in making its plans for the future, not to the output expected for its industry as a whole. The proprietor of the corner filling station in Kansas City could not care less about how much gasoline will be consumed in his home town five years hence, let alone in the country as a whole, because there is nothing he can do about it one way or another. It is the firm with only a few rivals that keeps its eye on output projected for its industry, because it may be able to affect total output by its actions alone and hence influence price. Competitive firms acquire this power and interest only if they are banded effectively together in a cartel sponsored or protected by government. When we add to this consideration the fact that planners find it easier to deal with a few decision-making units than with many, we understand why central planning of a market economy has a natural tendency to evolve into a program of universal cartelization—a glorified National Recovery Administration (NRA) and Agricultural Adjustment Administration (AAA).

In his recent critique of French planning experience, Professor John Sheahan verifies this tendency in noting that

> a method which requires the [Planning] Commission to grant favors to corporations in return for cooperation is tantamount to making the commission a spokesman for business within government. In particular, the Commission acts as representative for the firms which it finds easiest to deal with: these are the largest companies with professional managements best able to understand and influence the plans. The Commission has almost automatically favored greater industrial concentration. This attitude has led to increased concentration both where it may mean greater efficiency and where it may entail disfunctional [*sic*] size. It has weakened

any chance of significant domestic competition. If ITT were a French corporation, the Planning Commission would be its natural ally.[10]

Professor Ryutaro Komiya reaches a similar conclusion about Japanese planning. He says that

> Japan's industrial parties tend to favor leading firms in the industries concerned. When the government makes plans or rations quotas, the usual criterion for each firm's share is its past record. This means that the status quo is frozen. Industry associations and councils are dominated by the presidents and board chairmen of the leading firms, which in turn have the largest shares in their respective industries. There is a good deal of talk about fairness and impartiality, but, by and large, the leading firms retain their lion's share of the government pie. This sometimes tends to discourage new entrants into the field and to inhibit aggressive expansion on the part of smaller, more vigorous firms.
>
> The industrial policy system also is often incompatible, in principle, with antitrust policy. Industrial policy encourages mutual persuasion, collaboration, and mergers among firms; antitrust legislation calls for the prosecution of those engaging in restraint of competition. In the 1950s and 1960s, the heyday of industrial policy, MITI [the Ministry of International Trade and Industry] was often in conflict with the Fair Trade Commission.[11]

While making the market function inefficiently, concerted forecasting also provides an erroneous picture of what lies ahead. In her detailed examination of how accurate French forecasts had been for specific products and industrial branches, Vera Lutz found that output actually achieved varied between 25 percent and 230 percent of output forecast by the Third and Fourth Plans.[12] The forecasting record was better for economic aggregates such as gross domestic production, gross investment, manufacturing output, and agricultural output. But it was quite bad for the price level, foreign trade, and employment.[13] Some important economic changes correctly foreseen by the French government were deliberately omitted from plans for political reasons. For example, the Fourth Plan took no account of repatriation from Algeria because, as the commissioner of planning explained, "it was impossible to build a Plan on such a disagreeable eventuality. The

[10] John Sheahan, "Planning in France," *Challenge,* March–April 1975, p. 18.

[11] Ryutaro Komiya, "Economic Planning in Japan," *Challenge,* May–June 1975, p. 19.

[12] Lutz, *Central Planning,* pp. 74–82.

[13] Ibid., pp. 82–84.

government might have been reproached for having precipitated the event by announcing it."[14]

In evaluating French experience, Vera Lutz concludes:

Whichever way we look at the Plans, whether we assume exogenous or endogenous instrumentation, or a mixture of both, there is nothing in the record of the 2nd, 3rd and 4th Plans to justify describing what was being done as central planning of the entire economy.

As regards the aspiration to "indicative" planning, the forecasting had not so far achieved the necessary accuracy for there to be effective planning of this kind. Nor have 20 years of French planning shown signs of any continuous improvement in the degree of accuracy, as the planning authorities acknowledge. Indeed their experience with the 4th Plan inclined them to take the opposite view and to assume that the forecasting was becoming less accurate. The 4th Plan did not perhaps look much worse than the 3rd, if we were considering the complete set of items taken as an undivided whole. But it did look distinctly worse for some of the more important sub-sets: for both power and steel the forecasting was definitely poorer under the 4th Plan than under the 3rd, and for steel it was also poorer than under the 2nd. The experience in these sectors was particularly significant, since they were the ones which advocates of French planning (outside as well as inside France) had most often cited when pointing to the cardinal importance of correct prediction of the overall growth rate as a factor enabling approximately accurate forecasts to be made of the demand for individual products.[15]

This is the French experience, of course, and some might argue that our government would be more successful in forecasting the economic structure if it undertook to do so. Perhaps so, but the one piece of evidence now available provides little reason for such optimism. In 1952 the Paley Commission published a voluminous report forecasting domestic demand that would prevail around 1975 for various basic materials.[16] These forecasts were based on projections of growth trends for economic aggregates, also published.

In a recent study of how well the commission did in its forecasts, Professor Richard N. Cooper finds that it

---

[14] Pierre Massé, "Le Plan et ses partenaires à l'heure du Ve Plan," *Jeune Patron*, October 1964, p. 102, as translated and cited in Lutz, *Central Planning*, p. 85.

[15] Lutz, *Central Planning*, p. 101.

[16] *Resources for Freedom*, A Report to the President's Materials Policy Commission, 5 vols. (1952).

understated the growth in population and the labor force, and its projection of growth in real gross national product implied a trend level for 1975 about 20 percent too low. Estimates of real expenditure on durable goods fell even further short of reality. . . . By 1972, gross investment had grown by 80 percent since 1950, twice the projected rate, and expenditure on producers' durables, which grew by 141 percent, almost tripled the expected rate.

Despite the substantial underestimation of growth in the U.S. economy, particularly in the demand for durables, the commission *over*estimated the consumption of most minerals. . . . For seventeen of the twenty-four minerals [for which actual and projected consumption were compared], the commission's projections were overstatements, even though the economy outstripped expectations. In some respects the projections were not too bad: half of them fell within 20 percent of actual consumption. But the mean error was 46 percent, most errors were on the high side, and the average error on the high side was much bigger than the average error on the low side.[17]

There is no mystery as to why efforts to forecast economic structure over the middle and long range should fail in complex Western economies. In the West, the great engine of progress has been innovation, which by its very nature cannot be foreseen or planned in detail. The best path of progress is the one that unfolds as the economy moves along, cutting its way through a jungle of ignorance and coming here and there onto places where the cutting proves easier. Such chance discoveries let the economy move more swiftly through the jungle if it is adventurous enough to explore for them in the first place and supple enough to exploit them when found. All the while, we remain in the jungle, seeing only a few feet ahead.

Perhaps the most generous appraisal of planning is the one rendered by Mark Spade. "The difference between an unplanned business and a planned one," he says, "is this: (1) In an unplanned business things just happen, i.e., they crop up. . . . (2) In a planned business things still happen and crop up and so on, but you know exactly what would have been the state of affairs if they hadn't."[18]

[17] Richard N. Cooper, "Resource Needs Revisited," *Brookings Papers on Economic Activity*, 1975, no. 1, pp. 239–41.

[18] This charming quotation comes from N. Balchin (Mark Spade), *Business for Pleasure* (London: H. Hamilton, 1956). I have lost the page reference and have not had time to relocate it.

The Proposal before Congress

The lackluster record of Western planning notwithstanding, a bill to establish central economic planning in the United States now lies before Congress. Introduced by Senators Hubert Humphrey and Jacob Javits, the Balanced Growth and Economic Planning Act of 1975[19] would create an elaborate apparatus for central planning and empower it to formulate, enact, and implement a comprehensive middle-range plan. The proposed legislation has received the blessing of the Initiative Committee for National Economic Planning, whose cochairmen are Wassily Leontief, Nobel laureate economist, and Leonard Woodcock, president of the United Automobile Workers, and whose distinguished membership includes John Kenneth Galbraith, Robert Heilbroner, Robert Roosa, Robert Nathan, and Abram Chayes.

Since the bill has been skillfully analyzed elsewhere, there is no need to go over its details here.[20] We shall focus instead on what kind of planning is envisaged and how it is likely to work.

An Economic Planning Board would be the agency charged with formulating, evaluating, and coordinating the plan. Drawn up every two years, the plan would, in the words of the bill:

(1) establish economic objectives for a period to be determined by the Board, paying particular attention to the attainment of the goals of full employment, price stability, balanced economic growth, an equitable distribution of income, the efficient utilization of both private and public resources, balanced regional and urban development, stable international relations, and meeting essential national needs in transportation, energy, agriculture, raw materials, housing, education, public services, and research and development;

(2) identify the resources required for achieving the economic objectives of the Plan by forecasting the level of production and investment by major industrial, agricultural, and other sectors, the levels of State, local, and Federal Government activity, for the duration of the Plan; and

(3) recommend legislative and administrative actions necessary or desirable to achieve the objectives of the Plan, including recommendations with respect to money supply growth, the Federal budget, credit needs,

[19] The bill was introduced into the Senate on May 21, 1975, as S. 1795 and into the House of Representatives on June 5 as H.R. 7678. It has been referred to the Joint Economic Committee.

[20] See Stein, *Economic Planning;* and *The Economic Planning Proposal,* Legislative Analysis No. 5, 94th Cong., 1st sess. (Washington, D.C.: American Enterprise Institute, 1975).

interest rates, taxes and subsidies, antitrust and merger policy, changes in industrial structure and regulation, international trade, and other policies and programs of economic significance.

The sweeping and permissive language of the bill hardly makes it easy to foresee what kind of economic system would emerge once the Economic Planning Board assumed its powers, but it is clear that sponsors envisage something more than French-style indicative planning. Just what they envisage is a mystery that cannot be solved by searching through statements made so far by Senators Humphrey and Javits. When one witness at the hearings of the Joint Economic Committee suggested that it would be useful to know the "initial philosophy" behind the bill, Senator Humphrey gave the strange response: "That is exactly the purpose of these hearings. . . . This is advisory and consultative and hopefully out of this dialogue and discussion . . . we will come down to a much more clear and precise understanding of exactly what we are talking about and what we mean."[21] In other words, maybe witnesses in the hearings will come up with some good ideas about what the sponsors would have had in mind when they introduced the bill if they had thought of them in the first place.

Backers of the bill outside Congress have been less backward in airing their initial philosophy, but their explanations have not been very helpful. Noting that "the bill was originally drafted by members of the Initiative Committee for National Economic Planning," Myron Sharpe, a spokesman for the committee, states that "the Initiative Committee didn't start with any foreign model at all," that "French planning leaves much to be desired," and that "the same may be said about Japanese planning."[22] In elaboration of this negative description, he says:

> A planning commission that makes forecasts to which nobody pays attention is not what we have in mind. Nor do we have in mind a tug of war

[21] U.S., Congress, *Notes from the Joint Economic Committee*, 94th Cong., 1st sess., vol. 1, no. 19, July 1, 1975, p. 2.

[22] MES [Myron E. Sharpe], "The Planning Bill," *Challenge,* May–June 1975, pp. 3, 7.

For one reason or another, Senators Humphrey and Javits have been careful to keep some distance between themselves and the Initiative Committee. In the hearings of June 11 and 12, 1975, Senator Javits says, "I reject completely any effort to tie their aspirations to our motivations, and their purposes to the effect of our bill." Senator Humphrey echoes this sentiment, while adding that "we have appreciated their initiative and their efforts, but we have written our own bill and may I say we have written it within the framework of our own thinking, and recognizing that it is subject to many adjustments." See *Notes from Joint Economic Committee,* p. 20.

between planning technocrats, the Finance Ministry, and the Prime Minister. Nor yet a summary of the investment intentions of all the businesses in the country. Nor a planning system that is boycotted by unions because they are aligned with opposition parties. Least of all do we have in mind a *pro forma* planning procedure that is rubber-stamped by parliament and actually negotiated by chairmen of the boards of the largest corporations.

What, then, is the committee in favor of? Myron Sharpe struggles to explain.

What we envisage is an effective planning agency, the Office of Balanced Growth and Economic Planning [now designated as the Economic Planning Board], that is the direct instrument of the President and that actually has the authority to plan. On the Congressional side, we envisage a complementary and equally effective planning agency, the Joint Economic Committee, supported by an expanded staff, working with the Budget Office, able to recommend planning legislation to Congress. The bill also encourages and supports planning agencies at the regional, state, and local levels. It is therefore inevitable that a continuous public discussion will take place about what planning should be and how it is working.

We expect that the normal American political process, through which the President, Congress, and state and local officials are elected, through which issues are discussed, and through which labor, business, farmers, minorities, and other parts of the public are heard, will determine how we plan.

This kind of planning consists neither in making elaborate forecasts spiced with wishful thinking, nor in issuing detailed orders to businesses about how to run their affairs. The detailed decisions about purchases, sales, production, employment, prices, and investment remain private. All the virtues of decentralized decision-making are kept intact. Undoubtedly many sectors of the economy which are in a state of good health, where projections look favorable, will not call for any planning action at all. But in a modern industrial economy, a collection of private decisions does not necessarily guarantee that private and social needs are met automatically. The purpose of planning is to provide, where it is lacking, the mechanism to relate needs to available labor, plant, and materials. The plan is a guide to the market.[23]

But what does it mean to be "a guide to the market"? Mr. Sharpe clarifies:

The plan will analyze and set general objectives for the allocation of resources, labor, and capital to specific sectors of the economy; and will

---

[23] Sharpe, "The Planning Bill," p. 7.

set general objectives for the goods and services produced by those sectors. It will also analyze and set strategic objectives for the future structure of production and consumption. It will incorporate special projects for the development of energy, transportation, housing, health, research, and numerous other requirements of pressing importance. It will take into account "the quality of life" and the environment. And—what monetary and fiscal policy is supposed to do now—it will deal with such familiar matters as employment, GNP, and the price level.[24]

How, then, can "detailed decisions about purchases, sales, production, employment, prices, and investment remain private"? The answer seems to be that they can remain private provided that they are brought into harmony with what the planners want. If individuals can be made to reach the right decisions, they will be permitted to make them. For, as Mr. Sharpe explains:

a plan not only allows us to look at the general picture, but at its details. Plans are guides to the relationships between different parts of the economy and allow us to adopt coherent policies for the separate parts as required. The means to implement these policies are not specified in the bill. Just as in the case of goals, the bill provides a framework. A wide range of instruments can be used to accomplish specific, interrelated aims. These instruments are already familiar in nonplanning contexts or where the planning has been applied *ad hoc*: they are tax incentives and penalties; capital and credit allocation; laws requiring or prohibiting definite actions, such as those specifying how air, water, and land may be used; and projects within the public sector itself—the space program, for example. Incomes policy, now under a cloud, is also a possible planning instrument. Whether or not it is used depends, like everything else, on the circumstances.[25]

If the new system were to work as envisaged in this description, one thing is certain: consumer sovereignty would go out the window. All important economic decisions would be made politically, and the market would be used merely as a convenient device for carrying them out, being manipulated this way or that by appropriate coercive "instruments." The plan would "guide the market," all right, in the direction of becoming the tool of government. Private enterprise might become so weakened and circumscribed that the market itself would cease to be an effective coordinative mechanism. If so, something else would apparently be put in its place. Set up enough planning agencies and give them enough power, this proponent says, and planning will emerge.

[24] Ibid., p. 6.
[25] Ibid., p. 7.

What happens to American society depends on the laws Congress passes to enable the plans to work. Since those laws will issue from a "continuous public discussion," they are bound to reflect the will of the people, and hence everything will be all right.

Senator Humphrey tells us not to worry because this is "a voluntary system of economic planning. No authority is planned in the Economic Planning Board or any other agency of government or in the Office of the President to order or direct the private sector of the economy to do anything as a result of a particular approved plan." He goes on to say:

> There has been considerable confusion on this plan, and there is under-standable suspicion on the part of some that the Federal government will seek to expand its control over the economy and seek to manage it.
>
> I can categorically state that it is not the intent of the authors of this bill or of the bill itself, and there is not a single word or phrase in this bill which could be used to expand the government's control over the economy.[26]

Senator Javits asserts further that "there is not a line in [the bill] that makes anybody do anything except make the Congress plan." The bill is merely a "methodology by which a plan can be produced and kept up to date." It is "a road map—that is all that it is."[27]

Perhaps so, but there is no way to get down the road without "expanding the government's control over the economy." How else is the Economic Planning Board to collect the masses of data it will deem necessary for drawing up the plan? What else can result from, as the bill puts it, "legislative and administrative actions necessary or desirable to achieve the objectives of the Plan"? Passage of the economic planning bill would set the stage for—at best—an enormously burdensome and costly government bureaucracy if plans are not implemented or for—at worst—a regimented society if they are. In addition, by virtue of the immunity from antitrust action provided in the bill for the furnishing of information requested by planning authorities,[28] the door would be opened for pervasive price fixing and cartelization that would put the NRA, once declared unconstitutional, to shame.

The Burden of Proof

The movement for planning has a disturbing air about it: the air of reckless experimentation. Look at the mess our economy is in, advo-

[26] *Notes from Joint Economic Committee*, p. 19.

[27] Ibid.

[28] S. 1795, Section 205 (c) (1).

cates of planning say. We've tried a lot of things but not central economic planning. Why not give it a try and see what happens? Never mind that it hasn't worked anywhere else: Americans have a way of getting things done. [Why then, one wonders, did we get into this mess in the first place?] "I think," Professor Leontief reflects, "we can do many things much better than other countries can do, we will succeed because we know where other countries are in planning and where other countries fail. I do not abide by the observation that because it failed in some other country that it is bound to fail here."[29]

Here's our scheme, the planners say. Now prove it won't work. But no fair to use history as evidence: just because planning hasn't solved the same problems elsewhere doesn't mean it won't solve them here. We are different. And the fact that government has been the biggest and fastest growing thing in our economy has nothing to do with the mess we are in. The problem is, too much has been left to the shrinking market economy. After all, government is spending only 40 percent of national income. We need to get 60 percent or 70 percent of national income under government control, as in England. Then we'll have an efficient economy.

The planners try to place the burden of proof on those who wish to preserve the traditional American economy—and then they rule out all possible proof. They cannot be permitted to shift the burden of proof, for it rests on them. In proposing such a profound and far-reaching transformation of American society, they bear the responsibility for proving that the new order will be better than the one to be displaced. They have ample and varied planning experience to draw upon. Yet the best examples they seem to be able to offer are Norway and Sweden, two tiny and uniquely homogeneous societies, the one less than 2 percent of the United States in size and the other less than 4 percent. Even so, are we to believe that the average American would rather live in those economies than in his own? If this is the best evidence that advocates have to present on how well planning works, the verdict must be "not proved."

The fact is that we already have the best system of democratic planning there is: the market economy based on private enterprise. Ours is easily the strongest, healthiest, wealthiest, most responsive economy on this planet. The serious economic pains now being experi-

---

[29] *Notes from Joint Economic Committee*, p. 13.

enced are symptoms of political ills, not of flaws in the economic system. The basic problem is too much government, not too little.

To plan or not to plan is not the question, but whether to regiment society or to leave it free. The question is whether we wish to be guided in our lives by the invisible hand of freedom or by the visible hand of coercion.

PART TWO

16

The Soviet Citizen: Today's Forgotten Man

As we contemplate the Soviet Union in today's world, our thoughts naturally turn to the posture assumed by this giant nation in the arena of world politics. We think of her military prowess, her industrial might, her subversive apparatus, her scientific excellence. On the mental scoreboard that we watch in these momentous times, we chalk up points for her performance: so and so many successful flights into space, such and such an industrial growth rate, so many missiles in place ready to fire, so many people under domination, and so on and on.

This outlook is reasonable enough when we find ourselves confronted with an unsought and unwanted contest for power, a tragic contest over which the individual has no control. We view nations as if they were beings unto themselves, each with a personality quite independent of the people who compose it. We match a being called the United States against another called the Soviet Union, and in doing so we even step outside our own society, so to speak, to observe the strangely dehumanized spectacle as if we were detached spectators rather than participants.

It is, in other words, easy to forget that, at base, human beings are involved in all this. If we are to judge a nation, we should at least take

This essay, which was originally given as one of the 1967/68 series of Town Hall Lectures at Memphis State University, is reprinted from Festus Justin Viser, ed., *The USSR in Today's World* (Memphis: Memphis State University Press, 1968), pp. 19–44.

a look at the people who make it up. For the greatness of a society, our democratic tradition tells us, does not come from the power and glory that the society enjoys or from the monuments that it erects in their name, but from the kind of people that it creates and the kind of life it enables them to lead. The ultimate test of Soviet society consists in how the people live and how well they fare.

It is in this sense that I wish to talk about the Soviet citizen, today's forgotten man. He is forgotten by those who govern him, of course. But he is forgotten by the outside world as well. My purpose is to bring him to the center of the stage and put him in the spotlight for a moment, so that he may be remembered as we watch the drama unfold in which he forms the supporting cast.

I

A Russian was once talking to an American tourist, so the story runs. "I don't see what the difference is between the way things are in your country and mine," he said. "I have a steady job, earn a good living, and enjoy a paid vacation every year. I can't complain." The American thought for a moment and then replied: "I have all those things, too. But I *can* complain. I suppose that's the difference."

For Ivan Ivanov, the ordinary Russian, the first commandment is silence. The constitution does not put it quite this way, for it states that freedom of speech and press is guaranteed to everyone "in conformity with the interests of the working people, and in order to strengthen the socialist system."[1] There is the rub, of course. Exactly what are the interests of the working people, and what strengthens the socialist system? Ivan's rulers have given a clear and firm answer: what we say and nothing else.

And so it must be in an authoritarian society, where truth depends on who says it and not on agreement. In Ivan's society, the word comes from his rulers, who consider themselves infallible. What is the point in inviting open discussion when the truth has already been revealed? To do so is to raise the danger that the masses will be misled by falsehood and calumny spread by enemies of the state. Dissension and treason mean the same thing in such a system, and to tolerate the one is to condone the other.

[1] As cited in John N. Hazard, *The Soviet System of Government*, 3rd ed. (Chicago: University of Chicago Press, 1964), p. 241.

Ivan has gotten the message and has learned not to express his thoughts in public when they might impinge on political matters. He hardly dares to grumble about how things are at work or in the office, for his employer is the state, and to grumble is to be disloyal. He surely will not openly dispute any action taken by his government or any proposal made by it. Not even his supposed representatives in parliament will dare to do that. From the first session of every so-called parliamentary body in his country to the latest one, there has never been a dissenting vote cast on any act placed before it.

Every citizen knows that the secret police maintain careful dossiers on suspected dissidents and that their network of informers reaches into the most unlikely places. He takes it for granted that, if he gives them cause, the secret police will read his mail and tap his phone. Indeed, there is no such thing as a privileged communication in Soviet society. The state claims a right to know everything, including what is said between parishioner and pastor, accused and legal counsel, or husband and wife.

What, then, is privacy, and where is it to be found? It is nothing more than the circle of closest family and most trusted friends. It is only in this precious company that the normal Russian will feel free to express himself, and then preferably on some crowded street or in some noisy public place. The ordinary Russian family lacks privacy even at home, for it will normally share at least kitchen and bathroom with other families, assigned by the authorities.

If the Soviet citizen must watch what he says, he must seek permission for what he wishes to publish. Here the government takes no chances. Private ownership or operation of reproductive equipment, even the simplest duplicating machine, is strictly forbidden. The only place to get something printed is a plant owned by the state. As if this were not enough, every manuscript must be examined and approved by the government censor before it may be printed. Once published, a work may later be condemned and ordered withdrawn from circulation.

The world has been made aware of these stringent controls by the recent sensational trial of Sinyavsky and Daniel, two well-known Russian authors. These two writers were sentenced to forced labor camps, for terms of five and seven years, for publishing their works abroad under assumed names. There is no Soviet law that explicitly prohibits the publishing of books in foreign lands, and their crime did not consist in doing so. Instead, they were found guilty of defaming the Soviet system and bringing their motherland into disrepute. In fact, the formal charge against them was sedition and subversion, a strange accusation since their countrymen could not even read what they had written.

This case has become the focal point for extraordinary protest from the Soviet intellectual community, but so far the official response has been adamant. A second trial was held for four young writers who had supplied the outside world with a transcript of the Sinyavsky-Daniel trial, and the principal defendants were dealt with as harshly as Sinyavsky and Daniel had been. Among the prominent intellectuals who protested this second action, one has been committed to an insane asylum and another has been dismissed from his university post.

The state not only censors and prints all published material but also maintains a complete monopoly over its distribution. There is no such thing as a private bookstore, library, or newsstand in the Soviet Union. Foreigners have been arrested and harshly punished for passing out publications, even literary works of no obvious political significance. The crime consists of disseminating written material outside the authorized state channels.

All news media rest exclusively in the hands of the state. The Party publishes one set of newspapers and the government another. The typical daily paper is four to six pages in size and is filled mainly with official propaganda. The scarcity of news is brought home to every visitor who spends any time in the Soviet Union, for he quickly feels cut off from the world he lives in.

Control over the airwaves is less complete since the jamming of foreign broadcasts was discontinued several years ago, but laws strictly regulate the kinds of receiving equipment that listeners are permitted to own. Of course, the only stations allowed to broadcast inside the Soviet Union are those owned by the government.

The natural counterpart to freedom of expression is the right to assemble for peaceable purposes. We should hardly expect to find the second without the first, and we do not in the Soviet Union. No crowd may legally convene for any purpose without official permission granted in advance. Under Soviet law, two or more persons constitute a crowd.

Individuals may not legally join together in an association of any kind without first obtaining a license from the state. Once formed, the association must obtain a separate license for each meeting it wishes to hold. When participants are to come from different parts of the country, the license must be obtained from the central Council of Ministers. In brief, voluntary association does not exist in the Soviet Union except illicitly. The only organizations to which Ivan may legally belong are those specially created by the state for various purposes, and his government is careful to provide only one of a kind at any time.

Each worker is automatically enrolled in the trade union officially assigned to his place of work, but he will not expect many benefits from membership except in the form of recreational activities. The principal obligation of each union is to mobilize greater effort on the part of the workers toward achievement of planned goals. There is no such thing as collective bargaining over wages or other conditions of work, and strikes are absolutely forbidden as a serious crime against the state. Unions are run by a bureaucracy ultimately selected by the Party apparatus, and rank-and-file members have no say in the choice of their officers or in the ordinary business affairs of the union.

If the Ivanov family lives in the countryside, as half the population does, it may belong to a collective farm, as a matter not of choice but of birth or circumstance. In the strange language of the Soviet world, a collective farm is called cooperative, but the members have no voice in whether they belong or not, or in how the farm is run.

Like the government itself, every authorized organization is controlled by a core of Party members so that general conformity of policy and action is assured. If Ivan belongs to the Party, he is an exceptional person, for only about one out of every ten adults does belong. Even if he is a member, he has virtually no voice in Party affairs. Here as elsewhere there is a mechanism to ensure that everything is controlled from the top. Whether the Ivanov parents belong to the Party or not, their children of school age will be enrolled as a matter of course in the Party affiliates for the young, first becoming Little Octobrists and then Pioneers. At the age of fifteen, the children may decide whether they will apply for membership in the Young Communist League, where activities take on a more political flavor. Since membership in the Young Communist League cannot hurt one's career, about 40 percent of the youth do join it.

Religious worship is one form of peaceable assembly that is particularly obnoxious to the Soviet leadership. Bowing to necessity, they have permitted churches to exist while keeping them under strict control and surveillance. Atheism is, of course, inherent in Communist doctrine, and antireligious propaganda is encouraged, protected, and fostered by the state. Although the Soviet constitution generally bears no relation to political reality, it is interesting to observe that it guarantees to everybody the right to disseminate antireligious propaganda, while it is silent on the right to propagate a faith. In fact, churches are not permitted to engage in religious education except to train clergy, and even here there are special restrictions.

A church serves almost exclusively, then, as a place of worship. In doing so, it makes use of property owned by the state and lent to it at the pleasure of political authorities. The property, including sacramental vestments and vessels, is placed under the supervision of a small parish council responsible for its proper use, and the government retains the power to close any church to worship whenever it might wish to do so.

Religious activity is controlled by the State Council for Religious Affairs, an agency apparently subordinate to the secret police and staffed by personnel drawn from those ranks. It maintains a registry of all approved clergy and records of the membership in every congregation. One important reason for keeping a close eye on those who profess a religious faith is to prevent them from becoming members of the Party or from holding any position of trust in or out of the government. Another reason is to single out those who are the best targets for atheistic propaganda.

Historically the church has always been subservient to the state in Russia, and in some respects the present is a continuance of the past. In tsarist times, the Russian Orthodox Church served not only to meet the spiritual needs of the population but also to provide an ideological justification for the regime and its policies, a dual role that it performed well. We should therefore not be surprised to see that the Soviet government prefers to have religious activities channeled as much as possible into the Orthodox Church, which it feels can be easily controlled.

We should also not be surprised to see that the Soviet people have different ideas. The Baptists are the most rapidly growing denomination, the congregation having grown fourfold over the last half century to reach half a million today. The Soviet government has shown its concern by stepping up the harassment and persecution of Baptists in recent months.

The constant campaign against all religion and the close restrictions placed on worship and religious indoctrination must have had an adverse effect on religious sentiment over the last fifty years. Yet the religious spirit seems to remain strong among many, and the authorities are obviously not willing to undertake the gamble of launching an all-out effort to eradicate organized religion. Moreover, there are signs of a religious reawakening among segments of the intelligentsia, seeking some faith to give meaning to their lives. For some, Communist dogma had served as that faith, but many of these have become disillusioned by the growing gap between myth and reality. The denunciation of Stalin and his fall as an idol had a profound effect on many, if only symbolic.

It is not beyond imagination that, in this autocratic world in which other forms of expression and assembly are so rigidly controlled, organized religion may offer the environment most conducive to independent social thought. Nowhere else in the society is a similar opportunity provided for people to congregate together and at least listen to ideas that do not descend from Party ideologues.

In this regard, *The New York Times* carried a story about an abortive political conspiracy with strong religious overtones. Although nothing has appeared on the affair in the Soviet press, word-of-mouth reports indicate that a group of about sixty intellectuals formed an underground organization called the All-Russian Social-Christian Union for Liberation of the People. Their program called for a socialist economy within a democracy that would be overseen by a theocratic council of the Russian Orthodox Church. According to the same reports, some twenty-one of the conspirators have been convicted of treason, the leaders receiving sentences of eight to fifteen years.

We must understand that Ivan lives in the closest thing to a totalitarian state that the world has yet seen. Totalitarianism, conceived and perfected by Lenin and his successors, differs from earlier forms of tyranny in that it attempts to control all aspects of social life and not merely to maintain the sovereign in power. Literally everything becomes a political question of greater or lesser importance, and the answers as to what is right and wrong or true and false are reserved to the self-appointed elite that rules through a dictatorship.

Lenin was a man of great cunning and perception, and he recognized quite early that the best way to get the people to take their medicine was to sugarcoat the pill. They will accept the dictatorship, he reasoned, if it is made to look like a democracy without being one. Give the people what they think they want: a constitution with a bill of rights, a parliament, a system of courts, a federal system, and above all elections. Sell the system on its form and not its substance, and then the rulers may do as they please once they have consolidated power.

And so Ivan has all those things, the trappings of democracy, but they have nothing to do with how the country is run. When he votes for members of parliament or other offices, he is confronted by a ballot containing a single candidate for each position to be filled, the candidate having been selected by the Communist Party. He may drop the unmarked ballot into a box in the presence of election officials, or he may retire to a polling booth to scratch out the names that he does not approve of. On election day he votes wherever he happens to be and for whatever slate of candidates he may be offered, even though he may be far removed from his place of residence. What difference does it make when elections are a mere ritual? Small wonder that more than 99 percent of the eligible voters cast their votes for the official list of candidates.

When the members of parliament assemble annually for the few days of each session, they never engage in any meaningful debate or cast any dissenting votes on matters put before them. They obediently enact such legislation as is requested of them by the actual ruling authorities, at the same time ratifying all decrees issued by the parliamentary presidiums in the interval between sessions.

The apparatus that actually rules the country is dual in structure, consisting of parallel offices of the Communist Party, on the one hand, and the formal government, on the other. Executive power resides in the presidium of the Council of Ministers, but that presidium is in turn wholly subservient to the Politburo of the Party, and their memberships are virtually identical. Ultimate political power is focused in the position of the secretary-general of the Party, who also serves as the effective head of the Politburo. That person today is Leonid Ilyich Brezhnev. His counterpart in the formal government is Aleksei Nikolayevich Kosygin, who serves as chairman of the presidium of the Council of Ministers. But Kosygin is subordinated to Brezhnev in any test of strength.

In a word, the Party is a state within the state, and it in turn is ruled by a party within the Party—a bureaucratic apparatus that is self-perpetuating for all practical purposes. The Party has, of course, a regular membership, now consisting of about thirteen million persons. Most of them are rather ordinary workers and peasants who have demonstrated a special dedication to the Communist system. In order to become a member, Ivan must submit to a rigorous screening process before he may become a candidate, and he must then perform successfully as a candidate member for a trial period of a year before he may be admitted to the Party. Once a member, he will fall heir to certain privileges in the ordinary course of life, and in exchange he will serve as a loyal soldier in the political ranks. Democratic rule is as absent within the Party as outside of it.

It is the professional apparatus of the Party—those who serve full time as officials—that constitutes, in conjunction with the secret police, the seat of power in the Soviet Union. That apparatus is dominated by a select elite, and the ultimate purpose of the entire Soviet system is to maintain that elite in power. The Party controls all aspects of government and prevents any competing base of power from arising.

II

We cannot blame Ivan if he is fatalistically resigned to his destiny. He is powerless to influence policies within his country, and he is forbidden to leave—he is denied the right to vote with his feet. Even his movements within the country are strictly controlled by a rigid internal passport system, and he may not depart from the country without an external passport that he can receive only as a privilege and not as a right. He sees his country ringed by a frontier zone, constantly patrolled by troops, into which entrance is forbidden except by special permission. If he manages to receive permission to leave his country and, after doing so, defects, his renunciation of citizenship has no validity in the eyes of his government. Once a Soviet citizen, always a Soviet citizen, unless the government should in its grace decree otherwise.

This tyrannical society was nurtured in terror, an instrument introduced by Lenin to consolidate power and perfected by Stalin. We shall no doubt never know the full toll of that terror—the untold thousands liquidated and millions imprisoned. Incredible as it may sound, one reliable estimate indicates that, at the height of terror, forced labor camps never held less than one out of every ten adults, and at times one out of every five.

The Soviet leaders of today would have their subjects and the world at large believe that those dreadful days of terror occurred because Stalin was a demented paranoiac. No doubt he was, but he was more than that. He was the product of an autocratic system that has survived him. Terror was merely the ultimate weapon of power, a weapon required to establish despotic control. He pushed it too far, but without this heritage the rulers of today could not be as secure as they are.

When Khrushchev was recounting Stalin's crimes before the Twentieth Party Congress in 1956, so the story goes, a voice suddenly called out from the audience: "And where, Nikita Sergeyevitch, were you when all this was going on?'' Khrushchev interrupted his speech, looked out over the audience, and asked: ''Will the person who said that please rise?''

A heavy silence hung over the hall, and no one stirred from his seat. Khrushchev surveyed the audience slowly and returned his eyes to the manuscript before him. Then, speaking deliberately, he said: ''That, my dear comrades, is where I was.''

The Soviet system rests on fear of government, on blind obedience to orders. There is no room for a rule of law, prescribing what citizens may not do. It is better that the citizen not know the law, that he beware of the state. Let him obey absolutely, doing what he is told and not what he believes he can get away with.

And so the Soviet judicial system, while seeming on the surface to be similar to those in the free world, has a character all its own. Judges are selected by the Party, and they may be removed at any time at the pleasure of the Party. Prosecutors are appointed by the central government and enjoy more discretion than their counterpart in the West. A distinction is maintained between crimes against the state—which include pilfering of state property—and crimes against persons, the former being far more serious and subject to more severe punishment.

A person charged with a crime in the Soviet Union is not presumed to be innocent until proven guilty. On the contrary, it is taken for granted that he would not be brought to trial unless the evidence pointed to his guilt. After being charged, he is first investigated at a lengthy pretrial hearing, conducted by the prosecutor's office for crimes against persons but always by the secret police for crimes against the state. Unless the defendant is a juvenile or mentally incompetent, he is not entitled to counsel during this hearing. He need not be informed of the charges against him for ten days, and he may be detained incommunicado for up to nine months. The trial must begin within the tenth month, but it may be dragged out over an indefinite period. For all practical purposes, the case is decided at the pretrial hearing, since the trial consists of little more than formal verification of the facts presented at the hearing.

Trials are not heard by a jury, but by a panel consisting of a judge and two lay assessors, the latter having been chosen from a list approved by the Party. The defendant may be represented by counsel, but all lawyers belong to collective agencies strictly controlled by the state, and their careers depend on not incurring the disfavor of the Party. They may be summarily disbarred by the provincial legislature of the Minister of Justice without right of appeal. The threat of disbarment is not idle, as the world learned when the lawyer who represented the defense in the recent case against four Soviet writers suffered this fate, for no apparent reason other than his defense of "disreputable elements."

In addition to the regular courts, there are quasi-judicial "social assemblies" that try cases of so-called "antisocial and parasitic" behavior. They consist in gatherings of workmen, colleagues, or neighbors convened by a committee for public order composed mainly of Party members. If convicted by a show of hands, the defendant may be sentenced to banishment to a remote region for up to five years.

Living in fear of dire punishment, Ivan readily accedes to the regimentation imposed on his life, which begins with the question of where he may live. Residence is controlled by a domestic passport system. Regular passports, valid for five years at a time, are issued only to adults who live in the cities, certain other urban areas, the frontier zone, and the regions neighboring Moscow, Leningrad, and Kiev. No inhabitant of the rest of the country, mainly rural, may have a passport. If a peasant is recruited to work in an enterprise by the special governmental agency for this purpose, he will be issued a temporary passport. The work contract runs for one year at a time on a renewable basis, and the temporary passport for three months.

Persons without passports—at least half of the population—are not legally permitted to spend more than five days at a time in an urban area. This exception is necessary to permit peasants to carry on the ordinary business of life: to bring their meager produce to the collective farm markets for sale to the public, to shop for important items not available in the village, and to attend to affairs with various branches of government located only in urban areas. A member of a collective farm may not even move from one farm to another without permission of the management, and then only by reason of marriage or participation in an official program to settle remote areas. He may leave the collective farm altogether only if officially recruited for labor elsewhere or admitted to a secondary school. In a word, the peasantry, or almost half of the Soviet nation, is tied to the land just as it was in the days of serfdom.

The passport is much more than a document of identity, for it contains a historical record of such matters as marital status, employment, residence both permanent and temporary, and so on. With the exception already noted for peasants, the law requires that every person who moves about within the passport region must register with the local militia within twenty-four hours after he arrives in a locality and once again when he leaves. He is legally entitled to lodging only if the registration has been entered in his passport.

Every able-bodied citizen of working age, whether he has a passport or not, is issued a workbook identifying him and containing a complete record of education and training, job history with reasons for all separations, and special commendations or rewards. The workbook must be turned over to the employer for as long as a job is held. In the case of certain sensitive jobs, the passport must be surrendered as well, a special identity card being issued in its place.

The Soviet constitution states that "work is the duty of every able-bodied citizen, according to the principle: 'he who does not work, neither shall he eat.' " That is to say, Ivan is obliged to work whether he wishes to or not. This obligation in enforced in several ways. For example, no one of working age is entitled to housing unless he is currently employed. Those who have no visible legal means of support are considered to be "parasites" and "antisocial elements," and they may be tried by social assemblies and sentenced to banishment in remote areas, as we have already mentioned. In practice, the obligation to work begins at the age of sixteen for all urban residents except students and the handicapped. In the countryside, those who reach the age of twelve must begin working at least fifty days a year.

Mobility is restrained not only horizontally but also vertically, for Soviet society is highly stratified. In the words of Orwell, all citizens are equal, but some are more equal than others. Movement up the ladder of classes and associated privileges is very difficult to achieve.

On the bottom rung stand the peasants, just below the working masses. Next come the skilled workers and technicians, followed by the professionals and bureaucrats. At the very top are the leading Party and governmental officials. These classes are separated by sharp income differentials, and the disparities among salaries and wages are greater than in our country. A form of sales tax—averaging half the retail price of consumer goods—is the principal source of governmental revenue, weighing proportionally more heavily on the poor than on the well-to-do and thereby increasing inequality of income.

A vast array of special privileges ascends over the upper levels of social status. Those at the top are accorded the best of everything: spacious housing, country villas, private automobiles, special stores to shop in, first choice of seats at the opera and ballet, and so on and on. They never stand in line. In a society as drab and thoroughly controlled as the Soviet Union, such privileges make an enormous difference, and they attach in lesser degrees to all the higher levels of the social scale. Ivan Ivanov, our ordinary Russian, knows that he will move into an entirely different world if he can escape from the peasantry into the urban working class, or from the unskilled into the skilled labor category. But everything seems to be against him, from the dead weight of the established social structure to the discriminatory system of education.

The atmosphere of conformity that overhangs Soviet society stifles individuality and creative diversity. One important manifestation is the persecution of minorities. Let me illustrate with the case of the Jews, who are suffering particularly at the moment. Anti-Semitism has deep roots in the Russian culture, and it therefore provides a rallying ground for the public support of the government in critical times like the present. In addition, there is the desire of the Communist leadership to eliminate all cohesive communities that might threaten the development of a homogeneous Soviet culture. The problem has loomed larger with the emergence of Israel as a Jewish nation, for the very national allegiance of Russian Jews has become suspect. Now that the Soviet Union has cast itself on the side of the Arabs in their conflict with Israel, internal policy toward the Jews seems to have become an integral part of foreign policy as well. For all these reasons, a rather definite campaign of persecution seems to be underway.

The Jews continue to be designated as a nationality within the Soviet Union even though they exhibit few of the characteristics officially associated with one: only a small fraction (perhaps a quarter) speaks Yiddish as a native tongue; an even smaller fraction actively practices the Jewish religion; and only some fourteen thousand are congregated in a separate territorial unit allegedly intended for Jews. Yet a person so designated is identified as a Jew in the space provided in his passport for nationality.

By official count, there are over two million Soviet Jews. The state permits them to have a total of sixty synagogues. By contrast, there are fifty-five hundred churches for the half million Baptists. No seminary is permitted for the training of rabbis, and no rabbis may study or even travel abroad. The existing congregations are not allowed to confederate into a national organization. Not since 1958, when 3,000 copies of a prayer book were issued, has any religious publication been permitted.

The official policy carries over into the realm of culture. Although there are many schools for other linguistic minorities—including some tiny ones—in which classes are conducted in native languages, the same privilege is not accorded to use of either Yiddish or Hebrew in a single school throughout the Soviet Union. The Yiddish Theater, which once flourished, has long been closed, and a formerly rich literature has all but vanished.

To a people with such a strong tradition of learning, the recent tightening of the quota for admission of Jews to higher education, limiting entrance to 3 percent of those eligible, is especially harsh. Similar discrimination has been increasingly apparent in declining opportunities to enter certain professions and to rise to prominent positions. For example, almost 11 percent of the Central Committee of the Communist Party was Jewish in 1939 as compared with less than 0.3 percent today, or one Jewish member out of 360.

Hovering above this undeniable set of discriminatory policies is the ugly specter of official anti-Semitism, always veiled but nonetheless real. In the campaign against so-called "economic crimes" carried out in the early 1960s, more than half of those who were publicly announced as having been executed bore conspicuously Jewish names. In the Ukraine, the fraction was 90 percent even though Jews constitute only 2 percent of the population.

We could go on documenting at length the mistreatment of the Jewish minority in the Soviet Union, but we have said enough to make the basic point. What is perhaps more important is that the same thing can happen at any time to other identifiable ethnic or racial groups incurring the displeasure of the state.

Where may a Soviet citizen turn who is oppressed by reason of race, color, or creed? There is only one legal employer: the state. Except for food, he has only one legal place to shop: the state stores. He has only one landlord to whom he can apply for housing: the state. The state schools provide his sole opportunity for education. And so on and on. How can minorities escape persecution by the all-powerful state? Only by turning to the generally illicit marketplaces, and then they must live the dangerous life of outlaws.

III

Having concentrated so far in this necessarily brief sketch on the political and social environment of the ordinary Soviet citizen, I should like to spend my remaining few minutes on the question of his material well-being.

Let us start with the cold figures on urban housing. The official statistics tell us that the amount of housing space per urban inhabitant is less than 70 square feet. On the average, there are about 2.3 persons living in each room. In this simple respect, urban housing is more crowded now than it was before the revolution half a century ago. But conditions have improved considerably from the low point just before World War II, when average living space was around 45 square feet, or hardly more than double the size of a grave site.

The average amount of urban housing space today is only 70 percent of the minimum sanitary norm set by the Soviet government more than a generation ago. Even if the urban population did not increase in the meantime, existing housing would have to be more than doubled in order to reach the ultimate goal of one person per room. And, since housing facilities are so unevenly distributed among the various classes of Soviet society, we must remember that half the urban residents live in even more crowded conditions than these figures show.

By normal international standards, it is considered excessive crowding to have more than 1.5 persons per room. A very tiny fraction of the housing units in the United States are overcrowded in that sense. Only 12 percent had more than one person per room according to the census of 1960. Living space per person is around 350 square feet, or five times the Soviet figure. It seems clear that the Ivanovs, our ordinary Russian family, reside in what is considered a slum in the United States.

This is even more apparent when we recognize that kitchen and bathroom facilites are, except for the privileged classes, shared by a number of families in Soviet apartment buildings. Even in the case of the newest apartments being built, about half have communal kitchens and bathrooms. And those fortunate enough to get one of these must normally have applied at least five years in advance.

The crowded condition of housing is not the only bad aspect of urban life in the Soviet Union. If we leave aside the specially favored cities, most streets are still dirt roads. In Novosibirsk, only 18 percent of the streets are paved, and in Sverdlovsk only 40 percent. Both have populations of almost a million. Water lines run less than half the length of city streets, and sewage lines less than half the length of water lines. Only about half the sewage and almost none of the industrial waste are treated before entering inland waterways.

If this is the way things are in the city, how are they in the villages? One may only suppose that they are much the same as they always have been. The peasants still live in their huts and cottages, more roomy than the apartments of the city but far less well provided with modern conveniences. Perhaps most have electricity, at least in the form of a light socket or two, and some will have a radio. But water will still be drawn mainly from the well, the toilet will be an outhouse, and heat will come from an oven, stove, or hearth. Life in the countryside remains primitive and miserable.

The standard of living of the average man is equally low in other respects. While Ivan's diet contains about as many calories as John Doe's in the United States, almost three-fifths come from starchy foods instead of a quarter, as is the case with John Doe. In per capita consumption, the Soviet Union ranks behind only Egypt and Yugoslavia for bread and only Poland for potatoes. The purchase of food accounts for about three-fifths of the average Soviet budget, as compared with one-fifth of the American budget.

Everything considered, how well does the ordinary Soviet family live relative to the ordinary American family? It would seem that the Soviet family's standard of living is only about a fifth as high, and the gap becomes even larger when we weigh the factor of freedom of consumer choice.

The disparity in living standards for John Doe and Ivan Ivanov is even greater if we take account of the important element of consumption within the household economy. The normal American family is so accustomed to its vast array of personal capital goods, yielding so many services in the household, that it can hardly imagine how poor Ivan is in this respect. In the Soviet Union, the number of privately owned automobiles is about 2 per thousand inhabitants, or 1 for every 135 families (0.007 per family). In the United States, the figures are 400 per thousand, or 1.4 per family. In rounded figures the stocks of other consumer durables per thousand persons are as follows for the Soviet Union and the United States, respectively: radios, 170 and 980; television sets, 70 and 330; telephones, 30 and 480; refrigerators, 30 and 290; washing machines, 50 and 220; and vacuum cleaners, 20 and 210. The stocks range from 5 to 200 times as large in the United States as in the Soviet Union.

The primitive state of household conveniences and market facilities means that Ivan and Anna Ivanov must spend most of their leisure time in shopping and performing household chores. Official surveys indicate that at least 70 percent of free time is spent in these ways, much of it standing in queues one place or another. In a usual store, Ivan must wait in three lines: to select his goods, to pay for them, and to pick them up.

Ivan's lot is indeed not an easy one. By our standards, he lives in a slum and enjoys a standard of living only halfway up to the poverty line. He is denied the simplest freedoms by his government and subjected to oppression unexceeded in the history of mankind. The Russian, hardened by centuries of despotism, has a remarkable capacity for enduring physical and spiritual hardship. Yet he, like every human being, has the spark of liberty in his breast.

IV

And so we witness today an uneasy stir in the land, a malaise and dissatisfaction that may one day burst forth into a sustained cry for reform and freedom. Spokesmen for the cause of freedom are emerging among the intellectuals on whom so much educational effort has been spent. In their vanguard, as is so often the case, stand poets, artists, and writers.

Let us listen to the courageous and eloquent words of Lidiya Chukovskaya, a respected literary figure and daughter of the renowned author. In an open letter addressed to Mikhail Sholokhov, the Russian Nobel laureate who supported the action against Sinyavsky and Daniel, she wrote:

> On the surface, the trial of Sinyavsky and Daniel was held with due regard to the legal formalities. For you this is a fault, and for me it is a good feature. Yet even so, I protest against the sentence pronounced by the court.
>
> Why?
>
> Because Sinyavsky's and Daniel's committal to trial was in itself illegal.
>
> Because a book, a piece of fiction, a story, a novel, in brief, a work of literature—whether good or bad, talented or untalented, truthful or untruthful—cannot be tried in any court, criminal, military or civil, except the court of literature. A writer, like any other Soviet citizen, can and should be tried by a criminal court for any misdemeanor he may have committed, but not for his books. Literature does not come under the jurisdiction of the criminal court. Ideas should be fought with ideas, not with camps and prisons.

This is what you should have said to your listeners if you had really gone to the rostrum as a spokesman of Soviet literature.

But you spoke as a renegade from it. Your shameful speech will not be forgotten by history.

And literature will take its own vengeance, as it always takes vengeance on those who betray the duty imposed by it. It has condemned you to the worst sentence to which an artist can be condemned—to creative sterility. And neither honors nor money nor prizes, given at home or abroad, can turn this shame from your head.[2]

Perhaps this spirit of freedom is destined to triumph some day. Then the Soviet citizen will no longer be forgotten.

[2] *New York Times,* Nov. 19, 1966, p. 6.

17

The Structure and Growth
of Soviet Industry:
A Comparison with the
United States

I. Introduction

Summaries are always treacherous, particularly when treating such a complex subject as the structure and growth of Soviet industry. One may present either a detailed picture of a narrow aspect of the topic or a bold sketch of the subject in the large. The latter approach seems most appropriate here, but it should not be undertaken or studied without an awareness of the importance of things left unsaid. Few topics of the day are more controversial than the question of Soviet economic growth. Scholars who have devoted their professional careers to this subject reach vastly different conclusions, on matters of both fact and interpretation. We are a long way from the scholarly ideal of agreement.

For this reason, it is as important to know how conclusions are reached as what they are. And there is the dilemma: full documentation, usually tedious and complex in this field, cannot be presented in a summary statement. Nor can all the necessary qualifications be kept constantly before the reader. This essay represents an effort to compress voluminous materials and qualifications, with all the un-

This essay is reprinted from *Journal of Law and Economics* 2 (October 1959): 147–74 by permission of The University of Chicago Press. Copyright 1959 by The University. It was also published in U.S., Congress, Joint Economic Committee, *Comparisons of the United States and Soviet Economies,* 86th Cong., 1st sess., 1960, pt. 1, pp. 95–120.

avoidable vices of a summary. It draws on preliminary findings of a broad study of Soviet economic growth sponsored during the last five and a half years by the National Bureau of Economic Research. Since the study has not yet been completed, the findings are subject to revision before the final report is published. That report will, of course, contain a documentation of the basic statistics.

Any summary of Soviet industrial performance must start with a few words on the difficulties of appraising it. The student of the Soviet economy takes his data from the official Soviet press, and therein lie unusual troubles. Some may find it hard to believe that Soviet statistics are "really" worse than others, because every specialist in no matter what field quickly becomes convinced that no data could be as bad as those he is forced to work with. Why call the kettle black when it is probably no grayer than the pot?

Let us acknowledge at once that all statistics contain faults and errors. Let us also acknowledge that no government or other agency resists the temptation to stretch figures to its own account if it feels it can get away with it. Representative government, competitive scholarship, and free public discourse are the Western institutions that have counteracted error and misrepresentation in statistics, imperfectly to be sure, but at least to some degree.

The peculiar difficulties with Soviet statistics stem, in the first instance, from the system of authoritarian, centralized planning—from what has been called a "command economy." Published statistics come from only one source: the state. There are no independent sources to restrain each other or to be used as checks against each other, except to the extent that related figures published by different state agencies might not be fully coordinated before publication. At the same time, the suppliers of data to the central authorities—the economic and administrative units—have a stake in the figures they report, since their performance is judged on the basis of them. The Soviet statistical authorities do not hide their concern over the misreporting that results from this feature of the economic system.

A second set of difficulties stems from the crusading nature of Soviet communism. Statistics are grist for the propaganda mill. Knowing the ideological views of Soviet leaders, one cannot expect them to dispense facts in a passive and detached manner.

For both broad reasons, Soviet statistics are selective and of varying reliability and ambiguity. The policy of selectivity has two rather opposing results as far as statistics on physical output are concerned. On the one hand, some areas of poor performance are shielded from view, being underrepresented in published data. On the other hand, some of the more rapidly expanding economic activities associated with the military sector are also not reported on. It is impossible to determine the net bias of the sample of published data: whether there is, on this count, a net over- or understatement of growth. [1]

A few broad generalizations can be made about the reliability of the published statistics. In the first place, absolute output is probably overstated in the case of most industries, particularly for the years within the plan period, though the degree of overstatement cannot be determined. In the second place, growth in output is also probably overstated relative to a prerevolutionary or an early Soviet base, but not necessarily over other parts of the Soviet period. Over some of the latter years growth may be overstated, over others understated, and over still others more or less accurately reported. This will vary from industry to industry and from one situation to another.

Whatever the faults of data on output of individual industries, they are more reliable than official aggregative measures, such as the official Soviet index of industrial production. Although the details underlying this index have not been made public, Western specialists are generally agreed that, from what they know about the construction and behavior of the index, it exaggerates industrial growth, though apparently less in recent than in earlier years.

There are other factors in addition to the defects in basic statistics that make it difficult to construct meaningful measures of aggregate industrial production. Soviet prices generally do not reflect relative costs of production; the industrial structure has shifted radically over short periods of time; growth rates have differed widely from sector to sector; growth has been interrupted at critical points by major disturbances; and so on. Finally, quantitative growth has not been accompanied by the general improvement in quality that has characterized industrial development in most Western countries.

These considerations make it difficult to summarize Soviet industrial performance in terms of mere numbers. But summaries are useful and necessary, and they cannot be fully qualified at every point without

[1] These brief comments apply to the condition of economic statistics since 1956. Between 1938 and 1956, statistics of physical output of individual industries were not published at all in the Soviet Union, with a few minor exceptions.

turning them into the voluminous reports they are supposed to summarize. In the summary to follow, the necessary qualifications are intended to be implicit throughout, and they should be kept in mind to dull the edge of deceptively sharp figures.

II. Soviet Industrial Growth

GROWTH IN OUTPUT

Soviet industrial output multiplied between five and six times over the period 1913–1955 (see Table 1 and Chart 1).[2] Performance varied widely among sectors, with output multiplying sixteen times in the case of machinery and equipment, nine times in the case of intermediate industrial products, but only three times in the case of consumer goods. The average annual growth rate was 4.2 percent for industry as a whole, 6.8 percent for machinery and equipment, 5.5 percent for intermediate industrial products, and 2.6 percent for consumer goods (see Table 2).

Some of this growth is attributable to the territorial expansion that took place during and after World War II. We have estimated that the acquired territories added about 11 percent to industrial output, and, if we suppose that this relation would also have held true in 1955, the average annual growth rate for all industry over the Soviet period would have to be reduced from 4.2 percent to 3.9 percent to eliminate the effects of territorial expansion. The assumptions underlying such an adjustment are, of course, somewhat arbitrary.

The dispersal of growth trends (unadjusted for territorial expansion) may be seen more clearly by examining a finer breakdown of industries. For a sample of seventy industries, growth rates ranged from an average annual decline of 0.9 percent to an average annual increase of 16.8 percent; the middle half of these growth rates ranged between increases of 2.5 percent and 8.5 percent. The median was 5 percent, which is higher than the weighted average of 4.2 percent shown by the production index. Industries producing consumer goods dominate a distinct lower region of growth and are essentially confined to it, while other industries are concentrated about a higher region.

---

[2] Industry includes manufacturing, mining, logging, fishing, and generating of electricity. For the purpose of this summary, aggregate Soviet output is measured by a comprehensive index based on moving Soviet weights. That index directly covers almost all categories of products except military end items and the more heterogeneous categories of machinery. Alternative indexes using different product coverages, weighting systems, and weight bases give results dispersed about those given by the comprehensive index with moving weights.

TABLE 1: Indexes of Industrial Production for Russia, Soviet Union, and United States: Benchmark Years, 1870−1955 (1913 = 100)

	Total output		Output per person engaged in industry[a]		Output per head of population	
	Russia or Soviet Union[b]	United States	Soviet Union	United States	Russia or Soviet Union	United States
1870	13	12			21	29
1875	17	14			25	30
1880	22	20			36	38
1885	28	23			36	39
1890	38	35			55	54
1895	52	39			59	56
1900	74	50			77	65
1905	72	74			69	91
1910	102	85			61	88
1913	118				99	100
1913	100	100	100	100	100	100
1920	20	125			20	113
1928	102	172	110	149	93	138
1933	150	119	85	139	123	91
1937	258	194	121	158	195	145
1940	265	213	117	169	178	156
1945	119	342			124	234
1950	384	365	138	215	252	232
1955	558	454	167	246	358	264

[a] Persons engaged measured in full-time equivalents.
[b] For 1913, first figure applies to tsarist territory; second, to interwar Soviet territory. Otherwise, current territory. Index covers civilian products only.

The overall growth rate is lower for the Soviet period than for the last forty-odd years of the tsarist period, when the growth rate was 5.3 percent a year according to our index (see Table 2). Although the latter is based on a weak foundation of data and might have come out differently if better data had been available, one may allow for substantial relative overstatement of tsarist growth, presuming all the error in that direction, and still conclude that it was faster than growth over the entire Soviet period. As to individual industries, higher growth rates in the one period are not systematically related with either higher or lower growth rates in the other. Here again, the sample is small, covering only twenty-three industries, and conclusions must therefore be tempered.

There has been a rather striking inverse relation between the rapidity

CHART 1: Industrial Production: Tsarist Russia, Soviet Union, and United States, 1870–1955

Index (1913 = 100)

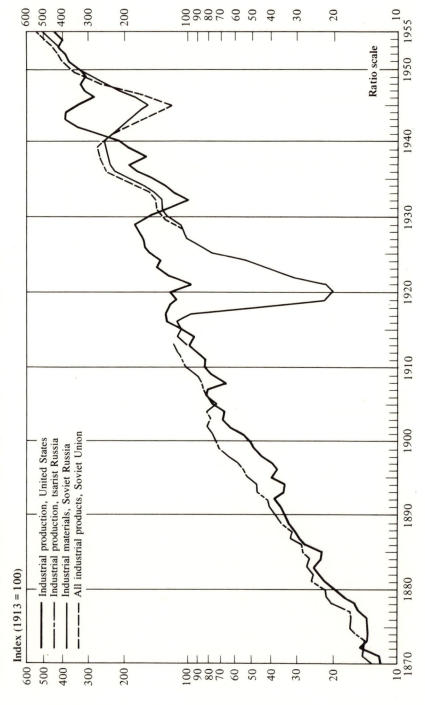

Industrial production, United States
Industrial production, tsarist Russia
Industrial materials, Soviet Russia
All industrial products, Soviet Union

Ratio scale

TABLE 2: Average Annual Growth Rates for Soviet Industry: Output, Labor Productivity, and per Capita Output, Selected Periods (percent)

Period	Industrial materials[a]	All civilian industrial products			
		Total	Intermediate products	Machinery[b]	Consumer goods
		OUTPUT			
1913–1955[c]	4.0	4.2	5.5	6.8	2.6
1913–1928	0.1	0.1	0.5	0.4	−0.2
1928–1955[c]	6.2	6.5	8.4	10.6	4.3
1928–1940[c]	8.0	8.3	11.9	15.7	4.8
1940–1955	4.7	5.1	5.6	6.7	3.7
1928–1937	9.6	10.9	15.0	26.3	5.5
1950–1955	9.6	7.7	9.0	2.6	10.0
		OUTPUT PER PERSON ENGAGED[d]			
1913–1955	1.0	1.2	0.2	1.4	1.2
1913–1928	0.7	0.7	1.4	−0.2	0.3
1928–1955	1.3	1.6	2.7	2.3	1.9
1928–1940	0.2	0.5	3.3	1.7	0.9
1940–1955	2.0	2.4	2.2	3.5	2.5
1928–1937	0.1	1.1	4.8	6.3	1.0
1950–1955	5.4	3.9	5.7	−1.5	5.9
		OUTPUT PER HEAD OF POPULATION			
1913–1955	3.1	3.3	4.6	5.8	1.7
1913–1928	−0.5	−0.5	−0.1	−0.2	−0.8
1928–1955	5.0	5.3	7.2	9.4	3.2
1928–1940	5.6	5.9	9.4	13.1	2.4
1940–1955	4.7	5.1	5.6	6.7	3.7
1928–1937	8.6	9.9	14.0	25.2	4.6
1950–1955	7.2	5.9	7.2	0.9	8.2

[a] Output per person engaged derived by dividing index for industrial materials by index for all persons engaged in industry. That is, for purposes of this calculation, the index of industrial materials is taken to represent an index of total industrial production.

[b] Output does not explicitly cover military end products while employment does. Hence growth in labor productivity is probably understated.

[c] Territorial gains may be approximately excluded from growth rates in the first two columns by subtracting the following percentage points: 1913–1955, 0.3; 1928–1955, 0.4; 1928–1940, 0.9.

[d] Persons engaged measured in full-time equivalents.

of growth in an industry over the Soviet period and its "stage of development" at the beginning of the period. For a sample of forty-eight industries, those whose outputs were smallest relative to the United States in 1913 have shown a strong tendency to grow fastest. The tendency is even more pronounced when the plan period is considered by itself, the stage of development in this case being measured as of 1928 and the growth over 1928–1955. A growth pattern of this sort is to be expected of any country undergoing rapid industrialization, but in the Soviet case the evidence suggests it has been accentuated by planned design, an effort to "overcome and surpass the leading capitalist economies."

Growth has varied widely not only among industries, but also over different spans of time. The early years were marked by external and internal wars, so that measurable industrial output dropped by 80 percent between 1913 and 1920. By 1927 or 1928 industrial output had roughly recovered to its 1913 level in quantitative terms, though a general deterioration in the quality of industrial goods over this period meant that the recovery was less complete. Moreover, it was uneven even if no allowance is made for deterioration in quality: the 1913 level of output was not achieved in the case of consumer goods, while it was somewhat exceeded in the case of all other products.

With the institution of the First Five-Year Plan at the end of 1928, growth accelerated rapidly and generally except in the area of consumer goods. The acceleration continued through the Second Five-Year Plan and extended into consumer goods. Against a background of political purges and partial wartime mobilization, the pace of industrial growth slackened in the succeeding three years of the short-lived Third Five-Year Plan, and such growth as took place may be attributed to territorial expansion. The growth of output over 1937–1940 is understated by our comprehensive index because it does not reflect the partial conversion of certain industries, principally chemicals and machinery, to military-type products. Output of industrial materials grew by 10 percent over this period, while output of all civilian products grew by only 3 percent. By the end of 1940, industrial output stood at about 2.6 times its level in 1913 and 1928; or, if territorial gains are excluded, at about 2.3 times its earlier level.

World War II brought with it a sharp decline in output—offset in large part by Lend-Lease shipments—and heavy losses in manpower and capital. Recovery was swift in the Fourth Five-Year Plan, being aided by collection of reparations and other economic policies in Eastern Europe, so that the prewar level of industrial output was apparently regained by 1948 or 1949. Rapid growth was maintained through the Fifth Five-Year Plan, where our study largely ends. Industrial output multiplied about 2.1 times between 1940 and 1955.

Over the plan period (1928–1955) the average annual rate of growth was 6.5 percent for all industry (6.1 percent if territorial gains are excluded), 8.4 percent for intermediate industrial products, 10.6 percent for machinery, and 4.3 percent for consumer goods. The growth rate has tended to slow down or retard: for all industry, it was 8.3 percent a year over 1928–1940 (7.4 percent if territorial gains are excluded) and 5.1 percent over 1940–1955; or, if the war years are removed from consideration, it was 10.9 percent a year for 1928–1937 and 7.7 percent for 1950–1955. There is a similar retardation in growth for each of the categories of intermediate industrial products, machinery, and consumer goods.

As in other countries, retardation in growth has been general for individual industries, narrowly defined. The available evidence indicates that most industries experienced a slower growth over the Soviet period than over the late tsarist period, and over the later Soviet years than over the earlier ones. Moreover, most of the industries with retardation in growth from the tsarist to the Soviet period also had retardation within the latter.

GROWTH IN OUTPUT AND EMPLOYMENT

The number of persons engaged in Soviet industry, expressed in full-time equivalents, multiplied 3.3 times between 1913 and 1955. Thus, 60 percent of the growth in output may be attributed to expanded employment and 40 percent to increased labor productivity. Put another way, persons engaged increased at an average annual rate of 2.9 percent; labor productivity increased only 1.2 percent, ranging from 0.7 percent a year for construction materials to 4.3 percent a year for electricity.

Growth in labor productivity, as we have measured it, has fluctuated from period to period, but there has been an underlying trend toward acceleration. Employment apparently grew slower than output between 1913 and 1928, 1933 and 1937, 1940 and 1950, and 1950 and 1955; it apparently grew faster between 1928 and 1933 and between 1937 and 1940, both periods of radical structural change in industry. The decline in labor productivity over 1937–1940 is overstated somewhat because growth in output is understated by our comprehensive output index. Chemicals and machinery are probably the major industries for which the decline is overstated. For industry as a whole, labor productivity would be shown as rising slightly if industrial materials were used to measure industrial output. The average annual growth rate in labor productivity rose from 0.7 percent for 1913–1928 to 1.6 percent for 1928–1955; from 0.5 percent for 1928–1940 to 2.4 percent for 1940–1955; and from 1.1 percent for 1928–1937 to 3.9 percent for 1950–1955 (see Table 2).

GROWTH IN OUTPUT AND POPULATION

While industrial employment was multiplying 3.3 times between 1913 and 1955, population multiplied only 1.4 times. Expansion of the industrial labor force has been achieved, particularly in the earlier phase of industrialization, by drawing upon a large supply of under-utilized labor, attached primarily to agriculture. It follows that growth in industrial output has been more rapid per head of population than per worker: 3.3 percent a year as compared with 1.2 percent.

Soviet demographic statistics are sketchy and subject to many doubts, so that it is particularly difficult to say anything with confidence about fluctuations in per capita output. According to Soviet data as modified and interpreted by Western scholars, population within Soviet boundaries grew at an average annual rate of 0.6 percent over 1913–1928, 0.9 percent over 1928–1937, 6.4 percent over 1937–1940 (because of territorial expansion), −0.9 percent over 1940–1950 (because of war and its aftermath), and 1.7 percent over 1950–1955. Despite a rather erratic relationship between growth in population and industrial output over different spans of years, growth rates have tended to move in the same direction for both total and per capita output. Thus the average annual growth in per capita output rose from −0.5 percent over 1913–1928 to 5.3 percent over 1928–1955; within the plan periods, it fell from 5.9 percent over 1928–1940 to 5.1 percent over 1950–1955, or from 9.9 percent over 1928–1937 to 5.9 percent over 1950–1955 (see Table 2). We therefore see a contrast between retarding growth in output per head of population and accelerating growth in output per worker.

III. Industrial Growth Compared: Soviet Union and United States

WHAT TO COMPARE

The Soviet record of industrial growth may be placed in perspective by comparing it with the record of other countries (see Charts 1 and 2). This is not so easy as it might seem, not only because it is difficult to

CHART 2: Industrial Production per Head of Population: Tsarist Russia, Soviet Union, and United States, 1870–1955

Index (1913 = 100)

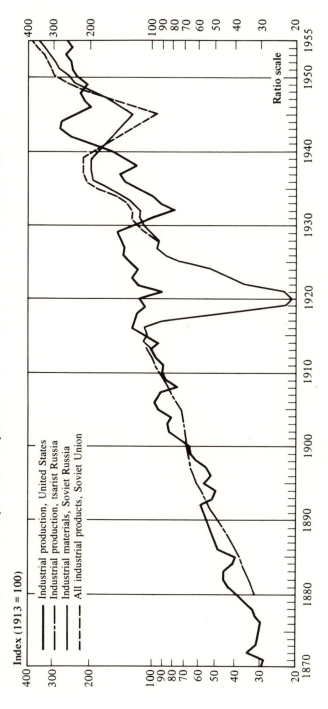

Industrial production, United States
Industrial production, tsarist Russia
Industrial materials, Soviet Russia
All industrial products, Soviet Union

Ratio scale

design relevant comparisons, but also because so little is known about the course of industrial development in most countries. The latter factor alone has forced us, with our limited time and resources, to concentrate on comparisons with the United States, a country with relatively, abundant historical statistics. The United States is an obvious first choice for comparative study in any case, since it presents a striking contrast in economic system while being similar in size and resource endowment. But while comparative study reasonably starts with the United States, it should not end there, and we may hope that others will take up where we have left off.

Comparative study may help us in answering two quite different questions. First, we are interested in knowing, for a variety of reasons associated with the current state of world affairs, which country has shown the more rapid industrial growth over recent years, so that we may have some basis for intelligent guesses about relative growth over the very near future. Second, we are interested in knowing which country has been able to generate the more rapid industrial growth under conditions in which "physical" capacities for growth have been roughly equivalent. Our quest here is for a more fundamental test of the growth-generating efficiency of vastly different economic systems under comparable circumstances, a matter of concern for the longer view.

The first question is obviously easier to deal with than the second, because it requires only a description of the "facts" of growth in the two countries over the same span of years. Of course, the facts are in dispute, and the quantitative evidence of growth is more representative and reliable for the United States than for the Soviet Union. But this problem must always be faced, whether the issues at hand are analytical or purely descriptive. The essential point is that, in making comparisons of concurrent growth trends, we are primarily concerned with what is or has been happening, not with why it is or has been happening. Our attention is focused on trends likely to be carried forward over an immediate future by their own momentum, in the absence of revolutionary change in conditioning factors.

The second question involves a complex problem of analysis that by its nature defies definitive solution. We try to find historical periods in two countries in which important determinants of growth are the same in both cases, while the economic systems differ. To do this we need to know, first, what factors affect growth in what degrees and, second, what periods of history in the two countries are comparable. Neither economic theory nor history blesses our task: theory is mute and history mischievous. At best, the periods chosen will be "comparable" only in some rather crude sense. Even so, the exercise is worth doing, as an early step in the successive approximations that mark the path to knowledge.

If industrial economies do undergo comparable stages of development in some meaningful sense, setting those American and Soviet periods side by side carries with it an important byproduct in addition to direct comparison of growth. It enables us to project Soviet developments into a context with which we are more familiar, and thereby to reason by analogy in directions where direct evidence is lacking. There are also great hazards in reasoning by analogy, but judiciously applied it enriches our knowledge of the likely growth and present status of Soviet industry. Our vision of Soviet industrial growth is clarified by associating it with American developments bracketing the turn of the century, but at the same time the analogy must not be taken too far. The sets of industrial conditions in the two periods abound with anachronisms relative to each other.

CONTEMPORANEOUS GROWTH

Over the same spans of years, industrial output has generally grown faster in the Soviet Union than in the United States (see Table 3 and Chart 1). This seems to be an old story since it was apparently true of the tsarist era as well: according to our indexes, Russian industry grew slightly faster than American industry over the period 1870–1913, the respective average annual rates being 5.3 and 5.1 percent. The differential is similar for the Soviet period as a whole: output grew over 1913–1955 at an average annual rate of 3.9 percent in the Soviet Union, when adjusted to remove territorial gains, as compared with 3.7 percent in the United States. Growth has apparently been faster in the Soviet Union than in the United States for all major sectors of industry except foods, textiles, and related products (see Chart 3).

Over the plan period Soviet growth in percentage terms has outdistanced American growth by a wider margin, making up for a differential in the other direction for the earlier years. American output grew at the same rate over both sets of years—namely, 3.7 percent a year— while the Soviet rate rose from 0.1 percent for the preplan years to 6.1 percent for the plan years, territorial gains excluded. In turn, relative performance has varied within the plan period itself. Over 1928–1940, industrial output grew 7.4 percent a year in the Soviet Union as compared with only 1.8 percent in the United States, reflecting accelerated

TABLE 3: Average Annual Growth Rates for Industry in Tsarist Russia, Soviet Union, and United States: Output, Labor Productivity, and Output per Capita, Selected Concurrent Periods (percent)

	Output		Output per unit of labor			Output per head of population	
				United States			
	Russia or Soviet Union[a]	United States	Soviet Union per person engaged[b]	Per person engaged[b]	Per man-hour	Russia or Soviet Union	United States
1870–1913	5.3	5.1	n.a.	n.a.	n.a.	3.7	2.9
1913–1955	3.9[c]	3.7	1.2	2.2	2.7	3.3	2.4
1913–1928	0.1	3.7	0.7	2.7	3.6	−0.5	2.3
1928–1955	6.1[c]	3.7	1.6	1.9	2.2	5.3	2.5
1928–1940	7.4[c]	1.8	0.5	1.1	2.4	5.9	1.0
1940–1955	5.1	5.2	2.4	2.5	2.0	5.1	3.6
1928–1937	10.9	1.3	1.1	0.7	2.4	9.9	0.5
1950–1955	7.7	4.5	3.9	2.7	2.2	5.9	2.8

n.a.: not available.

[a] For Soviet Union, measured by index for all civilian industrial products.

[b] Persons engaged measured in full-time equivalents.

[c] Adjusted to exclude territorial gains (see Table 2).

activity in the one case and depressed activity in the other. Over 1940–1955, on the other hand, the average annual growth rate was similar in both countries: 5.1 percent in the Soviet Union and 5.2 percent in the United States.

Moving to the recent postwar years 1950–1955, we find the Soviet growth rate of 7.7 percent a year exceeding the American rate of 4.5 percent by a significant margin. A discrepancy in favor of the Soviet Union has persisted through 1958, though the Soviet growth rate has tended to decline somewhat, as far as one can see from the defective published data. It is too early to say whether the decline is permanent or only temporary, whether this reflects a persistent retardation or a temporary fluctuation. It is also too early to say what is happening to the tempo of American industrial growth. In any case, the record for postwar years and for other peacetime years in the plan period suggests that Soviet industrial growth will continue to be more rapid than American growth over the near future.

The picture of comparative growth in output per head of population is much the same as what we have just sketched for total output (see Table 3 and Chart 2). But when we turn to output per unit of labor—or labor productivity—we find something quite different (see Table 3 and

CHART 3: Indexes of Output, Employment, and Labor Productivity by Industrial Groups: Soviet Union, 1913–1955, and United States, 1909–1953

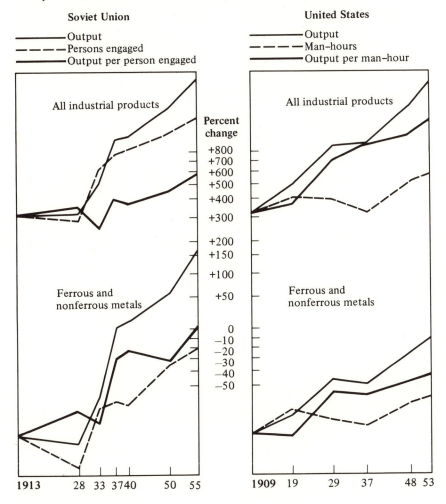

Chart 3). In all but one of the periods covered in our summary of comparative growth trends in output, labor productivity, as we have been able to measure it, grew faster in the United States than in the Soviet Union. This conclusion holds for output per person engaged in industry—the only extensive measure of labor productivity we have for the Soviet Union—and it probably holds for output per man-hour, since average hours of work did not change significantly in the Soviet Union, at least between 1928 and 1955.

CHART 3 (continued)

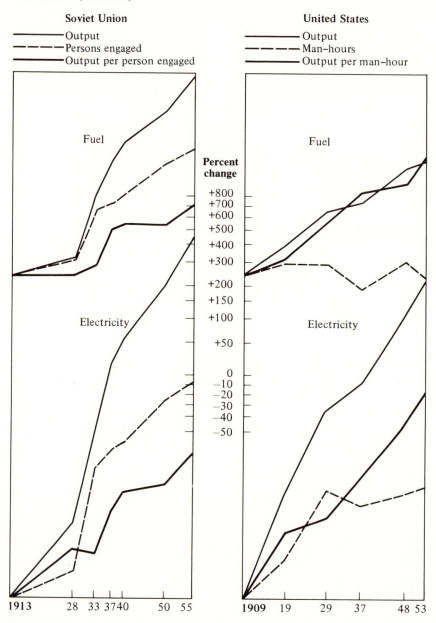

Soviet Union
— Output
--- Persons engaged
— Output per person engaged

United States
— Output
--- Man-hours
— Output per man-hour

In the United States, growth in industrial output has come mainly from improved labor productivity: over 1913–1955, output multiplied 4.5 times while employment multiplied only 1.8 times and man-hours

CHART 3 (continued)

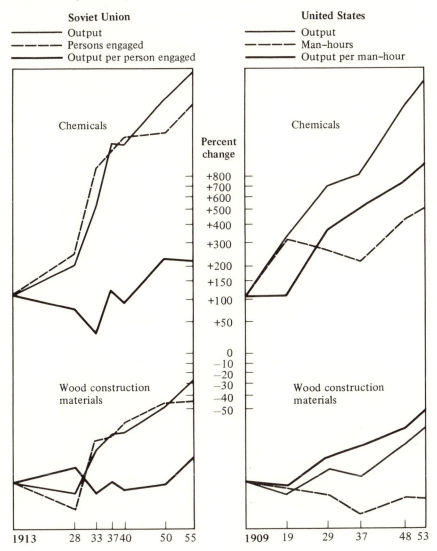

only 1.5 times. In the Soviet Union, on the other hand, growth in output has come mainly from expanded employment, as we have seen. The contrast is sharp: improved labor productivity accounted for 67 percent of the growth in output in the United States, but for only 40 percent in the Soviet Union. Labor productivity grew at 2.2 percent a year in the United States (2.7 percent based on man-hours) as contrasted with 1.2 percent in the Soviet Union.

CHART 3 (continued)

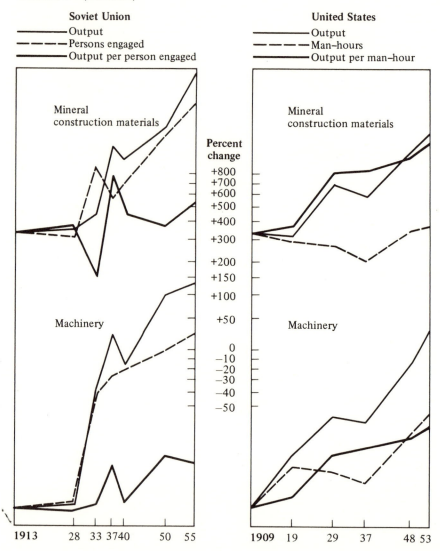

We should immediately note, however, that this conclusion applies to a long period of time and that growth in labor productivity seems to be drifting in opposite directions in the two countries, a development that could reverse the relations so far observed. The one period in which labor productivity grew faster in Soviet industry is the most recent covered by our study: 1950–1955. This is indicative of a broader

CHART 3   (concluded)

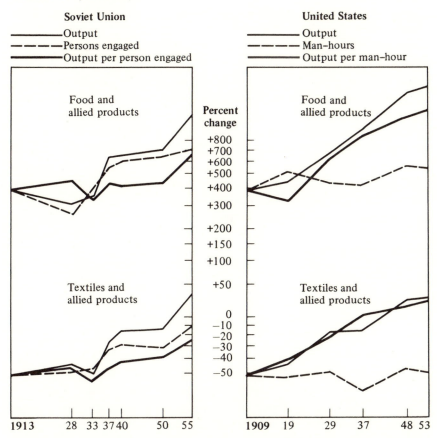

Soviet Union
—————Output
— — — —Persons engaged
—————Output per person engaged

United States
————— Output
— — — — Man–hours
————— Output per man–hour

phenomenon: growth in industrial labor productivity has been accelerating in the Soviet Union, but retarding in the United States.

The comparisons so far have been based on various indexes com-
puted directly for each country, and they can be roughly checked by
another, essentially independent set of estimates that, at the same time,
reveals some interesting information of its own. Evaluating Soviet
output of industrial materials in current American prices and adjusting
the figure to cover the whole of industry, we may estimate industrial
production in the Soviet Union as a fraction of the level in the United
States in 1913, 1928, and 1955. The estimates represent only rough
orders of magnitude; constructed in different ways and with better data,
they might vary as much as 10 percent, possibly more, in either direction. For example, American products are generally of better quality
than Russian counterparts, and the differential has tended to widen over

the Soviet period, except in special cases of machinery and ordnance. Yet both American and Soviet products are evaluated at the same prices, thus overstating Soviet production. Similarly, output of Soviet products tends to be overstated in official statistics. Other errors of unknown direction are introduced by estimating procedures. Despite such shortcomings, these estimates cannot be dismissed as inherently worse than other summary indexes calculated for the Soviet Union.

According to these estimates, Soviet industrial output rose from 15 percent of the American level in 1913 to 23 percent in 1955; similarly, output per head of population rose from 11 percent to 19 percent (see Table 4). On the other hand, output per worker fell from 25 percent to 21 percent, and output per man-hour from 23 percent to 18 percent. These findings are generally consistent with our more direct calculations, indicating that industrial output and output per capita grew faster in the Soviet Union than in the United States, while labor productivity grew more slowly.

At the same time, these estimates imply more rapid growth for Soviet industry than our direct indexes. In the case of total output, Soviet growth is indicated as 49 percent faster than American growth over 1913–1955; in the case of per capita output, 77 percent faster. Hence, if we calculate Soviet growth indirectly on the basis of the American production index, Soviet output is indicated as multiplying 6.8 times (6.1 times excluding territorial gains) and per capita output, 4.6 times.[3] By direct calculations, the two multiples are 5.6 (5.0 excluding territorial gains) and 3.9, respectively. Put alternatively, output is shown as growing at 4.7 percent a year when calculated indirectly as compared with 4.2 percent when calculated directly; excluding territorial gains, the two rates are 4.4 percent and 3.9 percent. Similarly, growth in per capita output is 3.7 percent a year when calculated indirectly, but 3.3 percent when calculated directly; growth in output per worker, 1.7 percent when calculated indirectly, but 1.2 percent when calculated directly.

We may pause here to note that our figures on the recent size of industry in the Soviet Union relative to the United States are rather lower than conventional Western estimates, which seem to place Soviet industrial output in 1955 at about 33 percent of the American level.[4] If

---

[3] Our index of industrial production in the United States is 454 for 1955 with 1913 = 100; on a per capita basis, 264 (see Table 1). The Soviet indexes calculated indirectly are taken as 149 percent and 176 percent of the respective American indexes.

[4] See, e.g., U.S., Congress, Joint Economic Committee, *Soviet Economic Growth: A Comparison with the United States,* 85th Cong., 1st sess., 1957, p. 11.

TABLE 4: Relative Value Added and Labor Productivity of Industry: Soviet Union as a Percentage of United States, 1913, 1928, 1955

	1913	1928	1955
Value added of industry[a]	15.2	8.8	22.7
Persons engaged[b]	60.8	48.7	109.6
Man-hours	64.7	53.1	129.2
Value added per person engaged	25.0	18.1	20.7
Value added per man-hour	23.4	16.6	17.6
Value added per head of population	10.8	7.0	19.1

[a] Evaluated in 1914 U.S. prices for 1913, 1929 U.S. prices for 1928, and 1954 U.S. prices for 1955.

[b] Measured in full-time equivalents.

there is no dispute over the relative size of Soviet industry in 1913, the conventional view implies that Soviet industrial output multiplied some ten times between 1913 and 1955, which would mean a growth rate of 5.6 percent a year on the average, substantially higher than the rate of 4.2 percent found in our study.

The industrial distribution of employment (Table 5) is the only information we have for comparing the changing structure of industry in the two countries. In both countries, the share of employment in the so-called heavy industries, particularly machinery and allied products, has been growing at the expense of the share in food processing and textiles and apparel. However, consumer durables account for a much larger fraction of machinery and equipment in the United States than in the Soviet Union. In the mid-1950s, the following major industrial groups accounted for a larger fraction of persons engaged in Soviet industry than in American industry: fuel, wood construction products, mineral construction products, and food and allied products. The following groups accounted for a smaller fraction: ferrous and nonferrous metals, electricity, chemicals, machinery and allied products, and textiles and allied products.[5]

---

[5] Employment in production of military products is included under machinery and equipment in the case of the Soviet Union and under both that category and metal products in the case of the United States. The relative importance of military production in the two countries has not been discussed in this paper because of the formidable difficulties in making estimates for the Soviet Union. By a very roundabout procedure, I have estimated that the value of Soviet military production (excluding atomic energy) in 1955 was about 42 billion rubles, or about $6 billion to $10 billion. The value of American production was around $13 billion in the same year (U.S., Department of Commerce, Bureau of the Census, *Statistical Abstract of the United States: 1958,* Washington, D.C.: Government Printing Office, 1958, p. 242).

TABLE 5: Percentage Distribution of Persons Engaged by Major Industrial Groups: Soviet Union and United States, Benchmark Years[a]

	Soviet Union[b]						United States[c]				
	1913	1927/28	1933	1937	1950	1955	1909	1929	1937	1948	1953
Ferrous and nonferrous metals	7.4	5.3	5.8	5.3	6.3	6.0	7.9	7.8	8.6	7.8	7.6
Fuel	5.5	7.6	7.3	6.3	8.0	8.0	10.2	9.1	8.4	6.8	5.3
Electricity	0.3	0.5	1.0	1.1	1.5	1.6	0.9	2.9	2.8	2.2	2.2
Chemicals	1.2	1.9	2.8	3.0	2.8	3.3	3.2	4.9	5.0	5.8	5.9
Wood construction materials[d]	18.7	14.6	18.2	16.5	17.8	15.3	13.3	9.6	8.4	7.3	6.6
Mineral construction materials	4.0	4.2	5.3	3.0	5.1	6.2	6.5	4.6	4.2	4.5	4.2
Machinery and allied products	12.0	14.2	28.4	30.3	31.5	32.4	21.1	27.8	28.0	35.3	41.5
Machinery and equipment	(5.1)	(7.4)	(8.2)		(16.1)[e]		(12.4)	(19.0)	(19.3)	(25.1)	(29.8)
Metal products[f]	(5.4)	(5.2)	(4.3)		(12.4)[e]		(8.7)	(8.8)	(8.7)	(10.2)	(11.7)
Repair shops[g]	(1.5)	(1.6)	(15.9)		(3.0)[e]		n.a.	n.a.	n.a.	n.a.	n.a.
Food and allied products	18.7	15.2	11.1	12.6	10.4	9.5	10.7	9.8	10.8	9.7	8.8
Textiles and allied products[h]	32.2	36.4	20.2	21.9	16.5	17.7	26.2	23.5	23.8	20.6	17.9
Total	100.0	99.9	100.1	100.0	99.9	100.0	100.0	100.0	100.0	100.0	100.0

n.a.: not applicable.

[a] Omits printing and publishing industries. Persons engaged measured in full-time equivalents.

[b] Breakdown for 1937–1955 applies to production workers only.

[c] Based on unpublished data of John W. Kendrick.

[d] For Soviet Union, includes paper and paper products.

[e] Broken down by percentage distribution implied by official Soviet data on gross production (*Promyshlennost SSSR* [Industry of the USSR], Moscow, 1957, p. 203).

[f] For the United States, includes ordnance in the narrow sense; other military products are covered by machinery and equipment. For the Soviet Union, all military products except ammunition and explosives seem to be covered by machinery and equipment.

[g] Repair shops are not covered by U.S. industry. They cannot be eliminated from Soviet data from 1937 onward.

[h] For the Soviet Union, includes furniture from 1937 onward.

"COMPARABLE" GROWTH

Once industrialization has gotten underway in a country, the pace of industrial growth at any moment would seem to depend on the resource potential, the state of industrial arts, the prevailing level of industrial output (i.e., the extent to which potential is being utilized), and that catchall, the economic system. The process of economic growth is mysteriously complex and cannot be summarized in these brief comments. But this is not the place to discuss the manifold preconditions and environmental factors essential for sustained economic growth. We take it for granted that industrialization and the accompanying process of growth are a fact in the Soviet Union, just as they were, more incipiently, in tsarist Russia. We are therefore concerned here only with the more fundamental conditioning factors, making that growth faster or slower than it would otherwise be. As far as such things can be quantified, the larger the resource potential, the more advanced the technology, and the smaller the output, the more rapid the growth in output will be, given the economic system. None of these factors can be clearly defined, but they can all be represented by certain more or less adequate indicators. Our immediate problem is to find indicators that will allow us to select periods in Soviet and American industrial history that are comparable except with respect to economic system.

What is a good indicator of resource potential? If we may judge from the general practice of comparing economies in per capita terms, it would seem that population is typically used as the indicator of resource potential. But it is often a poor indicator since populations grow in response to economic development and differently in different economies. Moreover and more importantly, population can grow from immigration as well as from natural increase. As a concrete example for the problem at hand, in the United States the expanding industrial labor force in the latter part of the nineteenth century was recruited in important measure from economically underutilized population in other countries, including Russia.[6] The expansion in the Soviet Union during the twentieth century came, on the other hand, from the large internal pool of underutilized population. Hence, as compared with the Soviet Union, population understates the resource potential of the nineteenth century United States.

[6] The foreign born accounted for about 18 percent of the net increase in total gainfully occupied population or labor force over 1870–1900. See Simon Kuznets and Ernest Rubin, *Immigration and Foreign Born*, Occasional Paper 46 (New York: National Bureau of Economic Research, 1954), p. 46.

The resource potential of an economy is more adequately described by the volume of natural resources at its disposal, including climate and terrain. If this can be precisely and accurately measured, it remains to be done. In the meantime, we are perhaps justified in making the impressionistic judgment that the Soviet Union and the United States have roughly similar resource potentials. Both countries are rich in natural resources, though the endowments of specific resources obviously differ. Against the larger size of the Soviet Union must be offset the substantial climatic and topographical disadvantages—at least in the present state of civilization. Although in total area the Soviet Union is about one and a half times larger than the United States, in inhabitable area it is probably no larger at all. Other relevant things the same—like tastes, technology, population, economic system, and so on—we suppose that the two countries would be able to support roughly equivalent levels of industrial production on the basis of resource endowments.

This leads us to suppose further that, if the state of industrial arts and the aggregate level of industrial output were the same in the two countries, differences in the rate of growth of industrial output should be attributable to differences in economic systems. Unfortunately, we cannot standardize both level of output and state of technology simultaneously in the two countries. To find dates at which output was roughly equivalent, one must go back a number of years in American history. Thus, as we shall see, the level of Russian output in 1913 within the interwar Soviet territory was reached in the United States around 1885 or earlier. But the state of industrial arts—at least the available body of technology—was less advanced in the United States of 1885 than in the Russia of 1913; the same body of technical knowledge, if not skills, has been available to the two countries at roughly the same dates in history. Therefore, when we standardize the level of output from which growth starts—as we are about to do—any difference that we observe between growth rates in the two countries must be attributed to differences in both technology and economic system. While the effects of each cannot be fully isolated, we can at least say in whose favor difference in technologies operates and thereby narrow the range of ignorance.

These remarks make the issues seem simpler than they are, because they presuppose that the periods to be compared represent normal times. This is, of course, not so for the Soviet Union, unless we view periodic disasters as a part of normal times there. Since the founding of the Soviet Union, no span of years longer than a decade has been free from major disturbances or recoveries from them. As we have emphasized before, we cannot possibly know which period has had a growth rate similar to what would be expected from a long stretch of normal years, and we must therefore choose several Soviet periods, representing differing circumstances, in making comparisons with American industrial growth.

Subject to the outlined qualifications, a Soviet period would have as its counterpart an American period whose terminal years had the same total industrial output, unadjusted for differences in population, as obtained in the Soviet Union in 1913 and 1955, or whatever years we might wish to choose. If industrial output is measured by weighted aggregates, the Soviet periods 1913–1955 and 1928–1955 are "comparable" with the American period 1877–1913; that is, for both countries industrial output started and ended at roughly the same levels within these periods, insofar as we are justified in making such broad intertemporal and international comparisons.[7] If output is measured by the median performance of a large group of individual industries, the Soviet periods are comparable to the American period 1885–1920. The dating of these periods implies that it took only thirty-four or thirty-five years in the United States to register the growth made over forty-two years in the Soviet Union—or, if the preplan years are ignored, over twenty-seven years.

We must remind ourselves that these periods are comparable only with respect to two of the factors influencing rate of growth: resource potential and prevailing level of industrial output. They are not comparable with respect to the state of the industrial arts. The advantage—a substantial one—is in favor of the Soviet Union, since it has had the technology of the twentieth century at its disposal in working out its industrialization. One can only dream about what difference it would have made to American industrial growth in the nineteenth century if it had proceeded under twentieth century technology.

The choice of comparable stages of development in the industries of the Soviet Union and the United States is, therefore, unavoidably hazy and arbitrary to some degree. We shall summarize here the records of industrial growth in the Soviet Union and the United States over periods

[7] The American dates are derived as follows: Soviet industrial output was 15 percent of the American level in 1913. Looking back into American industrial history, we find that output in 1877 was also around 15 percent of the level of 1913. A similar procedure gives the American date 1913 as roughly equivalent, in level of output, to the Soviet date 1955.

of equal length that are comparable in the sense that the beginning year in each case represents roughly the same level of output in the two countries.

We start with the longest period studied for the Soviet Union, 1913 –1955. The growth rate over this period—3.9 percent a year, excluding gains from territorial expansion—is slower than the rate for a comparable American period: 5.0 percent a year over 1877 –1919 or 4.8 percent over 1885 –1927 (see Table 6). On a per capita basis, the Soviet growth rate is higher: 3.3 percent a year as compared with 3.0 percent. But we must recall the misleading nature of comparisons of per capita rates, in view of the fact that population growth overstates growth in resource potential in the United States as compared with the Soviet Union.[8] For lack of data in both countries, we cannot compare growth in labor productivity.

If we turn to the plan period, 1928 –1955, we observe that the Soviet growth rate, again adjusted to exclude territorial gains, is higher than for a comparable American period: 6.1 percent a year as compared with 5.6 percent over 1877 –1904 and 5.3 percent over 1885 –1912. The difference in per capita rates is even larger in favor of the Soviet Union. We therefore do not observe comparable American periods in which the speed of industrial growth has matched that during the plan period in the Soviet Union.

For the shorter spurts of growth, the Soviet performance also seems to have the edge, although not so clearly. The Soviet growth rate over 1928 –1940 is almost matched by the American rate over 1877 –1889, but it exceeds by a wide margin the American rate over 1885 –1897. In a sense, this period of Soviet growth may be likened to the twelve years in the United States following the Great Depression; in both cases, growth was beginning again after a decade of depression and stagnation. The Soviet rate is faster in this comparison as well: 7.4 percent a year as compared with 6.3 percent.

We conclude this summary of growth over comparable periods on an exceptional note: Soviet industrial growth over 1950 –1955 may have been a bit slower than American growth over 1908 –1913. The point of

---

[8] If population were taken as a guide to industrial potential, we might identify as comparable "stages of development" those periods in which industrial output per head of population was the same in both countries. This procedure is not only difficult to justify for reasons just stated, but it is also impossible to apply. The Soviet level of industrial output per capita in 1955 corresponds roughly with the American level in 1887; the Soviet level in 1913 was lower than the American level in 1860, the earliest year for which aggregate industrial output can be calculated. Similar results are found by taking the median dates at which per capita output of a large group of industries was the same in both countries.

TABLE 6: Average Annual Growth Rates for Industry in Soviet Union and United States: Output and Output per Capita, Selected "Comparable" Periods[a]

Period for Soviet Union	Output		Output per head of population		Period for United States
	Soviet Union	United States	Soviet Union	United States	
1913–1955	3.9[b]	5.0	3.3	3.0	1877–1919
		4.8		3.0	1885–1927
1928–1955	6.1[b]	5.6	5.3	3.5	1877–1904
		5.3		3.3	1885–1912
1928–1940	7.4[b]	7.0	5.9	4.7	1877–1889
		4.5		2.6	1885–1897
		6.3		4.8	1939–1951
1950–1955	7.7	8.0	5.9	5.9	1908–1913

[a] Periods are comparable for growth in output only, not output per capita. See text.
[b] Adjusted to exclude territorial gains.

this is that it proves nothing. The experience of a five-year period, plucked from history, carries no permanent message with it.

IV. Some Tentative Observations

What can be said about Soviet industrial achievements? In the first place, they have been impressive. In terms of its ability to generate sheer growth in industrial output—leaving aside the question of how much the growth has cost, what product mix has evolved, and how the products have been put to use—the Soviet system of centralized direction has proved itself to be more or less the peer of the market economy, as exemplified by the United States. This much seems beyond dispute even in the face of the questionable reliability of Soviet statistics.

Of course, the character of Soviet industrial growth has not been the same as in other Western economies. Enhancement of state power has been the primary objective, the consumer being treated essentially as a residual claimant. Investment goods and ordnance have been emphasized at the expense of consumer goods; and other important sectors of the economy—agriculture, construction, and consumer services—have been relatively neglected to help foster industrial expansion. At times, large groups of the population have been sacrificed or made to work in forced labor to promote internal economic policies. Leisure has shown little tendency to grow. This is all well known but deserves repetition to place Soviet industrial achievements in perspective. The character of industrial growth being so different from elsewhere in the

West, there is a sense in which the two sets of achievements cannot be compared at all.

The last point should be underlined: the pattern of industrial growth observed in the Soviet Union would never be duplicated by a market economy. Sovereign consumers would not choose the paths of growth chosen by Soviet rulers. This raises the awkward question of whether a highly generalized measure of growth has much meaning even as an indicator of expansion in productive capacity available for whatever use it may be put to. It can be demonstrated that measures of economic growth, as they are conventionally made in the form of index numbers, depend in fact on the path of growth—on the uses to which productive capacity is put.[9] If we bowed to the stern dictates of logic, we would be able to compare Soviet and American industrial growth only if both economies served either consumer welfare or state power. But that is ruled out by the very difference in social order whose influence on growth we wish to assess. This dilemma can be mastered only by admitting it—by avoiding the delusion that there is some single-dimensioned, neutral measure of growth, equally meaningful for all types of economies.

The question of economic waste is a related matter and equally difficult to treat. Growth is measured in terms of things "produced," not in terms of things usefully consumed. In a market economy, the two magnitudes are similar but not at all identical: mistakes are made by both entrepreneurs and consumers, rendering some productive activities worthless. The same kinds of mistakes are made in the Soviet Union, probably on a larger scale since centralized planning is involved. In addition, because of the weak position of most buyers, substandard goods often pass for standard quality, goods are damaged and spoiled in transit beyond normal experience in a market economy, and so on. Although Soviet industry does not experience business cycles as they are known in market economies, it is periodically faced with the need to reallocate resources on a large scale, and the accompanying waste that would appear in the form of temporarily unemployed resources in a market economy will appear, at least in part, in the form of unwanted accumulation of inventories. It is difficult enough to say something sensible about which type of economy has the more waste inherent in it. It is even more difficult to say what all this has to do with problems of measuring growth. Unless wastage has, in

---

[9] See, e.g., my article, "On Measuring Economic Growth," *Journal of Political Economy* 65 (February 1957): 51.

some meaningful sense, been growing at different rates in American and Soviet industry, there is nothing to be gained by taking account of this factor as far as comparing growth of industrial output is concerned.

These qualifications serve as warnings against careless comparisons of either the relative size or the relative growth of Soviet and American industry. In particular, broad aggregative measures of industrial output tell us nothing about capacities for specific tasks, such as waging war or promoting consumer welfare. While Soviet industrial output in 1955 may have been, in the aggregate, less than a quarter of the American level, production directly available for military purposes was undoubtedly a larger fraction, and production available for consumers a smaller one. Similarly, growth in the two areas has differed in the same way in the two countries.

It remains also to be noted that the quantitative achievements of Soviet industry have not been understated by Soviet authorities. The official Soviet index of industrial production embodies a myth that should be dispelled from the popular mind. On this matter, Western scholars speak as one, though they may disagree as to the gravity of the myth. The official Soviet index shows industrial output as multiplying twenty-seven times between 1913 and 1955; the indexes presented here, based on official Soviet data on physical output and unit values and constructed according to conventional Western methods, show output as multiplying five to six times. If our indexes are taken as reasonably accurate, the official index contains a four- to fivefold exaggeration of growth over this period.

Somewhere in these generalizations and the mass of figures behind them lie lessons of history. The trick is to find them. The interesting lessons point to the future in one way or another, for the main purpose of history is as prologue: to help us foresee what is likely to come if things continue developing as they have been; or barring that—and it generally will be barred—at least to help us to understand why things are happening as they are.

My task is largely finished in providing the stuff from which the lessons will be drawn. But I cannot evade the responsibility for stating some opinions. And so I venture with great hesitation into the field of lesson drawing, leaving it quickly once my minimal obligation is fulfilled.

As one looks to the immediate future—the next five years, say—it seems reasonably certain that industrial growth will proceed more rapidly in the Soviet Union than in the United States, in the absence of radical institutional changes in either country. This conclusion does not seem to be in doubt even when all due allowance is made for the shortcomings of Soviet data. It is more doubtful that industrial growth in the Soviet Union will be faster than in other rapidly expanding economies, such as Western Germany, France, and Japan.

Over the more distant future—the next generation, say—the outlook is veiled, even if we might suppose there would be no important changes in the economic systems of either West or East, a most improbable assumption. There is no definitive evidence that the Soviet economic system has been able to generate more rapid industrial growth over the long run than the traditional private enterprise system of the West. Despite the fact that the Soviet Union was able to inherit an advanced Western technology at little cost, industrial growth over the entire Soviet period has been less rapid than in the United States over the forty years bracketing the turn of the century, a period more or less comparable in other important respects. It has also been less rapid than growth in the last half century of the tsarist era, a less comparable period.

On the other hand, if Soviet performance is best illustrated by achievements over the plan period, the Soviet record of industrial growth appears more exceptional. Which period is more representative of long-run growth trends: 1913–1955 or 1928–1955? There are good arguments to be made for both, and inevitable differences of opinion will be finally resolved by the course of history alone—which suggests the virtue of avoiding a dogmatic position one way or another.

In any case, the future will not be a simple reflection of the past. Growth has not been a mechanical process in either the United States or the Soviet Union. The driving force within the American economy has been private initiative mobilized by the incentives inherent in a free society. The trend of the day is in the direction of choking off incentives. One foreboding economic symptom is the slackening speed at which resource productivity has been growing in American industry. Incentives are being strangled and nothing is being put in their place to drive the machinery of growth. There is in fact only one thing to put in their place: the whiplash. The Soviet system has made clever use of both knout and honey, and the latter has been rapidly supplanting the former. If this evolution continues, the balance of economic growth will surely tip further in Russia's favor, since—fortunately, from the broader point of view—the West does not intend to take whip in hand.

18

The Soviet Stir:
Economic Crisis
and Response

The Soviet economy is passing through a time of troubles. The world has been made aware of this by the recent crop failure, but the troubles are more broadly and deeply rooted than this event might suggest by itself. They derive from growing pains intensified by accelerating obsolescence of the Soviet economic system and by excesses and neglects of policies over the years.

Under the best of circumstances the rate of growth should be expected to drift downward as an expanding economy matures. History shows few persistent exceptions to this rule, and the Soviet Union is not among them. In the case of industrial production, for example, the Soviet growth rate was slower in the postwar decade of the fifties than in the interwar decade of the first two five-year plans, slower in the second half of the fifties than in the first half, and slower so far in the sixties than in the second half of the fifties. In the last few years the annual growth rate has moved very close to the compound annual rate for the entire period since 1913, years of war and internal turbulence

This essay, which was originally written in 1964 as a contribution to the commemorative volume for Karl Wittfogel and was read at the meetings of the Mont Pelerin Society in September 1965, is reprinted from G. L. Ulmen, ed., *Society and History* (The Hague: Mouton, 1978), pp. 483–89. It closely resembles testimony given on February 18, 1964, to the House Committee on Foreign Affairs and reproduced in U.S., Congress, *Recent Developments in the Soviet Bloc: Hearings,* 88th Cong., 2d sess., 1964, pt. 2, pp. 179–85.

included. Finally, the rate is lower for the Soviet period as a whole than for the last half century of tsarist rule. A pattern similar to this is also traced out by intercity freight traffic.

Agricultural production has, on the other hand, behaved differently, growing faster in the postwar than in the interwar years. But this has been an abnormal and transitory development, reflecting the once-for-all plowing up of the virgin lands in the fifties. Peak agricultural production was probably reached in 1958, a year of exceptionally favorable weather. The rough plateau since then has now been broken by the serious crop failure of 1963, and it seems virtually certain that the future holds little prospect for sustained rapid growth. The virgin lands program of extensive cultivation, for example, has been essentially replaced by a crash program of intensive cultivation based on fertilizer and irrigation, an expedient unlikely to provide a tolerable solution to the basic agricultural problem in either the short or the long run.

Because the abnormal acceleration in agricultural growth temporarily offset deceleration elsewhere, the total product of the economy grew at an annual rate fluctuating around 6 percent in the fifties without any discernible trend one way or the other, and those who kept their eyes fixed on the overall rate lost sight of what was really happening. They even missed the significance of the drop in that rate to around 4 percent when agricultural expansion ran out of steam after 1958. It took the crop failure of 1963 to awaken most Western analysts to the weakening tempo of Soviet economic growth. Newspaper headlines announced to suprised readers in the United States and elsewhere that the Central Intelligence Agency had suddenly discovered a precipitous drop in the Soviet growth rate. This drop was quickly interpreted as evidence of a permanent slowdown.

By way of digression, it is interesting to look back at what this agency, along with so many other experts on the Soviet economy, had been saying earlier—and to see why the public was understandably shocked by the sharp change in opinion. When the American economy was in the midst of a recession in the spring of 1958, the director of the Central Intelligence Agency, Mr. Allen Dulles, gave a major public address in which he said:

> . . . the Soviet economy has been growing, and is expected to continue to grow through 1962, at a rate roughly twice that of the economy of the United States. Annual growth over-all has been running between 6 and 7 per cent, annual growth of industry between 10 and 12 per cent.

These rates of growth are exceedingly high. They have rarely been matched in other states except during limited periods of post-war rebuilding.[1]

Eighteen months later, in testimony before the Joint Economic Committee of the Congress, he estimated that "Soviet GNP will grow at the rate of 6 percent a year through 1965" and that "the Soviets will continue to grow industrially by 8 or 9 percent a year."[2] The message he left with the legislators was clear: unless something were done to speed up American growth dramatically, "the gap between our two economies by 1970 will be dangerously narrowed."[3]

These forecasts, as it turned out, were not entirely accurate. They had little basis at the time and less as the years went by. Why they were made in the first place would make an interesting chapter in the intellectual history of our times, but we must resist the temptation to dwell on that question here.

However all that might be, the Soviet economy has slowed down in its pace of growth while the ambitions of Soviet leaders remain undiminished. This is enough by itself to generate a crisis. The economy seems to have grown weary in the race for sheer growth and power, and it has to catch its wind before it can move ahead again. Costly attention must now be paid to the basic health of the economy, so long neglected.

It is in the nature of a highly centralized economy, particularly when driven by rulers with a mania for power, to make headway quickly by concentrating on easy tasks and neglecting difficult ones. Such a policy may work in the short run, but eventually the bill has to be paid, and it turns out to be bigger than it would have been if problems had been attended to as they arose. If critical tasks are neglected solely because they are hard to handle, problems gradually pile up until the system becomes overburdened.

In the Soviet case, industrialization has been pressed forward at the neglect of virtually everything else, including those parts of industry that would not have an impact on growth and power. Investment goods have been poured into areas that would yield more investment goods— steel has been used to produce more steel, and so on. In addition, swords have displaced plowshares. Housing, transportation, agricul-

---

[1] *New York Times,* Apr. 29, 1958, p. 8.

[2] U.S., Congress, Joint Economic Committee, *Comparisons of the United States and Soviet Economies: Hearings,* 86th Cong., 1st sess., November 13, 1959, p. 9.

[3] Ibid., p. 11.

ture, service trades, and light industry have been left to stagger along on scraps tossed to them from time to time.

A system too inefficient and inflexible to manage problems in an orderly sequence now faces the danger of breaking down under the cumulating weight of problems too long postponed. It is no longer merely a question of allocating resources and adapting the economy to rapidly changing conditions, basic tasks of growing complexity in themselves. It is also a question of providing a mechanism that will automatically generate progress and innovation over broad areas of the economy. That task, too, has been neglected because it has been easier to ride on the coattails of path-breaking economies. In brief, Soviet methods of economic organization have reached an advanced stage of obsolescence.

The manner in which a crisis has developed in recent years can be illustrated by tracing through the strains put on the economy by an expansionary military program coupled with a degenerating agricultural situation.

Military production had been sharply curtailed immediately after World War II as part of the general program of demobilization and reconstruction of the civilian economy. With the onset of the Korean War military production climbed rapidly upward, reaching a peak in 1953 and fluctuating down and up over the next three years as the new regime established itself in the wake of Stalin's death. Another cutback apparently took place in 1956 and 1957, most likely to accommodate to new economic policies forced by the Polish and Hungarian uprisings.

But the zig was soon followed by a sharper zag. Having weathered the storm in the satellite countries and having scored a great propaganda victory with the first satellite in space, Soviet leaders pressed ahead in 1958 and 1959 with a massive expansion in the output of military and space products, shifting a large volume of resources from investment and other uses. In the classical pattern for Soviet industrial mobilization, production of agricultural machinery was cut by 20 percent in 1958 and by an additional 15 percent in 1959, an action not destined to ease the smoldering agricultural crisis. Annual growth in civilian production as a whole was cut in half, falling from almost 10 percent in 1957 to around 5 percent in each succeeding year. Military production has continued to rise at a lessened pace over the last four years.

In the initial phase of the military-space buildup, Khrushchev might well have deluded himself into believing that he could borrow resources from agriculture without serious consequences. He was, in fact, so confident that he boasted of overtaking and surpassing the United States in per capita output of meat and milk within two or three years, while at the same time cutting the average workweek of the Soviet worker. Nature had smiled on the Soviet Union in 1958, bringing the most favorable weather and the most bountiful harvest of the century.

But nature was not long in exacting her price: winters became longer, more changeable, and more severe; droughts alternated in east and west and eventually struck simultaneously in both regions. Unfavorable weather now allied itself with bad management, inadequate investment, misdirection from the center, poor farming practices, and the general inefficiency of the agricultural system to impose a heavy toll. The agricultural problem rapidly deteriorated into a crisis culminating in the disastrous failure of the wheat crop in 1963.

As difficulties mounted on the farms, the Soviet leadership reversed the cutback in agricultural investment. Output of agricultural machinery was raised substantially in 1960 and even more in succeeding years, reaching its 1957 level once again in 1962. Far from bearing some of the military-space burden, the staggering agriculture sector piled a burden of its own on the economy. In the face of a cut in the workweek, industrial growth now had to suffer across the board despite undoubted efforts to confine effects to the consumer sector: growth in output was cut in the case of food and clothing and came to a virtual halt in the case of consumer durables. The growth rate for fuel and electricity, needed to turn the wheels of industry, fell from around 10 percent in 1958 to 7 percent in 1959 and 6 percent the next three years, rising only in 1963 to 8 percent. The fall was more precipitous in the case of construction materials, needed to maintain investment: the growth rate fell from 10 percent in 1958 to 1 percent in 1961, rising slightly thereafter. Industrial investment began paying some of the price of sustaining the military and agricultural programs, a payment increased in 1963 by the crash program of large-scale investment in chemical fertilizer and irrigation. It is no wonder that the compound annual rate of industrial growth dropped from around 7.5 percent for 1955–1960 to around 5.5 percent for 1960–1963, according to my calculations.

From this brief recital of recent difficulties, it is clear that Soviet leaders are being confronted with tough choices. Their major goal remains what it has always been: to enhance Soviet power—and, along with it, their own power. Again, as always, they must balance off policies to get the best mixture of short-run power, long-run power, and rising living standards. Since all three are interrelated, the job is not simple. It is made worse by the present economic crisis coupled with the Sino-Soviet rift.

Until recently, the normal response would have been to take as much as possible away from consumers and satellite countries in order to provide maximum relief from other pressures. Neither course is safe today. Aside from the fact that they have their own economic problems at the moment, the satellites are disgruntled and restless. So are Russian consumers. It is doubtful that much can be taken away from either group without a significant tightening of controls—perhaps without a reign of terror. Such a policy would impose costs in the form of reduced productivity that could easily offset any gains from shifting resources.

Another course of action, one discussed at length in Soviet circles over the last few years, would be to move in precisely the opposite direction: to introduce reforms relaxing centralized economic controls in favor of a more liberal system. Here the way has been blocked by a fundamental dilemma—what might be called the dilemma of the tsars: how to achieve the decentralization needed to improve economic efficiency without threatening survival of the autocratic political order. Soviet leaders are undoubtedly more interested in preserving their dictatorship and the supremacy of the Communist Party than in creating a more smoothly running economy. They will certainly not willingly sacrifice control for efficiency. Hence, on the question of reforms, we witness much talk and little action.

The basic question, of course, is to what extent markets and quasi markets are to be used in place of direct allocation of resources. Various proposals for reform are coming forth, all differing in detail but having in common the principle that production should be guided by prices and profits instead of quantitative goals. Nobody has seriously argued that prices should themselves be set by market forces, but it would seem to be a matter of time before logic forces such a conclusion.

So far Soviet leaders have moved cautiously and experimentally, introducing "work to order" in place of "work to plan" in isolated cases like manufacture of shoes and clothing. A piecemeal policy of this sort creates almost as many problems as it solves, and one may wonder how long it will be before it is either abandoned or broadened. For example, if shoes are to be produced to order from retail outlets while leather is to be produced and allocated by plan, and if prices are to be set for both at the center, how is the shoe factory to get more leather when its orders rise or less when they fall? There are obviously many headaches ahead in this kind of tightrope walking.

We therefore have little reason to wonder when the Soviet leadership begins looking to the outside world for help. Any relaxation of political pressures by the West would make it easier for the Communist world to hold what it has and even to expand when opportunities present themselves. Any disarmament by the West would make it easier to maintain a given rate of relative military expansion. Any trade concessions or other economic aid would make it easier to meet economic problems in general. Under existing world conditions, détente—or "relaxation of tensions" or "peaceful coexistence," as you will—is the tactical maneuver most likely to help the Communist world in the short run without disturbing long-run goals.

How should the West—and, in particular, the United States— respond to Soviet probing for a détente? There seems to be a growing body of opinion counseling that we seize the opportunity to develop more "friendly" relations. According to this view, one of the first steps should be to extend a helping hand to the Soviet economy on the ground that "fat Communists are less menacing than thin ones." In its more far-reaching version, this thesis maintains that the drift toward affluence in the Soviet system is sufficient in itself to guarantee the emergence of a liberal and less belligerent social order.

While such reasoning may be more or less valid if one is content to think in terms of millenniums, it promises nothing but ruin in the immediate strategic context. History seldom leads us blindly down one path or another. Where it takes us depends on how we respond to the opportunities it affords for guidance on our own part. At no other time in recent years have we had such a favorable opportunity to temper Soviet aggressiveness as we now find before us.

Our most promising allies at the moment are the thin Communists, not the fat ones. They have reason for discontent with their lot and will make it known to their leaders, not to the outside world. Only by forcing Soviet leaders to solve problems of their own making can we have much hope for reforms internally and disengagement externally. To rescue the Soviet system at the very moment when internal pressures are mounting would be perilous folly.

A similar argument can be made negatively. How have Soviet leaders responded to growing affluence in the immediate past? It is true that economic improvements in the post-Stalin period have been accompanied by a relative liberalization of the system, but it was the liberalization that brought about the improvement, not the other way around. It is also clear that the response of leaders to economic success was to push forward with a massive military and space program, substituting sputniks and rockets for capital and consumer goods, trips to the moon for food and clothing, rockets in Cuba for relaxation of tensions. Contrary to the "affluence causes liberalization" thesis, ambitions for power have been curbed only by resulting economic failures, by an inability to provide simultaneously the gradual enrichment the Soviet people have come to expect.

Our policy should be guided by the goal of preserving our own free system. Where sympathy plays a role, it should apply to dominated peoples and not to dominating rulers. We must deal firmly—but pleasantly—with the rulers and leniently with their subjects. This is a time for hard bargaining, for insistence on a viable quid pro quo in the case of every action we might take to ease Soviet internal problems, whether it is the selling of wheat or chemical machinery, the expanding of trade in general, the extending of credit, or the doing of anything else. We are in a position to exchange economic help for bona fide political and economic concessions.

Soviet leaders are seeking a breathing spell to allow them to divert resources from strengthening power now to strengthening it over the longer pull. Whether they succeed in this tactical maneuver without being forced to change their ultimate strategy depends on how prudently we respond to the opportunities before us. Prudence demands that we engage in hardheaded horse trading. Only in this way can we be gentle with peoples subjected to Communist rule, and with ourselves.

19

Some Reflections
on the Growth of the
Soviet Economy

T he promise of any revolution is, one must suppose, to right the wrongs of the system being overthrown, fulfilling the hopes of the masses who overthrow it and carrying forward the historical forces that undermined and weakened existing institutions to the point where new ones could displace them.[1] The promise is implicit in the powerful social movement leading to revolution and becomes explicit in the slogans of those who seek to capture mass support and thereby channel and control the inevitably amorphous and chaotic revolutionary upheaval. The Russian Revolution did not, of course, take place in October 1917. As the culminating acts in the overthrow of an established social order, it unfolded over a dozen years beginning in 1905, the symbolic climax occurring in February 1917 when tsardom

This essay is reprinted from *Studies on the Soviet Union* 7, no. 1 (1967): 144–50. It was also published in Vladimir G. Treml, ed., *The Development of the Soviet Economy: Plan and Performance* (New York: Praeger, 1968), pp. 290–96.

[1] This paper is not intended to be a thorough exposition of the economic performance of the Soviet Union. It began as a set of comments on the papers by Dr. John Hardt and Professor Stanley Cohn and was designed for oral presentation at the Munich conference on the theme "The October Revolution: Promise and Realization." It has been expanded into a somewhat more coherent and self-contained essay at the request of the sponsors of the conference. For the published versions of the other papers, see John P. Hardt, "Soviet Economic Development and Policy Alternatives," and Stanley H. Cohn, "The Soviet Economy: Performance and Growth," *Studies on the Soviet Union* 6, no. 1 (1967): 1–23 and 24–54.

came to an end. The events of October marked the capture of leadership by an organized minority, the Bolshevik faction of the Social-Democratic Worker's Party.

The rhetoric of revolution seldom deserves careful analysis in retrospect, but it would be wrong to ignore the slogans put forth by the Bolsheviks as they engaged in the struggle for leadership. If Lenin did not take them seriously, the masses doubtless did, for they heard in them an echo of popular demands. Paraphrased, the slogans promised land to the peasants, bread to the workers, and freedom, peace, and brotherhood to all. In these terms, the achievements measure up poorly to say the least. Far from giving land to the peasants, the Communist government took it away. The people may finally, a half century later, have more to eat and wear, but this is primarily because more of them work harder and longer and live in the cities rather than the countryside. There is little reason to believe that either the rural or urban population enjoys a significantly higher standard of living on balance—that is, when all components of consumption are taken into account—than before the revolution, but the living standard is higher in the city than in the country now just as it was then, and a larger fraction of the population lives in the city. One hardly needs to comment on how little freedom, peace, or brotherhood the Soviet people have enjoyed or enjoy today, though this question is perhaps beyond the scope of my topic.

In appraising achievements, it is obviously not enough to look at conditions now, fifty years after the revolution. Let us agree that there has been impressive economic growth. Let us agree that the people as a whole are now materially better off than before the revolution. There still remains the question of what happened over the course of this half century, of how the people fared over the years. On that score we see a system stumbling from one crisis to another while the masses paid the price. It was not until the 1950s that growth of agricultural production began to outpace population growth, and in the intervening years it went as often down as up. Not even during the last decade has there been a reasonably steady upward trend. In the field of industrial consumer goods, the record is scarcely better.

Was this suffering "necessary"? Has there been some "higher" purpose or accomplishment to justify continual neglect of what one would suppose, for the ideals of the revolution, is the fundamental task: improvement of the welfare of the masses? As a matter of fact, the promise of the revolution has not been fulfilled, because the Soviet government has not had freedom and prosperity as its aim, but rather enhancement of Soviet power—more accurately, the power of the ruling elite. Such growth as has been achieved has come through forced saving and forced industrialization, through attending to easy tasks and neglecting difficult ones, through domination of the economy from the center.

So much for the matter of fact. But, as John Hardt asks in his paper: "Was Stalin necessary?" He suggests that he was, given the aims of the Soviet economy. To me, this is simply to say that Stalin was necessary for Stalin. There is no other imperative of history that required this kind of leadership or direction. Nor was there need for this kind of system in order "to overcome backwardness" or to meet the problems of development in an underdeveloped economy, as has been amply demonstrated throughout the rest of the world. Nor to create a powerful nation, if that is supposed to be a legitimate end in itself. The question to ask is not whether Stalin was necessary, but whether the things for which he was necessary were necessary themselves. If one goes back to the hopes and expectations of the Russian Revolution, the answer is clear: No, Stalin was not necessary—not then, not now, not ever. Even that statement is too weak. Stalin and the Soviet system were more than unnecessary; they were completely antithetical to the avowed aims of the revolution.

One could go on, as Dr. Hardt does, and ask whether the rigidities and inflexibilities of the Soviet economic system must persist beyond Stalin. He thinks so for two reasons: first, because an authoritarian system is implicitly inflexible; and, second, because the imbalances inherited from the Stalinist period make it virtually impossible to introduce more flexibility into the economy. I agree fully with the first reason but not the second. Greater flexibility and decentralization— more accurately, polycentricity—are essential if the imbalances are to be remedied. Yet they are slow to come. Why? Because the overriding objective of political leadership is to preserve the autocracy. We see, in modern dress, "the dilemma of the tsars." For more than a century, the last tsars were quite aware that the social and economic system over which they presided was rotten and bound to collapse some day. While recognizing the urgent need for reforms, they were reluctant to introduce them, because they knew that curing the patient would kill the doctor. The social order demanded by reason had no place for an autocratic ruler, and the tsars were more interested in keeping their jobs than in benefiting the masses. And so they let things drift, responding only to overwhelming pressures as they built up.

The same dilemma faces the Soviet rulers of today. To improve the efficiency of the economy, they must relinquish some of their control. Multiple centers for making economic decisions must be created and dispersed throughout the economy. Impersonal markets and forces of competition must displace administrative planning. Where does the process stop? How can one avoid the specter, dreadful to contemplate, of independent focuses of power, each competing with the other? What justification remains for a monopoly of power in the hands of a single party dominated by a self-perpetuating elite? How can the appetite for political freedom, once whetted, be suppressed? These are the questions running through the minds of Soviet leaders in their more candid moments.

But let us turn away from such speculations and ask how well the objectives actually pursued and the methods used have worked in generating economic development. How has the Soviet system compared in performance over a half century with other kinds of economic systems? Any discussion of this sort must be introduced with the usual words of warning about the extraordinary difficulties encountered in trying to measure Soviet economic performance. For a variety of well-known reasons, Soviet statistics leave much to be desired. It is therefore natural that scholars will differ in their evaluation of growth trends in the Soviet economy. I shall give here my own evaluation, indicating where it seems appropriate how my figures diverge from those of others.

If we look first at the economy as a whole, it seems reasonable to say that the average annual growth rate in the Soviet gross national product over the last half century has been around 3 percent, after proper adjustment is made to remove the effects of territorial expansion. On this matter, the calculations of Professor Abram Bergson in his comprehensive study of Soviet national income agree with mine.[2] While there is considerable room for dispute here, I doubt that the growth rate over the last four or five years has been significantly higher than the long-run average. A long-run rate of 3 percent a year is quite respectable but by

[2] See G. Warren Nutter, "The Effects of Economic Growth on Sino-Soviet Strategy," in David M. Abshire and Richard V. Allen, eds., *National Security: Political, Military, and Economic Strategies in the Decade Ahead* (New York: Praeger for Hoover Institution, 1963), p. 166, excerpts from which are reprinted in Essay 20 below.

no means exciting, particularly when one considers the relatively un-advanced stage of development from which the Soviet economy started and the extraordinary expansion in investment and employment under-taken under the policy of forced industrialization, so well summarized by Professor Cohn in his paper. One might well wonder whether the results have justified the cost, and whether some other economic sys-tem would not have done better.

Let us take a brief look at industry, the favored sector. The long-run growth rate for industrial production has been about 4.6 percent a year, again with the effects of territorial expansion removed. More disagree-ment is to be expected from other scholars on the accuracy of this figure, though the index of Kaplan and Moorsteen for 1928–1958 implies a similar result.[3] For the last five years or so, I would put the average annual growth rate at around 5 percent, while others would put it at around 7 percent.[4] If my figures are substantially correct, the performance of Soviet industry over the last half century, while im-pressive, is neither unusual nor unprecedented. Despite the all-out effort to industrialize, overall growth has been less rapid than it was in Russia or the United States in the period 1870–1913.[5] Most of the Soviet growth is attributable to expansion in inputs of capital and labor rather than to improved productivity of resources, by contrast with the situation in the United States, for example, over the last half century.[6] Indeed, the evidence indicates that the stock of industrial capital has actually grown considerably faster than production, so that growth in productivity of capital has been negative.[7]

One should also note that the growth rate for industry reflects the fact that the economy has, because of the inherent nature of administrative planning, followed the path of least resistance. Heavy emphasis has been placed on those tasks that are most easily accomplished, a process of natural selection operating in favor of those production targets most readily fulfilled. Any economy can generate a higher measured rate of

---

[3] Ibid., p. 167; and G. Warren Nutter, *Growth of Industrial Production in the Soviet Union* (Princeton: Princeton University Press for National Bureau of Economic Research, 1962), pp. 337–40.

[4] See U.S., Congress, Joint Economic Committee, *Current Economic Indicators for the U.S.S.R.*, 89th Cong., 1st sess., 1965, p. 45; and J. H. Noren, "Soviet Industry Trends in Output, Input, and Productivity," in U.S., Congress, Joint Economic Committee, *New Directions in the Soviet Economy,* 89th Cong., 2d sess., 1966, pt. 2-A, p. 281.

[5] Nutter, *Growth of Industrial Production,* p. 229.

[6] Ibid., p. 232.

[7] Ibid., p. 236.

growth if it concentrates on growth for growth's sake rather than on satisfaction of other values. There is much to be said for the characterization of the Soviet economy, attributed to Professor Wassily Leontief, as an "input-input system." This is the basic reason why the Soviet economy faces critical reallocative problems at the moment. The emphasis on growth and power has led to the various distortions so familiar in the Soviet economy: sophisticated weaponry and primitive plumbing; abundance of steel and shortage of grain; spacious subways and pitifully overcrowed housing; jet aircraft and dirt roads; complex machinery and shoddy consumer goods; and so on. As concern for consumer welfare mounts on the part of leaders as well as the masses, these distortions present formidable obstacles in the way of rapid orientation of the economy toward better fulfillment of consumer wants.

In commenting on Soviet economic performance, one must not leave out of account the almost unbroken string of catastrophes that has marked the course of Soviet history and hindered progress. Some were endemic in the system. Thus, the toll of radical and violent revolution levied during the period of so-called War Communism, in addition to immediate suffering, generated a population deficit of almost twenty million persons, along with a distorted age and sex distribution, both leaving their indelible mark on the course of events over the following decades. Scarcely had the economy recovered from its initial shock, thanks to the period of New Economic Policy, when a second blow was struck in the form of forced collectivization of agriculture, causing another large population deficit and destroying about half the capital in agriculture. Next came the great purge of the late 1930s, placing its own heavy burden on the economy.

The effects of World War II, even more disastrous, lie in another category in that this event cannot be blamed on the Soviet system itself. Soviet foreign policy no doubt played a role in helping to build up the tensions leading to World War II, and the Hitler-Stalin pact must bear a major responsibility as the proximate cause of the outbreak of hostilities in 1939, but it would be a gross distortion of history to suggest that this great conflict was essentially the product of the Communist revolution. Hence, due allowance must be made in Soviet economic performance for the catastrophic impact of World War II; however, it must be remembered that the Soviet Union was not the only country to suffer from the war and that Stalin was willing to resort to more drastic policies of postwar recovery than were available to other countries. For example, the Soviet Union collected at least twice as much in reparations as all of Europe received in the form of Marshall Plan aid from the United States.[8] As the years recede, World War II must be reckoned as less and less of a factor in explaining long-run Soviet economic performance.

As an incidental matter, I should like to record my disagreement with the general view, echoed by Professor Cohn in his paper, that preparation for war was the major reason for Soviet economic stagnation during the period 1937–1940. While the Soviet military program was very large by standards of the time, it had been underway since at least 1934, with few signs of acceleration in the later years except for expansion in the size of the armed forces. Intensive industrial mobilization was not undertaken until after the German invasion. Sluggishness of the economy during the Third Five-Year Plan is to be attributed primarily to the great purge and to the relaxation of effort that followed the signing of the Hitler-Stalin pact.[9]

If, then, we are to appraise how well the promise of the October Revolution has been realized, we must measure performance over the entire Soviet period and not merely over the most favorable years, while making due allowance for the adverse effects of events thrust upon the economy from the outside. At the back of our minds, of course, there always lurks the question of how much differently things would have been under another kind of economic system facing the same basic circumstances, but we can never give a definitive answer to that question since we lack the power to reconstruct history. I am, nevertheless, prepared to advance the speculative opinion that the economy would have grown at least as rapidly as it has while providing far more welfare for the masses if the revolution of 1917 had resulted in the establishment of a constitutional government and a private enterprise economy along Western lines. I view the Communist revolution, now marking its fiftieth anniversary, as one of the great reactionary events of all time. As I read the history of tsarist Russia, it is the story of a slow and tortuous movement over the centuries away from oriental despotism and toward a liberal order in the Western tradition. Reform of the system accelerated in the last half of the nineteenth century and the first decade of the twentieth, reaching a climax with the constitutional revolution of February 1917, but the Bolshevik coup of October and its ultimate aftermath threw the country back to conditions of

[8] Ibid., p. 215.
[9] Ibid., pp. 210–13.

despotism, terror, and serfdom unsurpassed under the worst of the tsars—all in the name of ''construction of socialism.'' The slow and tortuous movement toward liberalism continues to assert itself beneath all the turmoil, and we may perhaps expect reaction to be overcome eventually. As it is, the promise of the revolution may gradually be realized.

20

The Effects of
Economic Growth on
Sino-Soviet Strategy

Developments in Communist China and the satellites cannot be
ignored, for they clearly will affect future policies of the Sino-
Soviet bloc. While specific figures could be cited as measures
of economic growth in these countries, they are not sufficiently reliable
to warrant serious attention, being at best crudely adjusted official
indexes. Western scholars have not, for a variety of reasons, yet made
the same careful audit of basic data and recomputation of indexes for
these countries as they have for the Soviet Union. My remarks will
therefore be essentially qualitative in character.

Let us consider Communist China first. Through 1957, industrialization apparently proceeded at a very rapid pace, reminiscent in
important respects of developments in the Soviet Union during the first
two five-year plans. As is normal for a period of this kind, actual
industrial growth can be fully assessed only if one knows what happened to workshops as well as factories. Official statistics are limited
to factory production, and they reflect diversion of output from the
small-scale to the large-scale sector as well as net increases in output.
The question of what happened to the small-scale sector is particularly

This essay is reprinted from David M. Abshire and Richard V. Allen, eds., *National
Security: Political, Military, and Economic Strategies in the Decade Ahead*, pp. 149–68, with
the permission of the publishers, Hoover Institution Press. Copyright 1963 by the Board of
Trustees of the Leland Stanford Junior University.

important in the Chinese case because hand trades must have accounted for a very large fraction—perhaps half to three-quarters—of industrial production at the beginning of the Communist era. This means that, if nothing had happened except a shift of resources from hand trades to factories (statistically if not "really"), recorded output could have doubled or tripled. In fact, more seems to have happened than this: there was a real expansion in the industrial sector. But the magnitude of the expansion was undoubtedly significantly less than the statistics show, the question of their reliability aside.[1]

Whatever actually happened in the years up to 1958, there is little doubt that progress has since been largely undone. Joseph Alsop characterizes developments over the last three or four years as "China's descending spiral,"[2] and this phrase seems to be apt. Although problems had already accumulated under collectivization of agriculture, the turning point came with the drive to communize, which was mainly carried out in late 1958 and early 1959 as a major element in the Great Leap Forward. Bad harvests followed in three successive years: 1959, 1960, and 1961. The entire economic situation has progressively deteriorated. It is too weak to say that industrialization has slowed down; the program has actually been put in reverse. People are being forcibly removed from the cities and sent to rural areas. According to Chou En-lai, 30 percent of the urban population is to be relocated.[3]

Under these circumstances and in the absence of comprehensive and reliable statistics for the last few years, it is impossible to say whether current production in the Communist Chinese economy is, in any meaningful sense, larger than it was in 1950. Famine has been widespread for three years running. Industrial production may be no higher than 30 percent of capacity,[4] which would mean that the growth during 1950–1957 has vanished. Indeed, Joseph Alsop considers the present situation to be so desperate that he sees a massive uprising in prospect unless there was a good harvest last fall.[5]

Conditions may not be so desperate as Alsop believes, but they are

[1] For some comments on reliability of official data, see Kang Chao, "The Reliability of Industrial Output Data in Communist China," *Journal of Asian Studies* 22 (November 1962): 44–66, and the book review in the same issue by Sidney Klein (pp. 100–101).

[2] Joseph Alsop, "On China's Descending Spiral," *The China Quarterly,* July-September 1962, pp. 21–37. For a thoughtful and revealing discussion of the problems of agrarian crisis and its origins, see Karl A. Wittfogel, "Agrarian Problems and the Moscow-Peking Axis," *Slavic Review* 21 (December 1962): 678–98.

[3] Alsop, "China's Descending Spiral," p. 25.

[4] Ibid., p. 23.

[5] Ibid., pp. 33 ff.

bad enough to create a serious crisis. If an immediate uprising is averted, if the communal system of agriculture is completely abandoned, and if the current ideological breach within the Sino-Soviet bloc is narrowed, there could be a rapid recovery of the Chinese economy and a reestablishment of the earlier pace of growth. The foundation for such a recovery is there in the form of modern industrial plants and a trained industrial workforce, two undoubted contributions of the earlier industrialization drive.

On the other hand, there are no signs so far that events will take this course. The alternative route is for the leaders of Communist China to become increasingly obstinate about internal policy and to try to channel their internal difficulties into external conflicts with Communist as well as non-Communist countries, simultaneously attempting to maintain internal order through terror. If recent events suggest anything, it is that the latter route is being followed. The situation cannot be comforting to the Communist world. If the Chinese policies do not succeed, communism will be overthrown there. If they do succeed, the Communist camp will probably be split in two, perhaps irreparably.

While the European satellites have experienced their own critical times, the climax occurring around 1956, nothing resembling the Chinese debacle has taken place. On the contrary, as far as one can tell, the average pace and the general directions of economic growth have been roughly the same in the satellites as in the Soviet Union. Even the recent slowdown in Soviet economic growth, which we shall discuss at a later point, has been mirrored in the satellites. On the matter of economic policies, the satellites have become considerably more independent since 1956, and Soviet doctrine speaks now of the "many paths to socialism and communism." In some respects the satellites may be viewed as proving grounds for experiments with the Communist economic system.

As already indicated, the economic fortunes of the Soviet Union and the satellites seem to be closely interwoven. This will probably become increasingly true as the European Common Market develops and the bloc countries come to rely more and more on trade among themselves.

In some respects, the Soviet economy stands at a critical crossroads, and some ways seem to be barred. The old formula used to be: when in trouble, squeeze the consumer. As long as the system could follow this path with impunity, it could at least partially resolve conflicting demands on resources in other areas and it could stand a large amount of wasteful activity generally. But the man in the street is a more reluctant whipping boy these days, and there seem to be definite restrictive limits to what he will stand for in the absence of a reign of terror. Promises of future glory and paradise are much poorer substitutes for "more now" than they used to be.

The major goal of Soviet leaders has always been to enhance Soviet power, and the rate and directions of economic growth, along with the current allocation of resources, have been planned accordingly. Even with such an overriding goal, serious conflicts of interest are bound to arise. To achieve power in a hurry, strategically important kinds of economic growth must be achieved in a hurry. But this may lead, as it has in the Soviet Union, to distortions inhibiting longer-range growth. Similarly, the desire for military strength-in-being conflicts with the desire for rapid growth: armaments and investments compete with each other. In the Soviet Union as elsewhere, you can't have your cake and eat it. Finally, sustained rapid growth is important not only for what it means directly in terms of future power, but also for what it means indirectly in terms of immediate power by virtue of its propaganda value, by impressing outsiders with the alleged superiority of the Communist system.

In brief, Soviet leaders must be concerned with accommodating conflicts among three interrelated goals: short-run strengthening of power, long-run strengthening of power, and raising of living standards. While one may dominate depending on tactical decisions, none can any longer be neglected. Being caught in this position, the leaders must give increasing attention to improving the organizational efficiency of the economy, which they clearly recognize to be in critical need of improvement, and to relieving international tensions, which impose such a heavy burden on the economy.

The reason little decisive action has yet been taken on internal reform seems plain: the leaders are not convinced that they can decentralize decisions on the operating level of the economy without losing control over fundamental allocation of resources. From a short-run point of view, it is difficult to see why they are so worried. By budgetary powers a government can effectively control productive activity even in a full-fledged market economy. The real dilemma seems to be more deeply seated and to apply to the longer run, namely, whether autocratic rule can survive indefinitely within the atmosphere of a highly decentralized economy run by educated people. The Soviet leaders have good reason to believe that it cannot, as the history of their own country up to the Bolshevik Revolution cogently argues.

No doubt, ideology also plays a role. Turning Marxist economics upside down, as must be done if a workable decentralized economy is to be devised, is bound to be a painful process. It surely cannot be done overnight without introducing serious political disruptions.

The disturbing question is whether the Soviet Union may not already be embarked on a dangerous race between erosion of the internal Communist system and fulfillment of the Communist design of world domination. Such a race becomes more and more dangerous as Soviet leaders become increasingly aware of it, for they may be induced to take reckless gambles in order to forestall the steady march of internal events so distasteful to them. The accelerating tempo of armaments production, the intensive effort to dominate space science and technology, the resumption and continuation of nuclear tests, the Cuban adventure—all these recent developments are disturbing signs of a concerted effort to achieve world domination "before it is too late." This conclusion seems to force itself upon one in spite—or, perhaps, because—of Khrushchev's continuing protests that the Communist world, renouncing war as a normal instrument of policy, has taken on the rest of the world in a race of "peaceful economic competition."

Of course, Soviet leaders would prefer to achieve world domination through relaxation of Western effort rather than through intensification of Soviet effort. The ideal solution from their point of view would be unilateral disarmament by the West, and we should expect mounting enticements in this direction if Western policy encourages them to expect unilateral concessions.

The moral is that we must be on guard against the classic Communist seesaw of alternating "conciliation" and "negotiation," on the one hand, and bold power politics, on the other, which Soviet leaders will employ; not because they are confident of winning the economic race, but because they are not. Developments within the next few years will indicate to what extent internal problems will be externalized. Movement in the opposite direction would be signaled by significant decentralization of the economic system, by a relative reduction in the military and space program, by steps to increase the standard of living, by agricultural reforms leading to more rather than less private family farming, by a revival of the residential construction program, and so on. These things may all happen—and indeed ultimately will, in my firm opinion, if the world is not blown up in the meantime and if we follow a firm policy of our own that turns Soviet weaknesses to our benefit instead of harm. They will not happen if we actively appease or passively wait and see.

21

Trends in Eastern Europe

There are, an economist from Eastern Europe recently explained, three ways to ruin: women, gambling, and Czechoslovak economic reforms. Women, he said, are the most pleasant way, gambling the most gallant, and Czechoslovak reforms the most certain. The tide of events so far has not contradicted him.

In an age when no Western politician could expect to garner many votes through a platform dedicated to liberty, it may be encouraging to find peoples in Eastern Europe who are moved to revolt in the cause of freedom and democracy. For events in Czechoslovakia have amounted to nothing less than a popular revolt, and there can be no doubt about the significant role played by a revulsion against tyranny in its many forms. Trends elsewhere, though perhaps less dramatic, point in the same direction, and in some respects—surely in Yugoslavia and probably in Hungary—they have moved further along the way.

The thirst for freedom is apparent among many in the intellectual community thoughout Eastern Europe, who by and large do not hesitate to single out thought control as the most oppressive feature that they have had to endure under the regime imposed on their countries over the last two decades or so. Ironically, the reaction against Marxist

This essay, which was originally given as a paper at the Aviemore Conference of the Mont Pelerin Society in September 1968, is reprinted from *Economic Age* 1, no. 1 (November-December 1968): 8–12.

dogmatism has even raised mental barriers that block sound analysis of remedies for current economic problems, as we shall have occasion to note at a later point. In any event, there is a real demand for greater freedom of thought and expression, whether they imply greater material progress or not.

We shall never know how far this sentiment alone would have carried matters, since there have been other important sources of discontent, long abrooding and affecting the attitudes of the masses. These include nationalism (in its narrower as well as broader sense), a yearning for more just and representative government, dissatisfaction with foreign policy, and economic failures. The opportunity for translating the growing discontent into action has been provided by troubles besetting the Soviet Union, both internally and in its ideological conflict with the Chinese.

The country in the spotlight at the moment is, of course, Czechoslovakia, where the swift current of events continues to amaze observers who have typically viewed the Czechs as so cautious and conservative in temperament that they would never resort to radical measures in trying to solve their problems. Even more amazing to some has been the outspoken and candid nature of the critical discussion that burst forth the moment thought control was relaxed. It is not difficult to reconstruct why the revolt occurred from what the Czechs themselves are now openly saying.

Let us start with the economic scene without implying its primacy in determining the future course of events. The Czech economy was rapidly transformed after the Communist takeover of the country in 1948. Private enterprise was for all practical purposes eliminated, and the market was replaced as the coordinating mechanism by highly centralized administrative planning. Rapid industrialization became the basic objective, heavy industry receiving top priority. The structure of foreign trade was radically altered in the nature both of goods traded and of trading partners. Trade with capitalist countries fell from 60 percent of total turnover in 1948 to 22 percent in 1953. Machinery rose from 6 percent of exports in 1937 to 42 percent in 1953, while consumer goods fell from 37 percent to 12 percent. In brief, the economy had been thoroughly sovietized on the Stalinist model by the end of the First Five-Year Plan.

As these developments were taking place, economists and other professionals with "bourgeois" backgrounds were systematically removed from all positions of influence unless they actively and convincingly embraced communism. Almost all the recalcitrants were banned from practice of their professions, and those who survived did so by turning to manual labor or other menial tasks, where they could gradually cultivate a proletarian background that permitted a few of them to work their way back up the professional ladder much later. Almost all administrative and government positions were given to the hard-core Party faithful who were generally poorly qualified by either native intelligence or training. One of the most persistent and universal complaints voiced by intellectuals concerns the ineptness and low intelligence—even stupidity—of the government officials who entrenched themselves in this period and retained full command over the country until very recently. But equally strong is their condemnation of the system itself, about which more later.

The early 1950s were also marked by a ruthless political purge and an accompanying reign of terror, as part of Stalin's campaign to persuade others not to follow Tito's lead in breaking away from Soviet hegemony. Thousands were tortured, imprisoned, and liquidated, as we are beginning to learn in detail. Being focused on Rudolph Slansky and his associates, the purge had unmistakable anti-Semitic overtones not easily forgotten.

The death of Stalin in 1953 did not bring about any significant liberalization in Czechoslovakia. On the contrary, the next five years were a period in which absolute control, down to the minutest details, was wielded from the center. Imbalances and distortions became rigidly ingrained in the economy as the foundations for later crises were laid. Not even the ill-fated uprisings of 1956 in Poland and Hungary seemed to have any impact on Czech leaders, who stubbornly strengthened their grip over all aspects of life. For example, the most intensive collectivization of agriculture took place between 1956 and 1960.

It was not until 1958 that any moves were made to relax control from the center in favor of more autonomy for the enterprises. These modest reforms, which had become imperative, did improve conditions briefly, but they were too little and too late. The economy came under stress as foreign demand for exports slackened while the agricultural sector suffered from bad harvests two years running, both for reasons unconnected with the reform. Even by Communist standards and statistics, the economy experienced stagnation from 1961 through 1965, registering a measured decline in national product in 1963.

As the public grew increasingly restless, economists were enabled to become increasingly outspoken in their criticism of the system and their demands for fundamental reform. Ota Šik, a member of the presidium of the Central Committee of the Communist Party who had some rudimentary training in economics, cast his lot with the reformers and greatly strengthened their hand. The target of criticism was the very system of centralized administrative planning itself. The remedy proposed was introduction of "market socialism."

The first major step toward reform was taken in January 1965, when the Central Committee approved a draft program aimed at severing the direct administrative control of enterprises by the central government and at restructuring the price system as an interim measure in the move toward a fully operative market economy. The central determination of planned goals for output and input was eliminated in stages over a two-year period and replaced by contractual transactions. Price reform was accomplished through massive computerized calculations that attempted, with varying degrees of success and failure, to bring prices more closely in line with costs. Enterprises were subjected to taxes and other charges on capital to improve the accounting of costs—in defiance of Marxist doctrine.

Despite the significance of these changes in policy, the reform was implemented with less than full enthusiasm on the part of the entrenched government and bureaucracy. Their aim, it became clear, was to try to satisfy the clamor for reform with a series of half measures that would stop short of radical alteration of the basic nature of things. Virtually nothing was done to eliminate the pervasive network of administrative subsidies and protective devices. Enterprises were allowed to measure performance in terms of output instead of sales. And so on.

Economic conditions seemed to improve, but this was in large part an illusion. For example, increased inventories—mostly unsalable goods—accounted for half the growth in national income in 1966 and for two-thirds in 1967. The fraction rose even higher in the first two months of 1968.

One thing led to another, resulting in the climactic events familiar to us all from recent news reports. There seem to have been three sets of circumstances that triggered the crisis of January 1968.

The first was the obedient adoption by the Czech government of the belligerent Soviet policy toward Israel during and after the Arab-Israeli conflict in mid-1967. The rumblings of anti-Semitism carried an ominous sound to intellectuals and various Party leaders who could not easily forget the Slansky affair. For some Jews who had only recently been rehabilitated after years of imprisonment and reinstated in important Party posts, there was a clear note of personal danger. For others who were struggling for a more liberal political order, the threat of a sweeping reactionary program, in the name of "anti-Zionism," must have seemed equally real. Many writers who had become increasingly bold in protesting against the lack of free expression now attacked the government's policy toward the Middle East. Several were expelled from the Party, and the principal journal of the Writer's Union was taken over by the Ministry of Culture. In a display of solidarity, both authors and subscribers mounted an effective boycott of the journal. At the same time, considerable activity was no doubt taking place in the Party and government apparatus as the reformist faction attempted to outmaneuver the dominant hard-liners and prevent them from launching a purge. There seems to be compelling evidence that Novotny was preparing to call upon the armed forces to preserve his position and suppress the incipient rebellion.

The second set of circumstances concerned the treatment of student demonstrations in November. Annoyed by persistent disruptions in the electricity service to their dormitories, the students in Prague staged a seemingly innocent and peaceful demonstration in protest. Given the general state of tension, the police responded in an understandably nervous fashion, dispersing the demonstrators with unnecessary force. The cry of "police brutality" was raised, and students and professors joined ranks in protesting against this symbolic suppression of free speech.

The third set of circumstances, which turned out to have special significance, was the aggravation of longstanding grievances on the part of the Slovakian minority. The Slovaks have long complained of unfair discrimination against them and their region. Accounting for 31 percent of the population and inhabiting 39 percent of the territory of Czechoslovakia, they feel that they have been treated as hewers of wood and drawers of water, that their economy has been slighted, and that the members of their nationality have been poorly represented in the leading positions in Czechoslovakia. There has been special bitterness over the fact that the constitution of 1960 destroyed all vestiges of the Czechoslovak federation and effectively abolished the instruments of self-government by centralizing all power in Prague. While details are missing, it appears that Novotny paid a brief visit to Slovakia during the fall of 1967, in the course of which he managed to insult everybody with whom he came in contact and to convey the unmistakable impression that he had nothing but disdain for Slovakia, Slovaks, and their claims for autonomy. In doing so, he succeeded in welding a powerful coalition against his continued exercise of power.

This brief catalog of events leading to the overthrow of the Novotny regime in Czechoslovakia is of interest in showing how a particular conjuncture of history can bring about a fundamental political change even in a Communist country. But the specific events are less important than the underlying forces that enabled the events to take on significance. In this respect, the current situation in Czechoslovakia is symptomatic of conditions elsewhere in Eastern Europe. The facts of political geography prevent any liberalization in Poland or East Germany in response to underlying pressures, but the case is different in Yugoslavia and Hungary.

Yugoslavia has, of course, gone furthest on the path toward political and economic liberalization, although Hungary has quietly moved a long way as well. Now that Czechoslovakia has joined their ranks, Rumania may be next, although she has so far done little more than declare her political independence from Moscow.

There are certain common problems and attitudes. Foremost is the question of the "system of management," as it is usually put, and the main thrust of reform has been a total rejection of centralized administrative planning in favor of some kind of a market system combined with "indicative planning." Here the proponents of reform have had to move with great skill and caution, since the uncrossable line as far as the Soviet Union is concerned is the one that marks off "antisocialism."

A rather standard strategy of reform has emerged. First, a case for the market is argued in Marxian terms, to convince the authorities that no heresy is involved. Justification of the market system by means of Marxian economic theory is no mean feat, and we should take our hats off to those East European economists who have patiently worked it out. Second, practical measures are devised for a transitional stage between administrative planning and a market system. This task has been viewed as one of finding some way to sever control from the center and to restructure the price system without disruption of the economy. During the transitional stage, enterprises normally substitute contractual relations, based primarily on centrally determined prices, for administrative orders in organizing production. Third and finally, the problem is faced of establishing the foundations for a viable and feasible market economy.

The most critical problem has been figuring out how to endow enterprises with meaningful property rights—usually referred to as the problem of the "autonomy of enterprises" and "work incentives"—without at the same time creating private property. Put another way, the problem is to create private property without calling it that. While some economists have displayed great ingenuity in trying to resolve this dilemma, the ideological barrier is formidable. As we can see from the Yugoslav experience, it takes time to breach it significantly. The task is not made easier by impatient haranguing on the part of some Western observers, who would perform a better service by putting their talents to work in inventing feasible and fruitful ways of undoing a sovietized economy.

A closely related problem is to ensure competition in the markets once they are established. How, for example, can entry of firms into profitable activities and exit from unprofitable ones be ensured without creating a full-fledged regime of private property and capital markets? How can monopolistic firms now in existence be divided up into competing firms? The latter problem has been aggravated by the fact that, in virtually every sovietized economy, a favorite temporizing measure for ameliorating the costs of coordination has been to consolidate enterprises as a last-ditch effort to save the system. Further consolidation may be resorted to in the transitional stage. In Czechoslovakia, for example, 1,417 industrial enterprises were consolidated into 253 trusts in 1958 as part of the program to shore up centralized planning, and the 253 trusts were further combined into the present 100 in 1966 as part of the transitional program. The sentiment now is in favor of breaking the trust up into the original enterprises, but this task will not be easy.

Foreign trade is looked upon as one important way of introducing competition, but the problems of reestablishing normal trading relations are legion. Economists of Eastern Europe are also well aware of the need for open trading to extend their markets and develop gains from specialization. To accomplish this end, these countries must first alter the closed trading system of the Soviet bloc, whose primary purpose has been to facilitate exploitation by the Soviet Union. I recall a Polish economist once saying that the Soviet economy could afford to be inefficient because it was large enough to generate gains from specialization anyhow. On the other hand, the East European economies have to be efficient in allocating resources because they must bow to the rigors of the world trading market to achieve their gains. In particular, their internal prices must reflect costs of production and their currencies must become convertible.

These are momentous times in Eastern Europe. Those striving so hard and courageously to give their peoples a greater measure of freedom without any hope of assistance from outside deserve at least our sympathy, admiration, and respect. We should not make their task more difficult by demanding more of them than they can provide.

In a profound sense, the hope of the West lies today in the East. We may one day owe the preservation of our own free society to those striving for freedom elsewhere. We certainly have little to show so far for our own efforts.

22

Soviet Economic Thought:
Whence and Whither?

When your esteemed president asked me to speak before this assembly on recent trends in Soviet economic thought, I told him he was crazy. Might as well draw the speaker's name out of a hat, I said, since I lost track of virtually everything important, and certainly of intellectual life behind the iron curtain, in four years of public service spanning, I must add, the period between the Pentagon Papers and Watergate. Or so I thought.

Now that I have taken a quick look at what has been going on, I am not so sure that there was much to miss. For example, whatever happened to Professor Liberman and all that discussion of economic reform that made the news a decade ago? The best short answer is that this too has passed away, leaving little behind in memory. A professor suddenly propelled from obscurity into the limelight has returned whence he came, and the short-lived controversy about reform has accompanied him.

Perhaps there are many Westerners—this audience excepted—who believe that the reform movement was a typical academic happening of the sort we are accustomed to. A professor has a bright idea, it would seem, and one thing leads to another: he reads a paper at the December meetings of the Soviet Economic Association before a host of avid

These remarks were given before the Philadelphia Society in April 1974.

newsmen as well as scholars; he publishes a learned article in the Soviet Economic Review, which precipitates a flood of comments, replies, and rejoinders; he writes a column in the popular Newspeak; he appears on the television program Tomorrow to answer the questions of the interested layman; and so on. After all, we have our Milton Friedman, and they have their Evsei Liberman.

We in this room are more sophisticated. We know that things don't work quite that way in the Soviet Union. Turn back to mid-1962 when the Seven-Year Plan had run out of steam and other problems were piling up for Khrushchev. Perhaps he had a premonition of economic crisis—it came, in fact, the next year after a massive crop failure—and of his consequent fall from grace just two years off. He needed something to distract attention while hopefully providing a way out that preserved authoritarian rule and, in particular, his own neck. His eye lit on E. G. Liberman, an obscure professor at the obscure Kharkov Institute of Economic Engineers who had written a couple of articles on industrial management in the latter half of the 1950s.

Liberman's theses had a certain appeal to Khrushchev because their purpose was to save the system—that is, centralized administrative planning—by giving greater latitude to plant managers in their day-to-day affairs. Liberman came to be known in the West as an advocate of the profit motive, but what he proposed had little to do with a profit-seeking system as we know it. Central authorities were to determine what and how much to produce, what prices to charge, what average wages to pay, what labor norms to set, and the like, while plant managers were to be given both the incentive and leeway to find the most profitable way of fulfilling the centrally determined tasks. Just how this was to be done never became quite clear, but the object was to relieve central planning from concern for minutiae so that it could tighten its grip on the economy. The proposal sounded like the kind of conservative reformism that was sought.

And so the Party launched a carefully planned "debate" in the official press and Party apparatus. The debate lasted only a few months, however, because it threatened to get out of hand. The political authorities must have been shaken to discover how widespread and deep-seated the sentiment for reform was among economists and how difficult it was to keep discussion within permissible bounds. The concept of market socialism lay just beneath the surface of some proposals by respected scholars, and there was no telling where that would lead to if left unchecked. In November, on the eve of the plenary session of the

Central Committee and in the aftermath of the Cuban missile crisis, the debate was abruptly brought to a halt, and the negative was declared the winner. After a pause, some brief but intensive discussion emerged again in 1964, and the whole thing came to a formal end the next year when Kosygin, Khrushchev's successor as prime minister, announced his set of reforms, which for eight years have succeeded in keeping things the same.

I mention these episodes of public discussion not to reveal Soviet economic thought but to illustrate how little of that thought can be discerned by the outsider. What is going on in the minds of Soviet economists is only remotely related to what is said in the glare of publicity. Only the tip of an iceberg is seen, and great care is taken in deciding how much of the tip to reveal. We would know more about the thinking of economists if we could attend their professional meetings or read candid proceedings of them. We would still not know the thoughts confined to one's study.

There is no doubt that many Soviet economists have escaped the crippling confines of Marxist dogma without making it too obvious that they have done so. The mathematical route has provided one way to escape. From inexorable logic, a symbol crops up here and there that we might call marginal this or that. But what's in a name? "Shadow price" will do as well without raising ideological hackles. And the optimal properties of a system based on rational calculus can be demonstrated without directly challenging the principle of surplus value. Hence mathematical economics—or economic cybernetics, as it is called in the Soviet Union—attracts some of the best talent, exemplified by Kantorovich, Novozhilov, Aganbegian, and Fedorenko.

Some of these economists have been bold enough to suggest a complete overhaul of the planning system amounting to central determination of prices rather than outputs, economic units then adjusting to the prices on the basis of a system of incentives. They currently call their concept an "optimally functioning socialist economy." But they have also learned how to fall back to secondary and tertiary lines of defense, one of which is the efficiency of the computer. The question now being resolved is how far to go in using computers, not whether they should be used at all. For the time being, the head of Gosplan (the State Planning Committee) has tossed them a bone by decreeing that computers may be used in storing, retrieving, and analyzing information, but not in allocating resources. The traditional system of centralized administrative planning will remain in force.

The two basic factors restraining economic thought are obviously Marxist ideology and authoritarian rule. Of the two, Soviet leaders will struggle hardest to maintain the latter. The specter that haunts them is disintegration of absolute control by the Party, and each small step toward decentralized power in the economic arena is seen as leading inevitably to that disintegration. Why take a chance?

At the moment, the situation in Eastern Europe is probably of greatest concern. Let me call upon personal experience to amplify that point.

For a decade I have helped sponsor an annual conference of economists from Eastern Europe and the West. Russians have been invited every year, but they have attended only twice. The first time was the Florence conference in 1966, when the Soviet delegation was headed by Academician L. M. Gatovskii, then director of the Institute of Economics at the USSR Academy of Sciences and therefore a prestigious member of the economic bureaucracy. The main event at that conference was a spirited debate between Professor Oldrich Kyn, then at the University of Prague, and the entire Soviet delegation, carried on in full view of the Italian press and continued by Kyn briefly on Italian television. Kyn, joined by others, had no kind words to say about the Soviet economic system. Market socialism was the answer, he said, to the hopeless inefficiency of the Soviet system. Back home in Czechoslovakia, the same spirit led to the autumn of 1968, when the Russians demonstrated decisively who had won the debate.

After four years in which this lesson sank in, the second Soviet delegation appeared at Ermenonville in 1972. The Czechs had not yet rejoined the conference, and other Eastern Europeans displayed their new vocabulary, particularly neglecting the word "market." Only in private conversation were any interesting topics explored.

Western economic thought became contagious in Eastern Europe, and it has not been eradicated so far by brute force. Why should the situation be much different in the Soviet Union? I am confident that Western economic ideas are spreading and intensifying, but I see little likelihood that much will happen in the near future as a consequence.

Soviet leaders of today face the dilemma of the tsars. Like the tsars, they know the economy is sick, but, also like the tsars, they fear that curing the patient will kill the doctor. The fear will not simply fade away because it is rooted in reality. Economic thought will prosper in the Soviet Union only when the totalitarian regime is shaken by some process yet to evolve.

PART THREE

23

Economic Aspects of
National Strategy

I am pleased to have the honor of speaking to this Staff College once again. It is only fair to warn you at the beginning that much of what I have to say might well be called controversial, and I cannot guarantee that everything will accord with positions taken by the administration in Washington. I assume, however, that you are interested in hearing my views, and in any case I am accustomed, as a professional scholar, to speak the truth as I see it, whether this accords with popular opinion at the moment or not. I do not believe in truth by authority. Frank and open airing of disagreements is the essence of a free society, and it is in this spirit that I appear before you today.

Now to turn to my subject, the economic aspects of national strategy. The American economy is currently producing goods and services at the rate of about $550 billion a year. This amounts to $3,000 for every man, woman, and child in the United States, and to $7,700 for every member of the civilian labor force. This large volume of goods and services is being produced by a labor force constituting about 55 percent of the noninstitutional population fourteen years old and above, working on the average less than forty hours a week. Leisure is therefore an important element in the American economy, being voluntarily

These remarks were given at the U.S. Armed Forces Staff College, Norfolk, Va., in June 1962.

chosen by our citizens in place of the goods and services that might otherwise be produced and consumed. In an emergency, the civilian labor force could be expanded by as much as 15 percent without serious hardship, and hours of work by 20 percent—total employment in man-hours by 30 to 40 percent. Production could not rise as much, but it could rise considerably—perhaps, by 20 to 25 percent. This is just to say that there is substantial slack in our economy, available for emergencies.

A significant part of our annual production—almost 9 percent—is needed to replace capital equipment and structures used up in the process of production. Allowance being made for capital consumption, the net production of our economy—the so-called NNP as distinguished from the GNP—is currently running at around $500 billion, or $2,800 a person, $7,000 a worker.

Almost 33 percent of net production originates in industry, about 4 percent in agriculture, and about 5 percent in construction. Production of goods thus accounts for about 42 percent of total net production. The remaining 58 percent is accounted for by production of services of one sort or another, including the activities of government.

Private enterprise is the basic productive engine of our economy and profits are the fuel. The health of our economy depends on the health of the private sector. Private business currently accounts for around 87 percent of productive activity, but the private sector has been shrinking. In every decade since 1900 there has been a rise in the share of employment accounted for by government and government enterprises, federal, state, and local. In 1900 that share was 4 percent. Now it is about 15 percent. The share of profits is also shrinking. In 1929 corporate profits after taxes amounted to 9.5 percent of national income, in 1961 to 5.4 percent.

Taking another view of the economy, we may note that private decisions determine the uses made of about four-fifths of productive activity, while collective decisions made through governmental agencies determine the uses made of the remaining fifth. The role of collective decision making has also expanded markedly within the last three decades. In 1929 governmental decisions guided less than a tenth of our productive activity, as compared with a fifth today. A large part of this increase is accounted for by growing defense needs, but by no means all of it. Government expenditures on goods and services other than defense and space are currently running at 11.5 percent of GNP.

This leads us to consider the burden of defense. For convenience of later comparisons, let me consider the conditions in 1960. Total governmental expenditures on defense, including mutual assistance and the space program, amounted to $46.1 billion, or about 9 percent of GNP. Expenditures on hardware, research and development of military goods, atomic energy, and the space program came to $21 billion, or about 11.5 percent of the gross product of industry. The remaining $25 billion was spent on support of troops and military operations. The armed forces in that year totaled 2.5 million, about 4 percent of non-institutionalized males fourteen years of age or older. The defense burden does not seem excessive.

With this view of the American economy in the background, I should like to turn to the Soviet economy. Here we have an economy with a territory 150 percent larger than the United States, a population 18 percent larger, and a labor force 37 percent larger. Despite these advantages, the volume of goods and services produced is only a fraction of the U.S. level. According to the best estimates I have been able to make, Soviet industrial production is about 28 percent of the U.S. level, agricultural production about 60 percent, and commercial freight traffic about 50 percent. For the economy as a whole, Soviet production would be no more than a quarter of the U.S. level.

I must now point out that this is an area in which there has been a strong difference of opinion. Estimates emanating from our State Department and Central Intelligence Agency indicate that Soviet industrial production is around half our level, and GNP also. The only explanation I can offer is that they are wrong. Unfortunately, I cannot say why because the basis of their calculations has not been published.

The plain truth is that, despite many impressive accomplishments, the Soviet economy remains small and inefficient alongside the American economy. Industrial production is about the same level in the Soviet Union today as it was in the United States in the mid-1920s, or some thirty-six years ago. GNP stands at the U.S. level of the mid-1910s, or some forty-five years ago. At the same time, the Soviet military effort is much larger relative to our own and hence places a much larger burden on the Soviet economy than our effort does on our economy.

The predominance of economic power in the West over the Soviet bloc is shown by considering the economic achievements of Western Europe. The GNP of the eighteen European members of the OECD

(Organization for Economic Cooperation and Development) was around $333 billion in 1960, about two-thirds of the U.S. level and more than two and a half times the Soviet level. By contrast, it is doubtful that the Soviet bloc countries excluding Communist China produce more than a tenth of the U.S. output of goods and services, or around two-fifths of the Soviet output. In 1960 the GNP of Western Europe plus the United States ran about $840 billion, contrasted with about $180 billion for the Soviet bloc excluding Communist China. In terms of population, the European West outnumbers the European East by 527 million people to 294 million.

If Asia were included in such comparisons, the committed East would overweigh the committed West in population but would fall far short in production. It is fairly safe to say that the committed West enjoys a four-to-one advantage in economic power over the committed East.

But what of the future? Aren't the Communist economies growing much faster than the Western economies? The general answer is no.

The Soviet Union and its satellites do not enjoy a strategic advantage on the basis of economic power. On the contrary, economically they have only a quarter the strength of the West. Moreover, the West is generally growing faster economically than the Soviet bloc. This is surely true in absolute terms: the annual addition to Western output of goods and services is much larger than the addition to bloc output. Percentagewise the growth is also faster for most Western countries, the major exception being the United States. Our current rates of growth are considerably below historic rates, particularly in industry where we are growing at only about 2 percent a year as compared with a long-run growth rate closer to 4 percent. There are undoubtedly many reasons for this slowing down of growth in the U.S. In my opinion, a major cause has been curbed incentives. The primary engine of growth in the American economy has been improved knowledge applied to the organization of economic activity—technology, as we call it. It has not been growth of capital and increased employment of labor, as in the Soviet Union. Something has happened to slow down the tempo of growing resource productivity in the American economy.

Nevertheless, this is a cause for concern over the long run, not the short run. As of now, we enjoy an enormous balance of economic power over the Soviet Union. When I was in intelligence work, I was taught a first principle: "Never underestimate the enemy." I don't recall learning a second principle. So I'd like to propose one now: "Don't overestimate him either." More troubles than we like to remember have come from overestimating Soviet strength, from confusing bluffs with pat hands. In any case, our strategic troubles, whatever they are, do not derive from lack of economic power but from the way that power is put to work.

24

Economic Warfare

I note from your syllabus that this is the sixteenth lecture in the course on "Strategy and Warfare" and this is the first time the subject of economic warfare has been mentioned. If I may say so—and, being an economist, I have license to say so—the subject seems to have been put in its proper place.

I sometimes think that we throw in the subject of economic warfare merely to round out a trilogy. Three is a magic number. Only bad luck comes in pairs; everything else comes in threes: animal, vegetable, and mineral; wine, women, and song; military, political, and economic warfare; and so on.

In fact, warfare is always a political act. The weapons may vary, but the action is always a struggle, a power struggle among sovereign states. Economic warfare is a clumsy concept, meaning at the same time both an area and a method of combat. On the one hand, it seems to mean policies to weaken, by all expedient means, the relative economic strength of enemies, actual or potential. On the other hand, it also refers to use of economic means to promote military or political objectives. The common element in both notions is the subservience of economic activity to political goals—in particular, to the goals of warfare.

These remarks were given at the National War College, Washington, D.C., in December 1958.

These days, political struggles take place in an atmosphere of either hot or cold war. The times are tragic, and not through our own choosing. It is idle to look for an early return of what used to be called peace, when nations exercised their rivalries by making and breaking alliances and other diplomatic maneuverings. It is doubtful that this period of comparative bliss characterizes more than one century of man's history—the nineteenth—in any event. The present state of things is illustrated by our yearning for an age of so-called limited wars.

I scarcely need elaborate the role of economic warfare under conditions of actual military operations. Trade with the enemy is severed, ultimately by means of blockade. All feasible means are used to disrupt and damage his internal economy. In short, everything possible is done to weaken the economic base of the enemy's military power.

Under conditions of cold war as we have come to know them, the nature of economic warfare is not so clear. The struggle is as much to align sides as to settle issues. We try to "win friends and influence people" at the same time that we try to weaken the economies of the opposing camp and to strengthen our own. This means not only winning friends but also keeping those we have; the struggle is defensive as well as offensive. The big question, which I shall return to later, is whether we can buy friendship.

In this type of economic warfare, the basic weapons are rewards and penalties. We reward those who go along with us and try to penalize those who are committed against us. Both have a dual purpose: to influence behavior and to strengthen the relative economic position of our side. I fear that we are often less than frank with ourselves as to what we are trying to do in our international economic programs, and as a consequence our policies are often inconsistent and self-canceling. I have in mind our propensity to delude ourselves that promoting self-interest—which today means simply protecting our political system from destruction—means nothing more than "doing good" in the world, helping the less fortunate. Business is business, and charity is charity. Each has an important place in our way of life, but it is suicidal nowadays to mix them up in international affairs.

Some will argue that this view of economic tactics is crude and misleading, that the proper approach is more subtle and sophisticated. The real problem, they will argue, is to create an economic climate in the so-called uncommitted areas that will destroy the attractiveness of communism. Satisfy the economic ambitions of these countries and they will automatically join our cause. Our task is simply to obliterate poverty throughout the world. In this sense, so the argument runs, there is no conflict between business and charity.

Now, I think there is a great deal of wisdom in this line of argument, but I think the practical form it usually takes is naive. Most of the people in the world are poor and always have been. The causes of poverty are manifold and deeply rooted, and it is silly—one could almost say insane—to believe that they can be removed in a decade or even a generation, if we only bend our backs to the task. The result of trying will most likely be social disruption and chaos, which, more than poverty, is the breeding ground of communism. Development means much more than sheer economic growth, and overly rapid growth may very well mean backward development. But more of this later.

The single most important fact in the present international struggle is that the East stands for overthrow of the existing order in the civilized world, while the West stands, more or less, for preservation of that order. We of the West are in the same unfortunate circumstance as the conservators of the nineteenth century, who tried through the Congress of Vienna and ensuing alliances to restrain the surging radicalism unleashed by the French Revolution. The danger to civilization as they saw it was real enough, but it hardly compares with the latent catastrophe in our age of successful totalitarianism and nuclear weapons.

The second most important fact is that significant groups in the West are openly doubting the superiority of the established order. These doubts come from high offices in our own government. Thus, Mr. Allen Dulles, director of the Central Intelligence Agency, recently stated in a public address that:

> . . . the Soviet economy has been growing, and is expected to continue to grow through 1962, at a rate roughly twice that of the economy of the United States. Annual growth over-all has been running between 6 and 7 per cent, annual growth of industry between 10 and 12 per cent.
>
> These rates of growth are exceedingly high. They have rarely been matched in other states except during limited periods of post-war rebuilding.[1]

In this statement and in much of the remainder of the same speech, Mr. Dulles suggests, first, that we in the United States consider the rate of economic growth a critical test of the success of any political system and, second, that we do not measure up to the Soviet Union in this test. Who could have spoken with more authority, at least on the matter of

[1] *New York Times,* Apr. 29, 1958, p. 8.

Soviet performance relative to ours? If we are to accept these statements as true, what are we to expect of uncommitted countries who have their eyes fastened on economic, political, and military growth, with little serious concern over matters of personal freedom so precious to us? What course of action, economic or political, are we to follow if the wave of the future belongs to the Soviet world? It is surely idle to expect that the capitalistic system should suddenly perform better than it ever has in its history. And if, as Mr. Dulles says, "a recession is an expensive luxury," what lesson are we—and, more importantly, the uncommitted nations—to draw from that? These are, indeed, serious questions. As I shall mention later, I do not believe Mr. Dulles was correct in his facts, but that does not alter the impact of his statements.

The West, then, is on the defensive, with a weakening faith in what it is defending. The East is on the offensive, with a growing confidence in ultimate victory, at least among the leaders, which is what counts at the moment. The world is filled with restless people and ambitious leaders, most of them completely ignorant of the workings of Western democracy and the content of Western civilization. We now propose to buy their allegiance to our cause.

The East has a much simpler task. It needs only to help trouble along wherever it finds it. A few pennies here, a few pennies there— wherever unrest is brewing, a boost to the revolutionists, directly or indirectly. The East merely helps undermine a tottering order that nobody seems eager to save.

It is in this context that economic warfare of our time must be viewed. Let me now consider the courses of action open to us.

Trading policies are the traditional weapons of economic warfare. These may take three general forms: first, restraining trade to harm another country; second, granting special terms to court another country's favor or to create a dependency; and third, disrupting the normal course of commerce to stir up internal troubles in another country.

A good case can be made for selective trade controls aimed at the Soviet bloc. The most important thing we can deny the bloc countries is our industrial know-how. They should be made to bear the heavy cost of technological progress. In saying this, I am not arguing that Soviet scientists and engineers are inferior to their Western counterparts. It would be both foolish and irrelevant to say that. I am saying that the Soviet pool of technology is much smaller than ours—overall, not everywhere. We should, I believe, do our best to deny the bloc countries machinery embodying technical knowledge they do not now have.

For example, we should not help Khrushchev in his goal of modernizing the Soviet chemical industry, for which he has as much as asked our help.

I doubt that selective controls could be carried much farther into the areas of so-called critical materials, and I think effective general trade controls are largely beyond serious consideration. We may try to reduce the volume of trade being carried on by the Communist countries, but there really is not much we can do through this course of action. First of all, trade by the Communist bloc with the outside world is not very important to the bloc in a long-run sense. Imports from the outside amount at best to 2 percent of the gross product of the bloc. In this sense, imports are considerably less important to the bloc than our own imports are to the American economy.

In the second place, most of this bloc trade is with countries other than the United States. We can control it only as far as we can persuade other countries to control it. Since trade benefits both partners, we cannot easily persuade. We have had ample experience with efforts to restrict this trade, most of it discouraging in all respects.

Trade severance is best reserved for that unhappy time when military operations seem imminent. It is the immediate impact that is most severe. Given time to adjust the economy to the strains imposed by loss of trade, any country can soften the damage. Since the permanent effects would be relatively small in any event, we should be careful to use this weapon when it will be most immediately effective. We can meanwhile hope that time will never come.

While declaring myself against a policy of general trade controls, I must also oppose deliberate expansion of trade with the Soviet bloc. Some might argue that we should do this in an effort to soften communism. Others might argue that we have something to gain economically. I don't agree with either argument. Insisting on bilateral exchanges negotiated through governments, the Soviet Union can twist terms of trade to her benefit, so that we could gain virtually nothing from the trade itself. If I could believe that there has been a significant change of heart among the leaders of the Soviet Union, I might favor an effort to resume more normal trading relations. I have searched hard for signs of such a change and found very few. Things are stirring within the country, but we must wait for more developments, in my opinion, before strengthening the hand of current rulers through gifts of this nature.

If we can't accomplish much by way of manipulating trade with the bloc, perhaps we can use this general weapon to influence behavior in uncommitted areas. By granting special favorable terms of trade, we might make them more friendly to our side or more dependent on us, thus making them more susceptible to pressure. I won't discuss the first policy at this point, since it can be handled better under the topic of foreign aid. The second policy might be called the dope-addict approach: get a country hooked, and then drive a hard bargain for future supplies.

There are three difficulties with this approach as far as the West is concerned. In the first place, most trade is carried on by private parties. It would be virtually impossible, from an administrative point of view, to work out a large-scale system of preferential terms. This is to say nothing of the problem of coordinating such a complex policy with all our Western partners, so that there would be no friction.

In the second place, the uncommitted areas are already heavily dependent on the West. It hardly pays us to increase the dependence through artificial means. For example, 94 percent of the foreign trade of underdeveloped countries is with the West. Even in countries like Egypt and Yugoslavia, where trade with the bloc is relatively most important, more than 75 percent of the trade is with the West.

In the third place, we are severely limited in exploiting any dependency, if we should wish to do so, by the fact that the Soviet Union stands ready, in the pose of big brother, to counter any significant moves we might make. If anything, the danger lies in the other direction; uncommitted areas may try to blackmail us into giving aid by threatening to take help from the bloc.

Unfortunately, these restraints do not operate to the same degree on the Soviet bloc. Since all trade is controlled by the state, there are no great difficulties in setting preferential terms, though bureaucratic rigidities cause some serious problems. Since the bloc countries are essentially on the offensive, penetrating new markets, they are able to shift the dependence of trading partners in their direction. At the same time, we must recognize that the situation is not unreservedly favorable. Just as the bloc limits the power of the West to exploit trade dependencies, so also the West limits the bloc. Yugoslavia is a clear example of the shoe on the other foot. Moreover, there are abundant examples of Soviet bungling, where bargaining has been rigid and terms inflexible, and the Soviet Union could not resist opportunities to make a little profit. We have the classic rice-cement barter with Burma. The cement was delivered and unloaded on open docks in the monsoon season, and the rice was later dumped on other Burmese markets.

So far, the bloc trade offensive has been carried out on a relatively small, though gradually expanding, scale. While the total trade of bloc countries with underdeveloped areas has risen by around 90 percent from its postwar low in 1953, it has risen by only about 50 percent from its level in 1948. As already pointed out, trade with the bloc accounts for only 6 percent of the total foreign trade of underdeveloped areas.

The third tactic of trade warfare is disruption of the normal course of commerce to create internal disturbances. Here again, the Soviet bloc is in a better position than the West. Our aim in the uncommitted areas is to stabilize, not to disrupt. The Communist aim is precisely the reverse. We might wish to stir up trouble in Communist economies, but we can't do much to disrupt trade that scarcely exists. The bloc has something to work on, namely, the relatively free commerce among Western nations.

There have, in fact, been rumors that the Soviet Union engaged in this kind of practice last year in the markets for tin and aluminum by dumping large quantities of these metals onto a market already depressed by the American recession. I am not yet convinced that this was a case of deliberate dumping. It could have simply marked the first stages of Soviet participation in these markets as a permanent exporter. In any case, it is not yet clear that the reaction of affected countries to practices of this sort will be entirely favorable to the Soviet bloc. As far as tin is concerned, the country most hurt was Bolivia. The Communist cause within Bolivia was probably promoted by the internal economic problems generated by the depressed price of tin. On the other hand, considerable resentment toward the Communist bloc has arisen from the suspicion of deliberate dumping.

To summarize very briefly, I would say that the West has little to gain politically from trade warfare. The cards are stacked against us. The bloc does have something to gain, but not as much as might appear at first glance.

Perhaps we can accomplish more through economic aid in the form of gifts and loans. These would presumably be used to bolster our ties with friendly nations and to win over so-called uncommitted nations. The key question here is how much friendship can be bought at what price. Since economic aid has obviously become the cornerstone of our international economic policy, I want to spend the rest of my time discussing this program and its likely effectiveness.

Let me, first of all, draw a sharp distinction between economic aid and military assistance. Both are to some extent the same thing in that they amount to giving other countries extra resources. One might argue that military assistance from the United States simply means that a country can divert to other uses the resources it otherwise would have used for national defense. In part, this is undoubtedly true, but only in part. The countries receiving military assistance simply would not have built up the same military establishment in the absence of assistance. We are, in effect, purchasing our own national defense in other countries through this program, providing a small subsidy for their economies on the side. None of the remarks I am about to make should be taken as applying to this military assistance program.

If I may speak plainly, I would say that we should be fully prepared for failure of the economic aid program. We have, in fact, nothing but earnest hopes to be optimistic about. We have no concrete evidence that a country whose economic development has been speeded up by substantial gifts from outside will commit itself against the Communist bloc. We are acting on faith, and in some cases it is misguided.

I have crudely branded our economic aid program as an effort to buy friendship. Having spoken for effect, let me now be more accurate. There are three serious arguments for Western economic aid to underdeveloped countries, which I would put as follows: first, gratitude leads to friendship; second, poverty leads to communism; and third, if we don't, the Communists will. I ignore fallacious arguments popularly advanced, such as giving goods away prevents depressions, economic aid solves our problem of agricultural surpluses, and so on.

Now, I would say that the three serious arguments for economic aid, though not so crudely put, still boil down to the proposition that friendship can be bought, indirectly if not directly. I will try to explain what I mean while examining each of the arguments critically.

There is little trouble with the first. Simply put, it states that aid to underdeveloped countries will make them grateful to us, and this gratitude will gradually develop into true friendship. Before we put much faith in this proposition, we would do well to reflect on a homely saying: "Nobody loves a rich uncle." We know what this means. If he gives you nothing, he is stingy. If he gives you something, he is still stingy. If he gives you everything, he is merely correcting past injustices: he had no more right to the fortune than you in the first place.

The Communist bloc has been shrewd on this matter. Aid has taken the form of repayable loans. To be sure, the terms are very favorable to the borrower, with low interest charges and many years to repay. The loans are, to this extent, gifts. But an entirely different atmosphere is created: the recipient country feels that it is being treated as an equal, not as a poor country cousin. The favorable terms are viewed as evidence of the good faith of the lender: he is not taking advantage of the temporary poverty of the borrower by charging what the traffic will bear. At the same time, the borrower is expected to repay as he can. Any extension of time granted by the lender is an additional gesture of magnanimity. It is refreshing to note that our own policy is shifting more toward so-called loans and away from outright gifts.

In any case, I see no evidence that gratitude for aid, loans, or investments has pulled uncommitted countries into our camp, nor that it has significantly deterred them from any leanings they have toward the Communist camp. I am impressed and depressed by the fact that some of the areas we have helped most, directly and indirectly, seem to resent us most. It is instructive to note which Latin American countries had the greatest disturbances during Vice-President Nixon's recent visit. We might also take note of developments in Iraq.

The second argument—namely, that poverty leads to communism—is more complex. There is, of course, a great deal of truth in it: people are more receptive to revolution when hungry than when well-fed. But poverty alone is not a cause of revolution. Revolutions are triggered when the possibilities for improving one's lot have been concretely demonstrated and when the restraining forces of tradition and custom have been suddenly shattered. Greatest unrest comes in rapidly growing economies just emerging from poverty, not in poor and stagnant economies.

It is interesting that this is precisely the Communist attitude: they give aid because they believe rapid growth, not poverty, fosters communism. They want to stimulate deterioration of the established social order without putting a new one in its place. They want to urbanize and industrialize rural peoples overnight, to create the social problems of industrial revolution. As the established order degenerates into chaos, they stand on the sidelines with a well-disciplined group prepared to seize power at the appropriate time.

Development means much more than economic growth. Social and political institutions must move along with economic change, and this takes time—a painfully long time. What shall we do in regions of West Africa where there are laws requiring meat to be sold with the hide attached to make sure it is not human; where people are brought to trial for interfering with the weather and plead guilty to improve business?

I do not mean to argue that economic development should be stopped in these areas. By no means. It should proceed, but at the moderate pace the societies can tolerate. Moreover, there is no reason for government-to-government grants or loans. Private investment will do the job efficiently and generally adequately, and it is more compatible with the kind of system we stand for.

I am deeply disturbed by the growing belief in the West that private enterprise cannot develop the underdeveloped economies. We are constantly told that only central planning can do the job, that there are no examples of rapid growth in such areas under capitalism. This is the very opposite of the truth: the only examples we have are examples of capitalism. I cite Japan and Malaya as outstanding. On the other side, there is one country and one alone in recent history that has shown rapid growth under comprehensive central planning: the Soviet Union. And it did not start from a period of stagnation: Russian economic growth during the last half century of the tsarist period was extremely rapid by any modern standards.

To illustrate the sentiments I am talking about, let me read at length from a very influential Western book on economic aid, written by Professors Millikan and Rostow of the Center for International Studies at MIT.

> For any substantial expansion of international investment above existing levels it is essential that investment *programs* (not merely projects) be developed by the receiving countries. Such programs are necessary to insure: (1) that the various component projects interrelate and reinforce each other; (2) that the general objectives implied in the entire pattern of projects are ones which the people of the country will support; (3) that the collection of projects and measures undertaken will produce a faster growth of national product than any other which is consistent with the goals of society; (4) that the resources of the economy have been tapped for the maximum contribution they can make to its development; and (5) that foreign exchange requirements have been minimized.
>
> Such programs should include both the investment planned by public authorities and some estimate of what can reasonably be expected from the private sector. In other words, they should project forward for a reasonable period the total pattern of investment for the entire economy, together with estimates of the sources from which resources for investment, both

public and private, can be secured. Whether the economic philosophy of the country calls for close regulation of private investment or permits private capital very freely to seek its own outlets, some estimate of the pattern of private investment is essential to the planning of whatever supporting public activity is contemplated. The need for programming derives from the fact that, in the transition stage of development, the success of many particular investment projects depends upon the entire set of investments being undertaken simultaneously.

At the least, the existence of such a national development program is evidence that the country has explicitly faced certain fundamental choices about its development—such as the relative weight to be given to agriculture as against industry; the fraction of resources to be devoted to social overhead capital such as railroads or public utilities and the like; the importance to be placed on consumers' capital (like housing) as against more directly productive instruments. A national program will naturally reflect the values and goals of the people of the country for which it is drawn. The purpose of review by an agency outside the country is not to pass on those values but to insure the program's internal consistency, to make certain that all relevant issues have been faced, and, where the program rests strictly on economic or technical relations, to see that they have been correctly applied.

An important consideration must be the adequacy of the measures undertaken by the country to capture the maximum flow of savings from its own citizens. The financial mechanism and the tax structure must be so designed as to eliminate pockets of either unemployed or misapplied resources. Savings channels must be set up to maximize the flow of savings, both small and large, into developmental investment.[2]

In short, the government of an underdeveloped country should take over the role of saving and investing and run the economy in accord with a comprehensive, centrally directed economic plan. This should, in fact, be made a requirement for receipt of American aid. We could not give a stronger endorsement to the Soviet system, the system we are struggling against. The plain truth is that no economy in history has promoted growth through forced saving and comprehensive planning and still stopped short of the Soviet-type political order. We have no example of a successful "middle way." In the case of underdeveloped countries, I have no doubt that the consequence of following the advice of Professors Millikan and Rostow would be deliverance of these countries to the Communists, the only disciplined group prepared to

[2] Max F. Millikan and W. W. Rostow, *A Proposal: Key to an Effective Foreign Policy* (New York, Harper & Bros., 1957), pp. 72–74.

take over their direction in the recommended manner. Since we should have given our blessing to comprehensive planning, we could scarcely be indignant when the countries followed our advice to its logical conclusion.

This leads me to consider the weakest argument for foreign aid: that we must act in order to forestall Communist action. In the first place, there is no natural limit to the amount of aid a country wants or will accept. When we give aid, this does not reduce dollar-for-dollar the amount a country will take from the Soviet bloc. Most underdeveloped countries will accept all aid that is offered, depending only on the strings attached. In the second place, we would have to spread our aid thinly in all directions, almost without end, to promote such a policy. As in actual warfare, we ought to choose our battlegrounds carefully. At least, we should not put ourselves at the mercy of the enemy, fighting wherever and whenever he chooses. This is simply to say that our aid should be based on strategic considerations. We should give aid where it will do most good and give none where it will do no or very little good. We should try to counteract or forestall Soviet action only when and where it pays us to do so for some other reason.

Since the end of World War II the United States has provided about $60 billion in direct governmental foreign aid of one sort or another. If we deduct military assistance and other forms of aid to countries already committed to the West, we are left with $12.8 billion in grants and loans to uncommitted underdeveloped areas. This does not include indirect aid through international organizations or the gross investment of private American firms in those areas, which together were probably equally large. This total of around $25 billion in American expenditures may be compared with bloc commitments of $1.6 billion and deliveries of around $400 million. In other words, the United States has provided—through grants, loans, and investments—about sixty times as much foreign aid as the Soviet bloc deliveries to date, and about sixteen times as much as total bloc commitments, fulfilled and unfulfilled. If we limit our comparison to the sixteen underdeveloped countries receiving aid from the bloc, the United States government has contributed eight times as much as bloc deliveries and 1.6 times as much as total bloc commitments.

In 1957 alone, direct governmental aid from the United States amounted to around $1.6 billion, or as much as total bloc commitments to date. Since bloc deliveries in that year ran around $200 million, American direct aid was eight times bloc aid. In the sixteen countries courted by the bloc, American aid was one and a half times bloc aid.

Not even this is the whole story. If we add together all grants, loans, and investments provided to underdeveloped countries by the West, the total is between $5 and $6 billion in 1957 alone, or twenty-five to thirty times bloc deliveries in that year.

I do not mean to say that the Soviet venture into economic warfare need not be taken seriously. Quite the contrary, it poses a grave challenge. Its effectiveness in stirring up trouble for the West cannot be doubted. But the big question is: Can we meet the challenge merely by increasing the flood of American and Western foreign aid? The enormous discrepancy between our and their expenditures to date points up the terrible handicap we suffer, as far as buying allegiance is concerned.

What am I trying to say by all this? Am I just taking an inflexible and doctrinaire position against all varieties of foreign aid? I do not mean to be or think I am. I merely ask that we restrain our sentiments and recognize the brutal certainty that foreign aid will not work miracles or near miracles. I think we should be psychologically prepared for the loss of areas into which we have poured large sums of money, particularly in Asia and the Middle East. I think we should recognize that our strength in the cold war does not lie primarily in weapons of economic warfare. If we draw the lesson from that, we will put less faith in untested economic schemes and more faith in tried political and military tactics, including the crucial area of psychological warfare.

I have been very negative this morning, and I want to close with a few remarks on a more positive level. To save time, I will be categorical in my statements, but you should all realize that I sound more confident about the wisdom of my proposals than I am.

First of all, we should continually ask ourselves what it is we are trying to save. What is the struggle all about? Each of us will have a slightly different answer, but that doesn't matter. The important thing is that we have a reasonably clear idea of the end we are seeking so that we don't choose means that in themselves forfeit the end. As we think these matters through, we are certain to realize that development means much more than growth, and perhaps we may tone down our awed praise of Soviet accomplishments.

Second, we must get the facts straight. While we should never underestimate the enemy, we should not overestimate him either—particularly if we are going to broadcast the estimate over the globe.

Many of our critical troubles of the day can be traced to a serious overestimation of the power of our military enemies in World War II. If I had time today, I would challenge in detail the official American assessment of the strength and growth of the Soviet economy. This is not to say that Soviet economic growth has been unimpressive. It has been impressive, indeed. But it has not been unprecedented, and it is currently being matched in other Western economies such as France, West Germany, and Japan. I fear that many recent statements on Soviet growth made by government officials are intended primarily to stir the American people into action, to drive away complacency. There is real danger in complacency, and a strong dose of fright serves a good cause. But overstimulation of fear may backfire with serious consequences. We need to be made to understand something quite different, namely, that a country can have enormous military strength without great economic wealth. In all matters, we must keep our heads when we examine the facts.

Third, we should always keep our eyes on the committed nations. A bird in hand is worth two in the bush. Our European allies are the great reservoir of strength for us now and over the next few decades. In 1956 the OEEC (Organization for European Economic Cooperation) countries had a total population of 287 million, over 100 million larger than ours, and a combined gross national product of $240 billion, about 57 percent of ours. Both population and GNP are larger than for the Soviet Union. From 1953 through 1957 their combined industrial production increased by 31 percent, which is not far below the Soviet performance—for some individual countries, the performance is above the Soviet level.

Our Asian allies—Formosa, South Korea, and Vietnam—are the second reservoir of strength. We must, of course, continue supporting their economic and military development.

The other committed countries are those in the bloc. It is reasonable to say that the people who want least to be ruled by Communists are those who are. The problems here are tragic, as we know from the Hungarian uprising, and I cannot prescribe foolproof ways to utilize this great body of discontent. At a minimum, we can play the Soviet game and take every opportunity to stir up discontent. As with them, it would not cost much.

Fourth, we should pick and choose carefully among the uncommitted countries. We should focus on countries of most strategic location and with the most stable political orders. There is no point in giving the historically unstable government that extra shove into the chasm of communism.

Fifth, we should liberalize our trade with all countries in the free world. This move alone would be a very large contribution to the economic well-being of our trading partners, committed and uncommitted, developed and underdeveloped. More importantly, it would show the world that we practice what we preach, that we really believe in private competitive enterprise. The rest of the world has good ground for calling us hypocrites on this score.

Finally, we should not sell ourselves short. The development of Western civilization is a feat unparalleled in man's history. We have had our sweeping periods of exciting and rapid economic growth. Even as late as the Civil War, this country was underdeveloped by modern standards. Forty years later we were a prosperous and powerful country. We must be careful not to boast, but we should not let Communist propaganda about unprecedented economic achievements go unchallenged. Nor should we fail to remind others of what other things went along with sheer growth and how empty and meaningless growth is without those other things.

25

Economic Influence
of the Middle East on
the World Community

I suppose this topic has been assigned to me as a practitioner of the dismal science because it isn't a very pleasant subject. It has all the characteristics of that well-known flight in which the pilot suddenly announced to the passengers that he had some bad news and some good news. The bad news was that he was lost; the good news was that he was making record speed.

There have been few events in this country that provided the opportunity to get lost so quickly as the energy crisis. I don't want to rake over old coals today by going back to the beginning, except to make it clear that the drastic action we took after the embargo was unprecedented. We have never done anything quite like it in our history. As a matter of fact, we had gone through a long war that we didn't want to declare and had studiously avoided normal wartime economic controls in order to give the appearance that it really wasn't a war. Then, almost as soon as some semblance of peace had broken out, we imposed rigid controls on our economy.

The embargo was a serious problem to which we reacted in an almost hysterical way. We continue to have an energy problem but it is a tractable one, and we shouldn't lose our heads. If we keep cool, we can solve it. So let me start with some good news.

These remarks were given at The Citadel, Charleston, S. C., in December 1974.

First of all, the sky has not fallen down on the world as a result of the Arab embargo and cartel. Despite reports to the contrary from many "chicken littles," the world is not becoming impoverished as a consequence of the oil cartel. The effect is significant but not disastrous. The world is consuming about twenty-two billion barrels of crude oil a year; the United States about six out of the twenty-two. Before the embargo, the price of that crude oil was about $3 a barrel, so that the total expenditure was $66 billion. The price per barrel was much higher than it had been a few years earlier, and the actual cost of producing a barrel of oil in the Middle East was far below the price. The world expenditure on crude oil amounted to about 2 percent of world GNP as best we can calculate these things. In the United States, the expenditure on crude oil was $18 billion or so, which was a little over 1 percent of our GNP. Now, after the embargo and the strengthening of the cartel, the price has roughly tripled, a quite amazing performance. It has more than tripled throughout most of the world, but not in the United States, because we have imposed strict controls on the pricing and allocation of domestic crude oil—a serious mistake, in my opinion, for reasons I shall get to in a moment. The annual worldwide expenditure on crude oil has risen from $66 billion a year ago to about $180 billion today. Instead of being 2 percent of world GNP, it is 6 percent. In the United States, the percentage has risen from a little over 1 to about 3 percent of our GNP. We import about 40 percent of the crude oil we use, and the cost of imported oil has risen from about $7 billion to $23 billion. Now that's what has happened. Restrictions by the OPEC (Organization of Petroleum Exporting Countries) cartel have cost the world an extra 4 percent of its GNP for oil. But let's keep that figure in mind: it is 4 percent, not 40. And, in the long run, the impact will certainly be less than that.

The second thing to keep in mind is that our inflation was not caused by the energy crisis. We and the rest of the West had inflation with us a long time before the embargo took place. Our inflationary period goes back at least a decade and is very closely related to what I mentioned before: our effort to fight a war without really trying. The oil cartel has, however, affected the price level in a significant way. The embargo and subsequent restrictions of supply probably had the effect of raising the U.S. price level in one year by about 3 percentage points, so that we ended up with an inflation of 12 percent instead of, say, 9 percent in 1974. That was a one-shot effect, showing up only in this year's rise in the price level. Whether the oil cartel will increase future rates of inflation will depend on its ability to continue raising the price of oil faster than other prices rise on the average.

The third piece of good news is that we are not running out of energy. It is just going to become more costly. There are many things from which we can get energy, including abundant coal, and we have no idea of how much energy is ultimately recoverable in an economically feasible way. We tend to get alarmed about running out of energy because we are aware only of what we call proven reserves, or what we know we can profitably pump or dig out of the ground at present prices and costs of production. As the cost and price go up, we look around for more and we find it. At least we have found it so far in our history. The problem is that it's going to cost us more and more for a unit of energy unless we achieve a spectacular technological breakthrough, and we may have to open up some areas for exploration that we have kept closed, like most of Alaska. At first, we will just probe and dig, but after a while oil will come bubbling up from a lot of places—the North Sea, Alaska, Vietnam, and so on.

Fourth, market forces are not to blame for the energy crisis. I get very annoyed at people like Senator Henry Jackson who are constantly pointing the finger of blame at the oil industry or the market in general. As a matter of fact, most problems have been created because political forces have interfered with the market and not permitted it to work. Price controls and administrative regulations, particularly such things as the ceiling price on natural gas, have created serious problems for us and have solved nothing. None of this gadgetry changes the basic reality—that less oil is being supplied and therefore more will be paid for each barrel, whether price is kept artificially low or not. The effect of keeping price down is to inhibit companies from searching for more fuel and increasing production. Hence we make the problem worse.

Finally, on the more or less good-news side, there is no long-run problem in where the Arabs are going to invest their newly acquired wealth. It will not pay them to hold that wealth indefinitely in the form of liquid assets. Now we shall face some special problems that we haven't thought about for a long time and need to give some attention to, such as whether or not we want Lockheed to be owned by some sheik or other. That is a problem, and we should have thought about that kind of thing a long time ago, with regard not only to the Arabs but also to anyone else that is a potential enemy.

That's the good news. Now let me talk about the bad.

Of course, the most serious impact has come from the sudden shock that the United States and the rest of the world have experienced as a result of the reduced supply of oil. The blow came out of the blue, so to speak. We were unprepared for it and hence the shock was violent. We had to adjust quickly without having any emergency resources to draw on. It takes time for people to adjust their consumption habits when something becomes more costly, so that the initial shock of such a cutback in supply has an impact on price. Price is the shock absorber. But if the market is allowed to work, the initial rise in price will generate both a reduction in consumption and an expansion in production that will bring about the needed adjustment. The greater the shock effect on price in the short run, the faster the long-run adjustment will take place. Unfortunately we tried to deaden the shock and as a consequence the adjustment period is going to be dragged out longer than it need be. Meanwhile, we are being confronted with all kinds of unpleasant choices, such as whether people should be forced to consume less through various devices like rationing. I think consumption should be reduced, but that should be done by letting price go, by removing controls on the domestic price of oil and gas, and by getting rid of compulsory allocation and all that.

I might point out, as Admiral Thomas Moorer did last night, that we should not have been caught by surprise. We were, but we should not have been. We were because nobody was listening to the Pentagon. We knew there was going to be a problem and tried without success to get attention in this question. Despite what our secretary of state now says, there was ample warning from the Arabs. They told us they were going to embargo oil the next time there was a war in the Middle East. Those in charge of our government just didn't listen.

The second piece of bad news is that, as a result of the shock, the international financial system has been under severe stress. The initial effect of the cutback in the supply of oil was, as I have said, to cause all consuming countries to pay more rather than consume less. Therefore, the bill rose enormously for many countries. Even though it might not be that large a fraction of national income, as I pointed out, it is a large fraction of trade transactions. It will take some time for the financial shock to be transmitted into a change in real income through a reorientation of imports and exports. In the meantime, particularly because our world order is in such a mess, a serious financial problem exists. Some countries like Italy that are already tottering on the brink of insolvency because of political weakness at home may be pushed into resolving the problem in a way that will not be in our best interest or in the best interest of the world as a whole.

Third, there is a threat that the vast Arab funds that have been accumulated from the tripled oil price may hang over us as a potential weapon in economic warfare. They may hold a large part of these funds as money to be used in disrupting the financial community in the same way that the embargo was used. That is a serious problem and one we have to think about and try to do something about. There is bound to be, as long as the cartel remains strong, a substantial transfer of real income from the rest of the world to the Arabs. The Arabs—we have got to accept this fact—are now going to be richer than they were before, and everybody else is going to be a little poorer. That's all there is to it, unless there is some way the cartel can be broken.

Incidentally, I am not so pessimistic about that as some people are. I think that the best way to break the cartel is to permit the development of alternative sources of oil through more exploration, allowing price to clear the market. It is puzzling to me how the Arabs have managed to keep the price so high for so long—why the market doesn't break. I think one of the answers is our stupidity in putting a ceiling on the price of domestic oil, an act that has given the Arabs an opportunity to raise the price that much more, because Americans don't feel the full impact and hence don't cut consumption as much as they otherwise would. So the Arabs collect more than they otherwise could. Another reason is that, having been once bitten, the world has become twice shy, and all available barrels and tanks and other storage facilities are being filled with oil. When everything is full, demand will drop. Sooner or later, it's going to be very hard for the Arabs to keep price as high as it now is. In any event, as long as they do manage to hold the cartel together—as long as they do manage to restrict production— they are going to get richer and the rest of the world is going to get poorer. That's a fact of life.

There is another even more discouraging fact, and that is that the regions really dependent on Arab oil, such as Europe and Japan, are going to become increasingly vulnerable to economic warfare. Their foreign policy will be accordingly influenced and the power balance of the world upset. The influence of the United States will continue to weaken as long as we retain the posture we have maintained in the Middle East. We have a problem that has always been with us and that we have not focused on sufficiently in the past, and that is the question of how much reliability we wish to have in the long-run supply of energy so that we can be prepared for emergencies such as last year's embargo or a sudden war. We have ducked this question for a long time, and it is time that we quit ducking. It's going to cost us something to get reliability. If we want reliability, we had better begin to pay the cost. We have to begin paying a little extra for our domestic supplies and protecting them from foreign competition, one way or another.

Finally—I'm not sure that this is bad news—this particular crisis, as we call it, has, I hope, finally made us aware of the fact that we live in a world in which we have to pay attention to the problem of economic warfare. We cannot think of foreign commerce and international trade in the classic terms of an exchange of goods in which everybody benefits because only private individuals are involved. We live in a world in which many economies are run by governments and are run for political purposes. Economic forces are used for political ends. We have to adapt to that world, and we have to begin thinking about how we can play that game. Living in such a world is unfortunate, just as a rainy day is unfortunate—it would be much nicer if the day were sunny. But if we have learned a lesson from our recent experiences and act accordingly, we can consider ourselves fortunate.

26

Power and Peace

The scholar is constantly frustrated and embarrassed, a revered mentor of mine used to say, by finding it necessary to prove that water runs downhill. I feel that way today as I speak to a subject best addressed by history: the role of power in keeping the peace. Yet the message of history is often unlearned, and I will not apologize for repeating it, familiar as it may be, from my point of view.

We have come to one of those times in which many earnest citizens set all things military on one side and peace on the other. Since war is waged by the military, they conclude that peace will be achieved only when the military disappears. What, aside from logic, is wrong with this line of reasoning?

First, we should take a look at what we mean by peace. Perhaps the only thing more difficult than maintaining peace is defining it. But we need not be concerned with philosophical niceties here, for the basic problem before us is one of relations among nations. Of course, nations are at peace in the trite sense when they are not in combat. In a more fundamental sense, they are at peace when some are not threatening to

This essay, which was originally presented at a conference commemorating the fiftieth anniversary of the Hoover Institution on War, Revolution and Peace, in November 1969, is reprinted, with minor omissions, from E. Berkeley Tompkins, ed., *Peaceful Change in Modern Society,* pp. 64–70, with the permission of the publishers, Hoover Institution Press. Copyright 1971 by the Board of Trustees of the Leland Stanford Junior University.

use open force against others in order to alter the existing order of things, either within or among them.

To go much farther in defining peace would rob the word of content and relevance. It would be utopian, for instance, to describe peace as a state of affairs in which all parties are satisfied with the status quo, or to equate peace with universal bliss or with the absence of implicit threats of violence. Men and nations being what they are, there will always be conflicts of interest of all sorts, and the important question is how they will be resolved, whether through coercion or agreement.

What makes nations choose the path of violence? Why does one nation go to war against another? One could obviously catalog many reasons, and I would not presume to lecture on them before an institution celebrating its golden anniversary of inquiry into this arcane subject. I will instead focus on one specific condition that has characterized much of history.

Let there be a powerful nation, and let it be governed by whatever group holds the reins of power. Let those in power be determined, for one reason or another, to change the state of affairs in the surrounding world; in a word, to be committed to altering the accepted status quo in other societies. The stage is then obviously set for conquest and violence.

Violence need not ensue, of course, if the threatened nations do not value the prevailing culture enough to fight for it. It need not ensue for two other reasons: because the threatened nations are too weak to resist or because they are too strong to be attacked. The only difference in the last two cases is the outcome. In both cases there is no war, but in the one there is conquest and in the other repulse. That is the sole difference.

For this characterization to make sense, the nations in question obviously must not be mutually threatening one another. Such a situation is not unknown, but we are not discussing it now. We are instead talking about one nation or group of nations that is minding its own business without harming anyone else and another that is aggressively meddling.

This is surely not to say that the peaceful nations are, if we may speak of their collective mentalities, fully satisfied with the existing state of affairs either within or beyond their boundaries. Quite the contrary is normally the case. The difference comes in the means used, first, to decide on desirable change and, second, to effect it.

We now come straight to the issue of deterrent power. A deterrent is relevant only if there is a deteree, or somebody who must be discouraged or restrained from committing forceful harm. Just as beauty is in the eye of the beholder, so also is deterrence in the mind of the deteree.

A story is told of an ancient Chinese strategist whose skills were legendary. The enemy mounted a large force against him and marched upon the citadel that formed the strong point of his defenses. Unfortunately, he had dispatched his troops to another field of battle and found himself undefended as the hordes gathered to attack. Sizing up the situation quickly, he ordered the gates of the citadel thrown open and a large banquet spread upon the ramparts. As the enemy approached, he sat majestically at the table, partaking of the feast and beckoning the enemy to enter the gates. Mindful of his genius, the attacking generals would not believe what their eyes told them. They saw no defenders on the battlements or within the city, but they were not to be so easily deceived. Taking counsel, they quickly decided that an attack was doomed to failure, and so they withdrew.

We cannot, of course, carry the moral of this story too far, but it illustrates, through an extreme example, the point being made. If the enemy bent on attack is to be deterred, he must assess in his own mind that the party he threatens is both able and willing to deliver a crippling blow. Manifest power need not be employed openly to be effective.

This principle applies equally to nations that threaten others. There is no need to engage in violence as long as the threat to do so will work as well. Diplomacy is therefore a useful instrument of power politics.

It is surely correct that the antithesis of conflict is rational discourse with the view to resolving problems through voluntary agreement. This is what we mean when we speak of government by discussion. Yet we must be careful to recognize that bargaining, negotiating, and compromising often go beyond the bounds of rational discourse among friends bent on reaching peaceful consensus, particularly in the area of international diplomacy.

Given the international scene we have postulated, with some nations determined to change the exising state of affairs, we cannot expect that agreements will be reached at the negotiating table solely on the basis of logic, reason, and persuasion. The threat of force stands waiting in the wings, just visible to the negotiating parties. Leaders of a powerful country determined to have their way will not be satisfied with resting their case on its intellectual, historical, and ethical merits. They will be prepared to do more than offer inducements and concessions of one kind or another to achieve their basic goals. They will not shrink from the threat, implicit or explicit, of forcibly denying legitimate rights or of imposing harmful consequences.

Those nations innocent of designs on others and desirous of settling international problems without coercion must face this reality. If they renounce military strength, as their instincts urge, they place themselves at the mercy of aggressors at the negotiating table as well as on the battlefield. Indeed, the one is merely another form of the other. The innocent nations must have sufficient armed strength to deter the use of aggressive force in either case.

One hardly needs to be reminded that this is a sorry and tragic state of affairs. How much more desirable it would be if good will and peaceful intent prevailed everywhere. But does it make sense for a lamb to bargain with a wolf? President Nixon drove this point home in his speech before the Air Force Academy in June 1969, when he said:

> . . . there is one school of thought that holds that the road to understanding with the Soviet Union and Communist China lies through a downgrading of our own alliances and what amounts to a unilateral reduction of our arms in order to demonstrate our good faith.
>
> They believe that we can be conciliatory and accommodating only if we do not have the strength to be otherwise. They believe that America will be able to deal with the possibility of peace only when we are unable to cope with the threat of war.
>
> Those who think that way have grown weary of the weight of free world leadership that fell upon us in the wake of World War II.
>
> They argue that the United States is as much responsible for the tensions in the world as the adversary we face.[1]

Nations can negotiate on many things, including limits on their respective armed power. We face the paradox, however, that a nation must be strong before it can negotiate with a powerful antagonist on mutual reduction of strength.

Having all this in mind, we need to be clear about one thing: confrontation is always to be avoided in favor of meaningful negotiations, whenever the choice is open. Wise diplomacy on the part of a reasonable government, when backed by sufficient strength, offers far more hope for peaceful resolution of problems than a policy of unyielding confrontation.

[1] *New York Times,* June 5, 1969, p. 30.

But we must not expect too much of diplomacy. In particular, we must guard against the illusion that a stable pattern of relations, once successfully negotiated from properly balanced strength, will endure forever. If nothing else, relative power changes over time, destabilizing the initial order. We need look no farther than the tragic interwar period in Europe and Asia to draw this lesson. As has been so often noted, the problem is one of continually balancing power rather than achieving a balance. In mapping foreign policy based on negotiation, one must keep a step ahead of the times to be successful in the deeper sense.

The dynamic demands of international politics can easily lead to frustration, and frustration in turn to the urge to withdraw. Thence flows the philosophy of the Maginot line or fortress America, which is even less relevant to changing conditions than the worst international order it is designed to replace. Here is a case of excessive reliance on a particular variety of strength: defensive, passive, and inflexible. It can succeed only if every powerful nation retreats into its own fortress, a situation hardly consistent with the reasons for withdrawal in the first place.

How, then, does a country of peaceful intent make its way through the maze of world politics? How does it protect its own legitimate interests when it must reckon with hostile designs on the part of other nations of varying identity and power?

It makes sure, first of all, that it has sufficient strength and resolution to cope with the rigors of world politics. It seeks, secondly, the path of negotiation as far as other nations will go along. And it prepares itself, finally, to deter and, if necessary, to repulse hostilities. To neglect any one of these elements of foreign policy is to invite disaster.

As I speak today, negotiators from the United States and the Soviet Union are gathered in Helsinki for preliminary talks on how we can curb the nuclear arms race. No negotiations in recent times have been more critical, and we in your government are determined to pursue them seriously, soberly, and realistically, with the objective of reaching a successful outcome. To do so, we must fully appreciate the realities of power confronting us. Let me give you some of the specifics, already reviewed in many public forums but perhaps worth repeating.

As we come to the bargaining table, we find that the Soviets are continuing a rapid buildup of strategic forces that seems to reach beyond their defensive needs and presents a potential menace to our own deterrent of nuclear warfare. I speak here not of surmise or speculation on our part, but of simple fact. It is a simple and unassailable fact, attested by hard evidence, that the Soviet Union is extending its deployment of the SS-9 intercontinental ballistic missile. This enormous missile is capable of delivering a 25-megaton warhead and possibly could carry three separate 5-megaton warheads.

Reflect, if you will, on the destructive power of such a weapon. A 25-megaton warhead is 1250 times as powerful as the atomic weapon released on Hiroshima. What possible need is there for such a weapon in the arsenal of deterrence? The only prudent assumption is that it could be designed to destroy our retaliatory Minuteman missile in its hardened silo.

Simultaneously, the Soviet Union is expanding its Polaris-type submarine fleet at the rate of seven or eight submarines a year, and that rate could be accelerated on the basis of installed capacity. This development could threaten the safety of our strategic bombing force if it were to be caught on the ground.

We cannot, of course, know what Soviet leaders intend to do, but we can appreciate what they are capable of doing. And it is the responsibility of the Defense Department to guard against the capabilities of an adversary. In fulfilling this responsibility, we cannot blink at the fact that, if the present Soviet weapons buildup continues at its current pace and if improvements are made that are already technically feasible, our strategic deterrent and retaliatory force could be in jeopardy by the mid-1970s.

As Secretary Laird has emphasized, the Defense Department would be gambling irresponsibly with our nation's security if it were to assume that Soviet leaders have no intention of using the capability they are now developing. I am confident that the American public agrees with the secretary. We all recall the peril of the Cuban missile crisis in 1962, when this country was caught by surprise. Up to the very time photographic evidence demonstrated that Soviet offensive missiles were installed in Cuba, it was widely assumed that the Soviet Union had no such intentions.

The Defense Department will focus on the capabilities rather than the intentions of the enemy, first, to do everything possible to avoid a similar crisis in the future and, second, to ensure that we are able to cope with one if it should nevertheless arise. We mastered the Cuban crisis because we had a credible deterrent. It is sobering to reflect on what the outcome could otherwise have been.

Let me be absolutely clear on one point: there is no doubt that we have a credible deterrent today. That point is not at issue. What is at issue is whether we maintain that deterrent unimpaired—not today, not tomorrow, but in the period beginning in the mid-1970s. What is at issue, too, is whether we discourage efforts to erode the credibility of our deterrent by demonstrating our will and ability to maintain it.

If we take no countering action now and simply permit our Minuteman missiles and strategic bombers to become vulnerable, the credibility of our deterrent would be diminished with serious consequences for our national security and our hopes for peace.

In preparing our defenses, we must think ahead for two reasons: first, because technological progress moves at a rapid pace; and, second, because complex weapons often require as long as five to ten years of development before becoming operational. Our defensive posture of the mid-1970s and beyond depends on decisions made now.

Our hopes for peace and our desire to build a better America may lead some to disregard the international arena and the challenges to our very existence that we face there. Those same hopes and desires may also lead some to conclude that we should sharply and immediately diminish the burdens of our national defense.

It is because I have those hopes and desires that I cannot agree with these conclusions. Together with Secretary Laird, I have pledged all my effort to the true mission of the Department of Defense: restoration and preservation of peace and tranquillity. If we do not weaken in our resolve to achieve this goal now that it may not be too far from our grasp, we can look forward to early fulfillment of our desire to build a better America. If we do otherwise, we might have no America to build.

27

The Political Environment
of National Strategy

T he task assigned to me is to survey the political environment in which a national strategy must be formulated and implemented. It is, unfortunately, not a happy one. And so let me begin by summarizing what I have to say in the form of a parable contained in a favorite letter of mine, written once upon a time by a workman in the Bahamas to his workman's compensation board. The letter runs as follows:

Respected Sir:

When I got to the building, I found that the hurricane had knocked some bricks off the top. So I rigged up a beam with a pulley at the top of the building and hoisted up a couple of barrels full of bricks. When I had fixed the building, there was a lot of bricks left over.

I hoisted the barrel back up again and secured the line at the bottom, and then went up and filled the barrel with extra bricks. Then I went to the bottom and cast off the line.

Unfortunately, the barrel of bricks was heavier than I was and before I knew what was happening, the barrel started down, jerking me off the ground. I decided to hang on and halfway up I met the barrel coming down and received a severe blow on the shoulder.

This piece is excerpted from remarks given at the U.S. Armed Forces Staff College, Norfolk, Va., in March 1976.

250

I then continued to the top, banging my head against the beam and getting my finger jammed in the pulley. When the barrel hit the ground it bursted its bottom, allowing all the bricks to spill out.

I was heavier than the empty barrel and so started down again at high speed. Halfway down, I met the barrel coming up and received severe injuries to my shins. When I hit the ground, I landed on the bricks getting several painful cuts from the sharp edges.

At this point I must have lost my presence of mind, because I let go of the line. The barrel then came down giving me another heavy blow on the head and putting me in the hospital.

There is little doubt that political events in recent years have given us a heavy blow on the head and put us in the hospital. Within the last two years, first a vice-president and then a president have been forced to resign in disgrace. Each was replaced in turn by someone selected by Congress, not elected by popular vote. The longest and most unpopular war in our history ended in defeat, as we renounced our solemn commitment to the cause of self-determination and abandoned South Vietnam to foreign domination by withholding a comparatively trivial amount of supplies that could well have permitted it to defend itself. Our economy has been rocked by an oil embargo and double-digit inflation. Two attempts were made within a matter of days to assassinate our new president. Terrorism has become commonplace here at home as well as elsewhere and crime rates have continued to soar. We have created an international spectacle by tearing our intelligence establishment to pieces in public view. And so on.

Shaken by one crisis after another, we are bound to wonder what in the world is going on. Living through the times, we run the risk of being overwhelmed by spectacular events and failing to discern underlying trends. I want, therefore, to turn away from those spectaculars and to share with you my speculation on what fundamental political and social forces are at work in shaping the course of history.

At some remote time in the future, when historians can view our experiences with detachment, I believe that they will characterize our period as the age of collectivization. They will describe the crises of recent years as eruptions caused by a steady erosion of the individualistic ethic in the West over preceding decades and even generations. Let me illustrate what I have in mind by sketching how the welfare state has evolved, how it has brought big government into being in democratic nations throughout the West, and what galloping government has wrought.

Let me start the story four and a half decades ago, when a momentous turning point occurred in our political and social history. We stood at the pinnacle of prosperity then, at the conclusion of the halcyon twenties. In that seeming golden age of free enterprise, who would have predicted the cataclysm of the thirties and the social revolution that erupted in that brief span of time?

Those who did not live through the Great Depression may find it hard to imagine that the events of a decade would work such profound and lasting change in social attitudes developed over centuries. Those of us who experienced those years don't have the same difficulty. Perhaps because it was not yet my good fortune to live in Charlottesville, the view from where I stood was not so idyllic as it seems to have been from Walton's Mountain. What I recall most vividly is the sense of shock and despair that colored social thought. The hardship of the moment was bad enough, but even worse was fear of what the uncertain future would bring.

Confidence was hardly inspired by looking elsewhere. Bad times were spread throughout the world, and societies most akin to ours were coping badly. There was Britain, for example, stuck in the rut of unemployment through the twenties as well as the thirties. Other nations of Europe had scarcely escaped inflation and even hyperinflation before being plunged into depression. The strains had proven too strong in Italy, and democracy had crumbled. A decade later, a more gruesome course was to be followed by Germany. Meanwhile, the Soviet Union was building the very model of the totalitarian state, that most modern of political inventions. A variety of isms sprang into being, and it began to look as if one or another might be the wave of the future.

In a word, things were a mess, and we sought a way out by creating a welfare state at record speed. The size of government, measured by its power to command the nation's resources, doubled virtually overnight in the reckoning of history. That is, the fraction of national income accounted for by government spending at all levels—federal, state, and local—rose from 12 percent in 1929 to 24 percent in 1939, when the real national product had roughly recovered to its 1929 level. If spending is divided into two parts, defense and all other (which I shall call domestic), the fraction of national income attributable to each doubled, although defense spending still amounted to less than 2 percent of national income in 1939. We did not sense any grave threat to national security.

During the next decade, the size of government moved up and down with the demands of war, demobilization, and subsequent threats to national security. At its peak in 1944, government spending had risen to 56 percent of national income; at its low point in 1947, it had fallen to 21 percent. While defense spending was rising relative to national income, domestic spending was falling, and vice versa. In 1944, for example, domestic spending accounted for only 8 percent of national income as compared with 11 percent in 1929. Between 1929 and 1949, the fraction of national income attributable to total government spending rose by 3 percentage points, but that net rise encompassed a decline of 1.4 percentage points for domestic spending. In other words, the growth of government was more than accounted for by expansion of the defense effort.

Over the fifties, the ups and downs of defense once again set the trend. Until 1958, domestic spending by government represented a smaller share of national income than in 1949.

To recapitulate, government doubled in relative size over the first decade after 1929 and grew by another third over the next two decades. But all the latter growth and then some came from the expanded defense effort. Domestic spending by government actually constituted a slightly smaller percentage of national income in 1959 than in 1939. The initial shock of the social revolution had been rather quickly absorbed, and a new state of equilibrium then seemed to prevail.

But not for long. Since the early sixties, a new trend has established itself: regardless of what happens to the defense effort, domestic spending by government steadily rises faster than national income. And the pace has accelerated: from 1961 through 1968, the percentage of national income represented by domestic spending of government rose from 24 to 27, or by 14 percent; from 1968 through 1975, it rose from 27 to 36, or by 33 percent. Despite the Vietnam War, despite introduction of the all-volunteer armed forces, and despite mounting problems of national security, the fraction of national income spent for defense has never again reached its level of 1959, when it was 11.5 percent. Today, the fraction is below 7 percent, or lower than in any year since 1950.

How big is government today? Government spending amounts to more than 40 percent of national income—to 43 percent in 1975, to be exact. If the prevailing trend continues, it will pass 50 percent by the early 1980s. Transfer payments alone—the personal income taken from one set of pockets and put in another—have averaged over 12 percent of national income in the last three years, or as much as total government spending amounted to in 1929. If those transfer payments last year were paid only to our ten million poor families and individuals, each would have received almost $17,000. More than four-fifths of government spending is for domestic purposes and less than a fifth for defense. Over the last four and a half decades, the fraction of national income attributable to domestic spending has more than tripled. A third of that expansion has come in the last fifteen years.

These figures symbolize, of course, the growth of the welfare state, a growth that has been even more pronounced in other democracies like Great Britain, France, West Germany, Italy, the Netherlands, and the Scandinavian countries. Consider the fourteen countries in the Organization for Economic Cooperation and Development. If for each of them we measure government spending as a percentage of national income and array the percentages from smallest to largest, we find that the median percentage—the percentage in the middle of the array—rose from 30 in the early 1950s to almost 50 in the early 1970s and to more than that today. That is, on the average for these democracies, government spending amounts to more than half of national income today. It amounts to more than 60 percent in some of them.

I cite these figures not to draw any moral or pass any judgment, but simply to lay out the facts. The point I am leading up to is that democratic governments have come to rest on a more and more precarious base of popular support as they have become bigger and bigger. Democracies are therefore being governed with diminishing authority and confidence. In other words, the bigger a democratic government becomes, the weaker it tends to be in this sense.

As proof, I offer the current state of affairs in democracies throughout the world. Look at the parliamentary governments. In case after case, the leading party is managing to stay in power by the skin of its teeth. If it has a majority of seats, it is a slim one, often based on a minority of the popular vote. Governments frequently must be built through formal or informal coalitions that permit factions or splinter parties to wield power far in excess of their popular vote. Governments rise and fall in close elections in which a small swing vote makes the difference. Thus the British Labour Party is said to have scored a big victory in the most recent election because it acquired a paper-thin majority in the new parliament. In the old one, it held only the largest minority of seats. But it won its majority of seats by capturing less than

40 percent of the popular vote. In Germany, the tiny Free Democratic Party holds the balance of power in an uneasy coalition, whose major partner—the Social Democratic Party—gets fewer votes than the opposition. In Italy, it seems proper to say that there is no government at all, only a succession of caretakers. And so on.

The presidential democracies have their close elections, too. Witness France in 1974 and our own country in 1960 and 1968. We had our landslides in the presidential elections of 1964 and 1972, and in the congressional election of 1974. But they have not exactly conveyed lasting power to the winners and hence are symptoms of the same basic instability. In both 1964 and 1972, the overriding issue was ideological, as one candidate in each case called for radical change in the role of the welfare state. The electorate convincingly rejected both candidates. And the cloud of Watergate hung over the recent congressional election. Our landslides have been against, not for, something.

If weak government is so widespread among democracies, one naturally suspects that there is a common reason. I would argue that one important cause has been the who-whom dilemma raised by big government. Who is to benefit at the expense of whom? Who is to receive what from whom? The answer is fairly simple when the welfare state is small enough. If, say, a quarter or less of national income is flowing through the hands of government, it may seem plausible to a large majority that needed taxes can be collected from the remaining minority. Politicians can credibly campaign on the platform of "soaking the rich." But not when the tax take rises to 30, 40, or 50 percent of national income. Voters promised growing benefits from the welfare state must begin wondering whether they will receive more than will be taken from them. A politician who puts together a successful coalition of the electorate by promising everybody pie in the sky and accordingly gets elected by a handsome majority is bound to lose support when the bill comes due. Even with the most skillful use of hidden taxes, he will find it increasingly difficult to persuade the public that mutual exploitation is beneficial to us all. The margin of voters who have more taken from them than they receive must grow with the welfare state. Eventually, the margin must rise to half the electorate. The natural result will be for elections to become close and for minorities to coalesce into powerful third forces.

There are, after all, only two conditions under which a welfare state can achieve a stable natural equilibrium: either the majority must be benefiting at the expense of a minority, or vice versa—a minority must be benefiting at the expense of the majority. When the welfare state grows past a certain size, it simply becomes impossible for government to take away from any minority what is required to provide net benefits to more than half the public. The equilibrium in which the majority benefits at the expense of a minority therefore gets ruled out by the facts of life when government becomes too big. And the other alternative— in which a minority exploits the majority—is ruled out by the nature of democracy. That leaves only an unstable borderline situation in which half the electorate tries to gain at the expense of the other half, a circumstance that weakens and demoralizes government. No elected authorities can govern firmly and effectively if they must constantly look over their shoulders to see whether they still have a majority of voters behind them. Margins of victory at the polls become so small and fleeting that politicians, struggling to survive reelection, curry favor from all manner of factions and special interests thought to be of marginal help in winning an election. The demagogue has his day.

It is this weakening of democratic government, taken together with the underlying who-whom dilemma, that largely explains, I believe, why inflation has erupted virtually everywhere in the democratic world. Governments are driven to spend without visibly taxing. Inflation becomes the easiest way out, and it acquires a momentum of its own. Once started, it cannot be stopped without endangering the holy of holies: full employment. The insecurities of unemployment are in part replaced and in part supplemented by those of inflation. Mixing inflation and unemployment means, in effect, that neither can be controlled without straining democratic institutions.

The emergence of gigantic but weak government in Western countries has brought about social instability in other respects as well. The increasingly collectivized nature of society comes into growing conflict with the traditional individualistic ethic of the West, and more and more people are torn loose from moral moorings. One result is growing lawlessness and antisocial behavior. The system and the establishment become popular targets of attack, and for a growing group of dissidents the traditional search for reform turns into a call for revolution.

As government becomes burdened with far more than it can confidently handle, it loses its grip over those affairs that can be well managed only by strong government. Thus we witness growing confusion and disorder throughout the West in the area of foreign policy and national security. What is happening in the United States is a particularly tragic example.

Far be it from me to be a prophet of doom, but I do believe that we may face a social crisis as serious as the thirties unless a way is quickly found out of this vicious circle. A democratic public will endure many hardships, but it cannot live with the prospect of perpetual insecurity. If the sense of insecurity is not removed by democratic means, the public will seek another political solution. A few years might well mark another momentous turning point in social history.

Once I had the experience of being in an honest-to-goodness train wreck. It happened one January morning in 1953, when the Federal Limited plowed into the anteroom of the Washington Union Station and crashed through the floor. I remember watching a television report that evening. The commentator was questioning eyewitnesses, and at one stage he asked a redcap whether it had crossed his mind that, if the train had not crashed through the floor, it might have broken through the columns holding up the ceiling, torn through the crowd in the waiting room, and run out into the street. The redcap scratched his head and said, "Well, I don't know. But now that you mention it, it sure enough was headed in that direction."

Well, I don't know whether there will be a wreck. I hope and trust not. But the inflation express sure enough is headed in that direction. If we at least comprehend that fact, perhaps we shall be able to do something about it.

28

Moralism, Morality,
and Trade

Vents of the last few years leave no doubt that the international economy is a mess. As we move from one foreign-exchange crisis to another and grapple with a perennial deficit in our balance of payments, we are finally coming to realize the need to put our own foreign-trade policy in order and to fashion a more sensible international system of commerce and finance. We are propelled to do so by strictly economic considerations, but it would be wrong to believe that they alone will shape the policy that emerges.

There was a time when economic interests, rightly or wrongly perceived, determined trade policy almost exclusively, but that was a generation ago. As World War II and its aftermath thrust us into an active and powerful role in world affairs, political factors came inevitably to exert influence. Our actions were, in large measure, dictated by the realities of the cold war. In response to the serious threat posed by Soviet expansionism, we placed restrictions on our trade with Communist countries, including special controls over exports contributing directly to their military power. Such restraints made sense on the ground that it is unwise to conduct unrestricted trade with the enemy, in a cold as well as a hot war.

This essay was commissioned by *New York Times Magazine* in May 1973 but was never published.

National security has not, however, been the only rationale for politicizing trade with other nations. Our government has reacted to concern over political and social conditions inside certain countries by controlling trade with them. In such cases as South Africa, Portugal, Greece, and the whole of Latin America, those controls have been confined to sale of arms. In one notable case, Rhodesia, they have applied across the board. All have one factor in common: morality is the issue, not national security. The purpose has been to bring about internal reforms elsewhere by applying economic pressure ranging in intensity from reprimand to retribution.

In view of this history, it is not surprising to find the current debate over trade policy colored by political and moral considerations. One strand of the debate has taken an interesting twist now that the administration advocates liberalization of trade with the Soviet Union on pragmatic grounds while many members of Congress, led by Senator Henry Jackson, oppose such a move unless the Soviet government first liberalizes its policy on emigration. This expression of congressional sentiment, along with actions already taken toward other countries, signifies growing commitment to the view that trade should be used as a lever to induce political and social reforms in foreign countries.

The question of what goals should be served by trade can be addressed only within the broader context of what ends and means are appropriate to foreign policy in general. Our foreign policy may be oriented in either of two general directions: toward promotion of national interests or toward pursuit of some transcendent mission. We promote national interests by safeguarding our system of government against manifest external threats, by creating a peaceful world order in which conflicts among nations can be resolved without resort to arms, and by promoting the welfare of our citizens within that context. Any foreign policy that reaches beyond these specific objectives is mission oriented.

It is, of course, not difficult to take a view of national interests so broad that the distinction between security-oriented and mission-oriented policies vanishes. One might, for example, argue that the best way to promote peace and security is to create governments everywhere patterned after our own. Aside from being impossible to achieve, such an objective so broadens the concept of national security as to deprive it of meaning. No policy can be constructed on the all-embracing principle that everything depends on everything else. Those cause-and-effect relations that are immediate and direct must be distinguished from those that are remote, indirect, and generally unpredictable. In that sense, a security-oriented policy should be conceived as one designed to cope with clear and present external forces directly threatening preservation of our form of government and way of life.

To go beyond this specific purpose is to take upon ourselves a moral duty beyond our borders, whether to right wrongs as we perceive them, to spread freedom and democracy as we conceive them, or to liberate others from oppressive forces as we see them. It is to presume that we have a right or obligation to intervene directly in the internal affairs of other nations, provided only that our cause is just. If that presumption were warranted, other nations would have a similar right or obligation, and the only point of contention would be justness of cause, an issue not easily settled by consensus.

There is great merit, from both moral and pragmatic points of view, in espousing and following a foreign policy based on nonintervention. We would do well to heed the warning of Dean Acheson.

> By painful experience over the centuries there has come an understanding that each state should respect the autonomy, with respect to internal affairs, of every other state existing in the vast realm external to its own boundaries. That precept is basic to whatever hope there is for peace and order in the world. That it is occasionally violated is no reproach to its validity.[1]

Nonintervention obviously does not rule out expressions of concern or efforts at persuasion. Rather, as a principle, it proscribes use of power by one nation for the purpose of effecting change in the domestic conditions of another. It constitutes the negative aspect of a security-oriented foreign policy, since a nation adhering strictly to such a policy would not intervene in the internal affairs of others except under the most extreme circumstance, namely, when its very survival was at stake.

As far as the United States is concerned, the case for a mission-oriented foreign policy and for the interventionism necessarily associated with it rests on the argument that our government should exercise its power to move other nations toward a political order in accord with our ideals. We should, in this view, strive for perfection abroad as well

---

[1] U.S., Congress, House, Committee on Foreign Affairs, Subcommittee on Africa, *Rhodesia and the United States Foreign Policy: Hearings,* 91st Cong., 1st sess., Nov. 19, 1969, p. 124.

as at home. However worthy this aspiration, results are no more ideal than the processes through which they are achieved. This is the age-old problem of whether ends justify means, and the answer implicit in American political ideals is that they do not. Indeed, it is the process of discussion and deliberation leading to consent that forms the philosophical core of our traditional political system, the assumption being that the right process generates, by definition, the best possible results. Those results are bound at any moment to fall short of ideals, and concerned citizens must constantly stir and prod if progress is to be made toward them—but always through the proper process. Since this is the moral code we adhere to in trying to resolve our own domestic problems, it is difficult to see how we can justify applying another one to our involvement in the domestic affairs of foreign states.

Moral issues are fraught with dilemmas in any case. Our republic was founded by a revolution declared to be necessary in order to institute the democratic process. What stance should we take toward incipient revolution elsewhere if its presumed purpose is the same as ours? Do we encourage it, support it, or merely sympathize with it? In deciding what course to follow, we must be mindful of the integrity of an existing body politic, a principle established for us by a civil war. And then there is the principle of self-determination, long supported by this country but often less than clear in meaning and more endowed with pragmatic than with moral content. There is no point in elaborating on the myriad of precepts and scruples proclaimed at one time or another as guiding our relations with other nations, except to note that there is no obviously simple way of resolving conflicts among them.

In a perceptive introduction to a recent book on this complex of issues, Ernest W. Lefever contrasts morality and moralism.

> Moralism, soft or hard, tends toward a single-factor approach to political problems, while mainstream Western morality emphasizes multiple causation, multiple ends, and multiple responsibilities. . . . If one of several valued goals—peace, justice, or freedom—becomes the supreme political end, the other two are bound to suffer. Peace (order) without justice and freedom is tyranny. Justice without freedom is another form of tyranny.[2]

---

[2] Ernest W. Lefever, ed., *Ethics and World Politics* (Baltimore: Johns Hopkins University Press, 1972), p. 6.

His linkage of interventionism with moralism deserves extensive quotation.

> Some adherents of the moralistic approach advocate interventionist foreign policies designed to reshape the internal customs and institutions of other states. At the same time, they often downgrade or even deprecate the primary security role of foreign policy. This strange combination of reform-intervention and security-isolation turns foreign policy on its head. In the classical view, the first task of external policy is peace and security, and the first task of domestic policy is order and justice. The reform-interventionists, soft or hard, blur the salient distinction between what can and ought to be done by a government for its own people, and what can and ought to be done by a government in the vast external realm over which it has no legal jurisdiction and where its moral and political mandate is so severely limited. The insistence that the U.S. government employ extraordinary and sometimes coercive means to reshape the internal political, economic, or social structures in other sovereign communities is morally arrogant and flies in the face of the most basic international law which, in the words of the U.N. Charter, prohibits intervention "in matters which are essentially within the domestic jusrisdiction of any state."[3]

Beyond the moral issue, there remains the practical question of whether the goals of interventionism can be achieved. The world is a place of great diversity in every significant respect: culturally, historically, racially, politically, economically, socially. Diverse forces interact in diverse ways to mold the conjuncture and trend of events. We have at best a limited capability of exerting influence on conditions of life abroad through instruments of national power at our disposal, and that capability must be exercised sparingly if it is to have perceptible effect. Whatever we might accomplish, it is bound to be small relative to the product of internal forces at work.

Moreover, we must live and function in that diverse world. The first order of business is to attend to our own security, and to do so we must respect the realities of power and, regardless of what we may think about the internal state of affairs in other nations, maintain relations with them consistent with our national interests. If we were to confine our favorable attention to those countries whose political and social systems are congenial with our own, we would find ourselves dealing with a distressingly small segment of the globe. In the world in which

[3] Ibid., pp. 10–11.

we live, being the friend of another country depends as much on its willingness to reciprocate as on any standards we might set for its character. And we are not rich enough in friends to afford the luxury of throwing them away.

These broader considerations should give us pause in excessively degrading the traditional role of trade as a means of enriching the nation. This is not to say that trade should never serve any other purpose, as some of the more ardent free traders seem to imply. The classic case for free trade derives from a time in which the totalitarian state had not entered the scene and commerce was therefore overwhelmingly in private hands, regardless of the forms of government under which trading partners lived. Almost all economists, myself included, find it painful to admit that there are legitimate political arguments for controlling foreign trade, primarily because time-worn arguments based on spurious economic reasoning quickly masquerade as the newly justified political ones. But we cannot escape the fact that the spread of state trading, particularly as practiced by totalitarian states, makes it necessary for us to qualify the normal case for free trade.

More fundamentally, the state has as much right to employ trade policy as an instrument of national power as it has to employ anything else. Trade policy deserves no special immunity as long as it is a legitimate and effective means for achieving a legitimate end. Enough has been said for the moment on the question of legitimacy, so that we may focus on the question of effectiveness.

Let us start with the obvious: trade, in the sense of a genuine exchange of goods, imparts a perceived economic gain to both parties. Otherwise, it would not take place. It follows that restraint of trade hurts both parties, though it may hurt one more than the other. We should, therefore, restrain trade only if we expect a net gain, in terms of whatever political goals we are seeking, after taking account of the economic cost.

There is usually an asymmetry in the felt effects of punishment and reward or, in this case, of imposing and removing a given restraint. That is, the harm felt by imposition is likely to exceed the gain felt by removal. This asymmetry results in part from a real difference, because the immediate impact of a restraint will be more severe than the ultimate one, when adjustments to it have been made. But there is a psychological difference as well: the stick normally imparts a stronger message than the carrot. Or, to mix a metaphor, a bird in hand is worth two in the bush: we are seldom able or inclined to attribute the same value to a gain of what we have not yet experienced as we are to an equivalent loss of what we have grown accustomed to.

The impact of trade restrictions imposed by us on another country will depend on many things, including how important the two-way trade is to that country and to us, how many alternative trading partners join with us in the restrictions, what kind of economy the other country has, and what power it has to retaliate similarly or otherwise. The influence of each factor is largely self-evident, but that does not guarantee that we will give each its proper weight in the heat of zeal.

One danger with economic interventionism is that the intervener may treat it too cavalierly. On the one hand, restraint of trade hardly seems to be a hostile act in the same category as resort to arms. Why not give it a try? On the other hand, there is no point in fooling around with a powerful adversary capable of striking back in some dreadful way. Hence economic interventionism can easily become a means of browbeating the weak while looking the other way as far as the strong are concerned. The inequity of the double standard aside, the basic trouble is that the weak may prove to be recalcitrant, refusing to knuckle under to the allegedly gentle economic pressure. Whatever the government intervening may think, the one suffering intervention surely views any pressure as a hostile act. One thing can then lead to another until the ugly question arises of resort to force.

Having said this much in the abstract, we need to get down to concrete cases. The embargo of trade with Rhodesia would seem to be the best starting point, since it illustrates an extreme in terms of both objectives and means. There is hardly room here to reveal all the facets of the Rhodesian question, fortunately well covered in the literature,[4] but we can sketch its salient features.

The Rhodesian question derives from the declaration of independence issued in 1965 by the Ian Smith government. That declaration came after four years of fruitless negotiation with the United Kingdom on the issue of independence, following the granting of a new constitution in 1961. The government of Rhodesia argued that, inasmuch as the U.K. had never governed Rhodesia (an argument fully supported by history), the act of granting a new constitution relieved the U.K. of any further control over its destiny. The government of the United Kingdom argued to the contrary that Rhodesia had acted without authority in severing its ties with the U.K., since the latter had the sovereign right

---

[4] *Congressional Digest* of February 1973 contains an excellent summary of the controversy.

to grant independence. Hence the U.K. considered Rhodesia to be in a state of rebellion.

The root issue is not whether Rhodesia should be independent but what form of government it should have as an independent nation. Given the political history of other former African colonies, few have been so bold as to suppose that Western-type democracy was called for. Rather, the issue is which racial group shall rule: the small white minority as at present or the overwhelming black majority, constituting some 94 percent of the population. More precisely, the matter at dispute is the pace at which government can be turned over to the black majority while preserving civil rights for the white minority.

Not wishing to resort to arms as a means of preventing Rhodesian independence, the British government referred the matter to the United Nations. The Security Council thereupon passed a series of resolutions calling upon member states to refrain from recognizing and assisting the self-declared state and to impose voluntary restrictions on trade with it. When these measures showed little effect, the Security Council found the situation in Rhodesia to constitute a threat to the peace and, on that basis, invoked mandatory economic sanctions in the form of an embargo of trade with Rhodesia, first (in December 1966) for a selective list of commodities and finally (in May 1968) for all commodities. Our government endorsed these actions and then implemented them through appropriate executive orders.

The sanctions have been a subject of controversy from the start, with proponents and critics disputing the legal, moral, and practical merits of the case. In a concise and lively exchange with Dean Acheson in late 1966 and early 1967, Arthur Goldberg, then U.S. ambassador to the United Nations, defended the sanctions on all grounds. But the nub of his defense was a moral-political argument.

> Our country, founded on the proposition that all men are created equal—and currently engaged in a vigorous nationwide program to make that equality real for our own Negro citizens—cannot honorably adopt a double standard on what is happening in Rhodesia. . . .
>
> From a political standpoint, we have a practical interest in maintaining friendly relations with the newly independent countries of Africa for whom this Rhodesian issue is of the highest importance. Moreover, the success of a rebellion aimed at creating a new white minority state in southern Africa would inevitably harden the lines of political conflict and would tend to stir interracial violence on that continent.[5]

[5] *Washington Post*, Jan. 8, 1967, p. E3.

Dean Acheson dissented on all counts with characteristic vigor.

> International law does not proclaim the sanctity of British dominion over palm and pine. Certainly we Americans are in no position to declare it—we who conspired to instigate French aggression against British power in America and not only threatened but shattered international peace to achieve our independence. . . .
>
> Certainly Rhodesia's voting laws and system of popular representation in its legislature are not contrary to any international obligation. The one man, one vote deduction from the Fourteenth Amendment is not recognized in international law, as our friend King Faisal of Saudi Arabia can testify. Indeed, the present system in Rhodesia, broadly speaking, has been in effect and regarded with complacency in Great Britain for nearly half a century.[6]

This tiny sample of arguments can do no more than suggest the flavor of the controversy. Suffice it to say that a cloud hangs over the authority and wisdom of the Security Council—and hence the United States—in undertaking a responsibility that, by legal and historical precedent, rested with the United Kingdom. That our government has had serious second thoughts is demonstrated by the fact that we cast a veto, for the first time, against the Security Council resolution of March 17, 1970, calling upon member nations to impose a virtual blockade of Rhodesia and upon the United Kingdom to overthrow the Ian Smith government by military force.

Mandatory economic sanctions have, of course, proved to be ineffective in achieving either the intitial objective of overthrowing the Smith government or the later one of promoting fruitful negotiation between Rhodesia and the United Kingdom on a suitable basis for independence. The embargo has turned out to be a sieve because of widespread violations, particularly through use of the reexport channel provided by South Africa and Mozambique, friendly neighboring countries of Rhodesia. Moreover, loss of Rhodesian chrome caused us to become dependent on the Soviet Union for some 60 percent of our imports of that strategic material at prices about double those paid for Rhodesian ore, while there are grounds for believing that some of the Soviet ore originated in Rhodesia. As a consequence, Congress passed the Byrd Amendment in late 1971 permitting U.S. importation of chrome ore and other strategic materials from Rhodesia as long as they were also being imported from a Communist-dominated country. Our

---

[6] *Washington Post,* Dec. 11, 1966, p. E6.

total embargo has thereby been breached, and efforts to close the breach, led by Senator Gale McGee, have so far failed.

The Rhodesian question remains alive, and our nation will continue to face decisions on how to deal with it. As repugnant as racial inequality is to us today, we would do well to reflect on our own history as we make those decisions. When the United States gained its independence, many Americans were enslaved and many others did not enjoy the franchise. Such progress as we have made on human rights has come overwhelmingly from the working of internal forces, whereas we can well imagine that intervention by other nations in these affairs would have generated more resistance than progress.

Similar considerations apply to intervention elsewhere in southern Africa. Pressure has steadily mounted in the United Nations and various domestic circles for drastic economic actions against South Africa, for example. Our government has responded cautiously, so far imposing only an arms embargo on the sound ground that more drastic action would create a beleaguered atmosphere hardly likely to make the whites more reasonable on the racial question while diminishing the opportunity for blacks to improve their lot, politically as well as economically, through economic advancement. We have wisely decided that we can do more good for all concerned by maintaining open political and economic relations.

Let me comment in passing on an ill-fated episode of a different nature in our recent foreign policy. During the 1960s, when nation building was in fashion, official attention was focused for a time on Latin America, and concern was expressed over the weakness of democratic institutions there. It became popular to treat military control as the cause rather than the consequence of this weakness, and the remedy seemed to be for us to do what we could to weaken military elements in those countries. The major step taken was to impose severe restrictions on the sale of modern arms to all countries in Latin America. During the ensuing years, those countries purchased large quantities of modern arms anyway, turning to sources outside the hemisphere, and the military remained as thoroughly in control as ever. The only apparent effect was a deterioration in our relations with most of those countries and a consequent erosion in our influence over the course of events in this hemisphere.

It is interesting that the moral case for trade restraints is sometimes turned upside down in application to the People's Republic of China. As long as five years ago, Senator Mike Mansfield called for abandonment of trade and other restrictions against the People's Republic of China on the ground that

> . . . the government on the mainland has not only survived, it has provided China with a functioning leadership. Under its direction, Chinese society has achieved a degree of economic and scientific progress, apparently sufficient for survival of an enormous and growing population and sophisticated enough to produce thermonuclear explosions.[7]

He summed the matter up by saying:

> . . . it seems to me that the basic adjustment which is needed in policies respecting China is to make crystal clear that this government does not anticipate, much less does it seek, the overthrow of the government of the Chinese mainland. In addition, there is a need to end the discrimination which consigns China to an inferior status as among the Communist countries in this nation's policies respecting travel and trade.[8]

In other words, out of respect for the realities of power, we should give up trying to do anything about the pervasive violation of human rights and international law on the part of the People's Republic of China. We have no choice but to look the other way, even on such matters as the conquest and repression of Tibet.

Whatever may have been the case for mainland China, our policy toward the Soviet Union over the last quarter century has surely not been based on anticipation that the government would be overthrown or that internal reforms could be induced. On the contrary, we have had few illusions about the reality and endurance of Soviet power. Hopefully, we have none now. If so, we will exercise great caution in moving away from a foreign policy based in all its aspects on national security.

If we were to embark instead on an interventionist course, it would hardly be possible to know where to begin. The Soviet Union is a totalitarian state ruled by a ruthless and oppressive regime. Freedom, as we know it, does not exist even, as Senator Jackson has pointed out, in the elemental sense of freedom to leave. No Soviet citizen has the right to a passport permitting travel abroad, and only half the citizens have the right to a passport permitting travel inside the country. And so on and on.

In addition to all the other reasons for avoiding interventionism, it is hardly likely to work in the fundamental sense that Soviet rulers can

[7] U.S., Congress, *Congressional Record,* 92d Cong., 1st sess., April 15, 1971, p. 10472.
[8] Ibid., p. 10473.

easily take away with one hand whatever they give with the other. They can nullify or impose an exit tax without the stroke of a pen, while we can grant or remove most-favored-nation treatment only through an act of Congress. Moreover, they could control emigration in countless unverifiable ways, as they do now, once they received what they want from us. What leverage would we then resort to? Before we go down this path, we should take full advantage of the pressure of external public opinion, which has been responsible for such liberalization of emigration as has taken place.

It is natural, at the same time, to sympathize with the view that we have little to gain by merely exchanging economic concessions with the Soviet Union. Given the nature of its economy, the Soviet Union can offer no counterpart to most-favored-nation (i.e., nondiscriminatory) treatment that means anything. Discrimination is inherent and pervasive in Soviet trading, applying to individual transactions as well as to nations, and no piece of paper or other formality will alter this fact of life. Put another way, we would gain very little relative to the Soviet Union from a liberalization of trade, and it would have to be brought about almost entirely by our actions.

The course of recent events and the reactions to them by Soviet leaders leave no doubt that the Soviet economy is the weakest link in Soviet power. Whatever we might do to help shore up that economy would not benefit the Soviet people in the near term, but would rather strengthen the hand of Soviet rulers who exercise tight control over the economy as well as everything else. This we would do at the very time when we are negotiating with those rulers to resolve issues critical to our national security. If we are to grant economic concessions, let us do so only in exchange for political concessions in the realm of Soviet external policy that would explicitly improve our national security.

When all is said, our trade policy is the product of our political process, just as any other policy is. In the pull and haul of domestic pressures, the squeaking wheel gets the grease. And so it would be too much to expect all aspects of foreign policy to be pure, consistent, and coherent. Yet we must constantly strive to bring order to the structure created by ad-hocism. Trade will be politicized, but perhaps we can at least pause from time to time to sort out all elements extraneous to national security and, in the process, relegate moralizing to the province of rhetoric.

29

The Ebb and Flow of
American Foreign Policy

Historically, security has been the dominant theme in our foreign relations, at least those reaching beyond our continent. Apart from such episodes as "manifest destiny" in the last century, "making the world safe for democracy" in the Wilsonian era, and "nation building" in the Kennedy period, crusades have not been our custom.

Oriented toward security, we sought protection over the bulk of our history by isolating ourselves from political strife abroad. Europe was the fountainhead of our culture, but it was also a place of constant squabbling and fighting in which we had no desire to become involved. Considering ourselves safe from invasion from across the seas, we forswore entangling alliances and warned countries of the Old World not to extend their sway over lands in the Western Hemisphere. It is fair to say that, until World War I, this policy kept us out of wars with powers outside the hemisphere. The two exceptions that come to mind are the War of 1812 and the Spanish-American War, and our hands were not exactly clean in either case.

Meanwhile, we and the world were changing. Despite the tragedy of the Civil War, we became a great power if only by territorial expansion and the amazing growth generated by our political economy. A net-

These remarks were given in the Greater Issues series at The Citadel, Charleston, S. C., in October 1975.

work of commerce linked us with the fortunes of nations virtually everywhere while technology was shrinking the globe. Most significantly of all, we burst out of our continental confinement, extending our territory into the Pacific. We could hardly fail to appreciate the role in world affairs being thrust upon us by history.

The message was driven home by World War I, as we watched the great powers of Europe sapping their strength in an utterly mad struggle. It is just as noteworthy that we waited almost three years to enter the war as it is that we finally went in. Overt acts attributable to the enemy-to-be were required to whip up the public spirit to fight, and an aura of righteousness, constantly replenished by President Woodrow Wilson, sustained us through the war—but not the peace. Our efforts had hardly made the world safe for democracy, nor had American blood shed in the cause of Wilsonian idealism redeemed the world. The facts of life revealed the Wilsonian cause for what it was: a visionary crusade. The cry became "back to normalcy," which in foreign affairs meant isolationism.

And so we stood by as an observer during the interwar interlude, our diplomatic efforts restricted to the peddling of unenforceable—and therefore meaningless—agreements to outlaw war and to disarm. We did nothing to counter German rearmament and ultimate aggression. That was a European problem, we said. We did virtually nothing to help stabilize the Pacific region, waiting until World War II had erupted to focus on the problem, and then we took such a radical diplomatic stance against Japanese policies that we aggravated instability.

In any event, once again we ended up in a worldwide conflict. We managed to stay out an even shorter period that time, and another overt act, horrendous and unmistakable, pulled us in. The America First sentiment was strong and pervasive. Remember that the draft law of 1941 was passed by a single vote in the House.

American opinion changed profoundly as a result of World War II, and for thirty years our foreign policy was shaped by three salient facts. The first was the dominating lesson we derived from World War II: much as we might wish otherwise, if a major war were to erupt in Europe or Asia, we would become involved. Hence we left occupation troops in both Europe and Asia and made ourselves party to a host of agreements and treaties designed to conclude the war and create a stable international order.

The second fact was the creation of nuclear weapons and their spread among the major powers. War has taken on dimensions of potential holocaust, and modern weapons combined with modern means of delivery have rendered obsolete the moat of seas surrounding the American island. Our mainland is subject to attack without warning at any time.

The third fact was that the Soviet Union hardly waited for the guns to fall silent before amassing a bloc of satellites and embarking on a series of conquests. The Potsdam Agreement was flagrantly violated as Eastern Europe was subjugated to Communist rule emanating ultimately from Moscow. The Soviet bloc was real and monolithic in the decade after the war.

In 1946 and 1947, the Soviet Union made menacing moves against the territory of neighboring Iran and Turkey. The bloc launched a Communist insurrection in Greece in 1947, and late that year and early the next it violently replaced the coalition government of Czechoslovakia, the only one in Communist-dominated Eastern Europe, with a full-fledged Communist dictatorship. The Soviet Union then made the boldest move of all by blockading Berlin for almost a year beginning in mid-1948 in an effort to throw out the Western powers, establish Berlin as the capital of East Germany, and solidify Communist control there. Thwarted in all probes outside its established sphere of influence in Europe, the Soviet Union turned next to a place far away, South Korea, where it unleashed a Communist invasion in mid-1950.

I recount these events because those who did not live through them need to appreciate that one thing was vividly clear at the time: namely, that the Soviet Union was engaged in a grand adventure of conquest by whatever means were feasible and required. Those who argue today that the cold war was the product of Western aggravation and intransigence—some even argue that it was a figment—make a mockery of history. They conveniently forget that we had hastily demobilized after V-J Day and that Defense Secretary Louis Johnson was busy slashing the defense budget to the bone when the Korean War erupted.

It was the resolute response of President Truman to Soviet adventures that checked them at every turn. The Truman Doctrine, the Marshall Plan, NATO, and the defense of South Korea by United Nations forces became the pillars of a concerted worldwide effort to contain Communist expansion. The policy became internationalized in the Eisenhower period in the form of a ring of alliances—NATO, SEATO (Southeast Asia Treaty Organization), CENTO (Central Treaty Organization), ANZUS (Australia, New Zealand, and the

United States), and a number of bilateral mutual defense pacts—combined with a military strategy of massive retaliation. Given our overwhelming nuclear superiority, that policy was both sensible and effective.

In the succeeding Kennedy-Johnson period, the essentially defensive stance of U.S. foreign policy shifted in a more positive direction with the proclaimed emphasis on nation building and counterinsurgency, both of which involved an interventionist outlook. Moreover, the concept of counterinsurgency envisaged use of mobile U.S. ground forces, always ready to be thrust as firefighters into any protected nation threatened by the flames of insurgency. It was a dangerous set of concepts, as later events were to prove, and it was particularly so because no ultimate strategy of deterrence had been constructed to replace the tottering one of massive retaliation. Cuba was to be at once the initial failure of interventionism and the final triumph of massive retaliation. The bankruptcy of our foreign and national security policy became tragically apparent in the Vietnam quagmire and the achievement of strategic nuclear parity by the Soviet Union.

And so we come to the most recent years, when it has been no longer possible to postpone overhaul of an anachronistic foreign policy. While the world was undergoing profound change over some two decades, the diplomatic foundation of our security posture and the philosophy of our foreign relations remained virtually the same. A host of commitments appropriate to the days when we were the only Western country capable of bearing the major burden of defense had persisted while Western Europe and Japan flourished and prospered. To our Asian friends, all with abundant manpower, we had continued to promise military assistance in the form of U.S. ground forces when needed to repel attack. The Soviet bloc had divided and subdivided without major impact on our diplomacy. And, worst of all, we had continued, at least implicitly, to rely on a strategic deterrent that lost its credibility when we permitted the Soviet Union to achieve strategic nuclear parity. The name had changed to mutual assured destruction—MAD—but the basic ingredient was the same: threat of massive retaliation. But the threat lost effect since to carry it out meant to commit suicide.

When the Nixon administration took office, it faced only unpleasant options in foreign policy and therefore decided to punt. Attention was focused on disengagement from Vietnam as justified by the Guam Doctrine. To help end our involvement in Vietnam, to set the stage for SALT (Strategic Arms Limitation Talks), and to buy time in general, we adopted the policy of détente toward the Soviet Union. Negotiation was heralded as replacing confrontation, and conferences were initiated on all sorts of East-West issues, the most serious effort being SALT. Relations were opened with Communist China to provide some counterweight to growing Soviet power while easing our disengagement from Vietnam. In Europe and the Middle East, we tried to serve our national interests as best we could with a diplomatic holding action.

It seems fair to say that the principal political objective of foreign policy during the first Nixon administration was to generate results, whether illusory or real, that would produce a landslide victory at the polls in 1972 and thereby convey a mandate enabling the second Nixon administration to undertake spectacular diplomatic initiatives. The evidence available so far demonstrates that preoccupation with winning a mandate at the polls caused the resulting foreign policy to serve merely as a brief transition to a set of world relations almost the opposite of those envisaged in President Nixon's grand design.

President Nixon won a mandate but lost power. We disengaged ourselves from Vietnam but lost Southeast Asia to Communist domination. Détente has helped erode Western resolve to resist Soviet expansion without producing any tangible gains for the West. Our diplomatic holding action was instrumental in setting the stage for renewed warfare in the Middle East, deepening our commitment to defend Israel, and preparing the way for use of the Arab oil embargo. The region is now set to explode in the most sophisticated kind of warfare under conditions in which there will be little capability or popular backing of U.S. intervention in fulfillment of implicit commitments. Europe has become far more disorganized and disunited than in 1969. The arms balance, both conventional and nuclear, has become more favorable to the Soviet Union. The American public has reverted to isolationism, and Congress has become almost domineering in day-to-day foreign affairs.

The picture is indeed frightening, and there is no simple or obvious way for us to preserve our influence in the world.

30

Aid to Vietnam: Keeping Our Word

Good money after bad, they say. Is there no end to Vietnam? Haven't we done more than enough? We sacrificed 46,000 lives, squandered $150 billion, and what do we have to show for it? The war goes on, and more American aid just means more killing. Why not call it quits and let the South Vietnamese fend for themselves? Peace will come only when we stop supplying arms, and the sooner the better.

So speak the critics of further aid to South Vietnam, and their words are persuasive to an American public still enduring the tragic consequences of an ill-conceived venture in Vietnam. There can be no quarrel about our epic mistakes of the past. But must we so brood over the past that we blind ourselves to responsibilities of the present and future? Must we be so zealous in avoiding repetition of old mistakes that we commit new ones at least equally perilous to national security?

We were not wrong to help South Vietnam resist naked foreign aggression. Our mistake of the past consisted instead in trying to do the whole thing ourselves. We assumed a task we could not meet even with half a million troops unless we overstepped the self-imposed moral bounds of warfare. We not only bled our nation needlessly but also lost precious time in preparing the South Vietnamese to defend themselves.

This essay was published in an edited version in *Washington Post,* Mar. 4, 1975.

Hurt and suffering of the past cannot be undone. It can only be brought to a halt, as it was through vietnamization. While our forces were being steadily withdrawn, the South Vietnamese were trained, armed, and psychologically prepared to undertake the full burden of defense. They assumed that burden as combat responsibility was thrust upon them and passed the test of fire when they decisively repulsed the full-scale invasion launched by the North Vietnamese in 1972.

The Paris Accords called for a cease-fire but, as we know all too well, the firing never ceased. One might disagree as to which side has been guilty of this or that incident, but there can be no doubt that North Vietnam has contemptuously ignored the accords from the start despite its signature to them. It has done so by persistent heavy attacks near the demilitarized zone and by relentless buildup of troops, supplies, and arms throughout South Vietnam. Whatever flimsy mask of respectability remained has now been torn away by the launching of a major offensive, supported by heavy artillery and tanks, that has resulted so far in capture of the entire province of Phuoclong.

The South Vietnamese face an enemy more strongly massed, far better supplied, and more heavily armed than it was at any time when we were doing the fighting. Having only a small part of our firepower and mobility, they must substitute guts and staying power. What was once a supply trail from Hanoi to the south, constantly harassed and interdicted by air, has become an unmolested freeway. Last year it brought eight times as many supplies into South Vietnam as the trail carried in the year of buildup and support for the all-out invasion of 1972. The iron triangle near Saigon is now menaced by tanks, heavy rockets and artillery, surface-to-air missiles, sophisticated antiaircraft artillery, and heavy mortars that were never in the area in the days of American defense.

The Paris Accords strictly forbade even the replacement of enemy troops then in South Vietnam, but Hanoi has since doubled its forces in the south. These are main-force units of the army of North Vietnam, filled out no more than a tenth by local Viet Cong. Seven additional regular divisions are stationed in reserve in North Vietnam. In resisting this powerful enemy, the South Vietnamese have suffered more combat deaths in the last two years than we did in our entire seven years of warfare. The South Vietnamese have earned their red badge of courage.

Make no mistake: the South Vietnamese are defending their homeland. Man for man and unit for unit, they have outfought the North Vietnamese. That may be hard to believe, but it is true. Those who argue otherwise rely on memory of an irrelevant past, not on facts as they now are. And those who say that South Vietnam's military cause is lost are dead wrong. The South Vietnamese are long on resolve, heroism, and fighting skill. They are short of bullets.

We cannot expect them to provide bullets as well as blood. They could if the invader were also fighting with its own weaponry. But North Vietnam is supplied in plenitude by the Soviet Union and the People's Republic of China.

Meanwhile, we have provided far less than the one-for-one replacement of consumed supplies permitted by the accords. In fact, Congress enacted a double-barreled cutback last year when it, first, reduced the authorized aid program by $400 million and, second, appropriated $300 million less than the authorization. Inflation cut real aid even further. Some wished to believe that cutting our aid would reduce the level of violence by forcing President Thieu to fight less and negotiate more, as if it were all up to him. The result has been quite the opposite. Sensing American abandonment of South Vietnam, Hanoi stiffened its negotiating stance while launching a military offensive. When military victory seems at hand, why should Hanoi negotiate for something less? If there is to be progress at the negotiating table, the south must be visibly able to defend itself militarily.

Of course, some opponents of military assistance don't care whether there is a political settlement in Vietnam or not. To them, the only important thing is for us to wash our hands of the whole affair as quickly as possible. They often go on to argue that the South Vietnamese economy is a mess and will collapse sooner or later anyhow. So communism will win out regardless of how things go politically and militarily.

This is a groundless myth. The South Vietnamese economy has suffered many strains, but it has responded with remarkable resilience and vigor. Recent performance is all the more admirable because we had patronized the South Vietnamese in economic as well as military affairs, doing for them what they needed to learn to do for themselves, and often doing it wrong. In addition, the economy became distorted in trying to serve Americans in the style to which they are accustomed. Fortunately, much progress was made during vietnamization in building the foundation for an ultimately self-reliant economy. Consequently, the brutal shock of the final American withdrawal and the 1972 invasion was quietly absorbed by the economy. So was the sharp rise in oil prices last year.

The standard of living has, of course, gone down while inflation and unemployment have gone up, but the economy is coping without complaint. The people tighten their belts and the policy makers keep a cool head. In current prices, imports fell by 45 percent in the second half of 1974 and by 10 percent in the year as a whole. This happened while import prices were rising by 35 percent, so that the reduction in real imports was much larger. At the same time, the rate of domestic inflation was cut by more than a third in 1974. In fact, the cost of living remained stable over the entire final quarter of the year. What other country can claim such a record?

Meanwhile South Vietnamese economic policy has not lost sight of the long-run objective of creating a self-reliant economy capable of generating a healthy and steady pace of growth. Workers are being attracted out of the cities into the countryside to boost agricultural development. The program has worked so far despite the deteriorating security situation, but it faces an increasingly difficult period. In a word, the economy has been performing extremely well under the circumstances, and it shows no signs of collapsing.

Having heard this much, many will ask: so what? So the South Vietnamese are making their own way. But what do we owe them? Well, we owe them no more than our heart tells us. We owe them neither more nor less than it means to our conscience to forsake the principle of self-determination and to acquiesce in a blood bath of innocents.

We should also ask what we owe ourselves, and that is a matter of the head. What we owe ourselves depends on how much difference it makes to live in a disintegrating world order. For nothing will diminish our ability to wield a stabilizing influence in world affairs so much as a well-deserved reputation for infidelity and unreliability in time of trouble.

There is no doubt where my sympathies lie. I was in charge of vietnamization from beginning to end, and I cannot forget its deeper meaning. That deeper meaning derived from the Guam Doctrine, which proclaimed to the world that we would provide material assistance to any nation that demonstrated the resolve to fight for itself in resisting aggression. This we would do instead of fighting others' battles for them. Vietnam was to be the first case of the new doctrine at work.

Well, they are fighting their own battle, and now the world waits to see whether we shall stick to our end of the bargain. Yes, it will be costly to do so, but if we don't, what message will be carried to the Middle East? And what nation will be next in line to defend itself against the unrelenting expansionary powers of the world?

Perhaps it doesn't really matter that powerful aggression will be resisted nowhere. Perhaps the wolf shall dwell with the lamb. Or perhaps resistance would fail in any case. If so, we can be content to let our Vietnamese friends eat cake.

31

Power in the Arena of International Politics

We must take a good look at where the power lies in the arena of international politics, for it is the powerful who have the capability of threatening our security. We protect ourselves by causing powerful nations and coalitions to side either with us or against potential enemies.

Many of the problems of today have their roots in the awful blunder we committed at the height of our power in World War II when we personified the threat. We saw Germany and Japan as our enemies of the future because they had been those of the past. We were blind to the threat of the Soviet Union and other Communist powers because of an unfortunate mixture of idealism, naiveté, and inexperience in the arena of power politics. We blundered in failing to appreciate the dynamics of power, and we should not do so again.

It has become commonplace to speak of five focuses of power, the pentagonal superpowers: the United States, Western Europe, the Soviet Union, Japan, and China. My vision of the world is rather different. For one thing, I would distinguish at least two types of inter-relationships: those involving prime powers, on the one hand, and those involving balancing powers, on the other. For another, I would

This piece is excerpted from remarks given at the Naval Aviation Executive Institute in June 1974.

give recognition to such nations as Thailand, Indonesia, Australia, and Brazil as stabilizing influences in specific regional contexts.

Perhaps the most significant interaction of power on the world scene is taking place at the moment within the triangular politics of the United States, the Soviet Union, and China. Each considers itself an adversary of the other two, but it has an interest in common with either insofar as it weakens the third. It is a spinning triangle: Russia seeking our favors against China; China seeking ours against Russia; we reciprocating; and, perhaps in the offing, China and the Russians coalescing against us. Managing such a triangular relation requires great art and balance. Things can get out of hand. But at the moment there need be no doubt on our part that Russia has replaced us as the most dangerous enemy in the eyes of Chinese rulers.

This delicate balancing act is complicated by an independent factor: the Soviet economy has run out of steam and must have help from the West to avoid serious consequences for all Soviet ambitions.

It is against this background of triangular politics and economic needs, coupled with the shifting strategic nuclear balance, that the so-called spirit of détente is most easily understood. Soviet leaders want a calm and quiet Western frontier so that they may muster strength to the East, where they confront China. They also want economic and technological assistance from Western Europe. At the same time, they recognize that achievement of strategic nuclear parity has created a certain military paralysis in Western Europe, where public opinion opposes defense spending in any event. Europeans have found a convenient solution to their worries: stick your head in the sand and pretend that there is no threat. Meanwhile, the Soviet Union turns a smiling face toward the West. Wish is father to the thought, and therefrom springs the spirit of détente, the Ostpolitik, and all the rest. The great danger in all this is that the NATO unity that has protected Europe so successfully these last two and a half decades will splinter, and each nation will take upon itself the task of striking its own accommodation with mighty Russia, the weak facing the strong. The threat is not so much that Russia will invade Europe as that it won't have to.

Much is said in official statements and the press of the great strides toward peaceful relations that have already been made in such agreements as the one on the status of Berlin. But those agreements have been reached because the West has acceded to positions consistently and persistently advanced by Soviet diplomacy in the postwar period. Perhaps that is just as well, but we should not delude ourselves that

commitment and thereby strengthened world order. We should not spoil these accomplishments by promising what is beyond our grasp, namely, peace in Southeast Asia. Nor should we destroy our self-respect and create a deserved reputation for perfidy by running out on our obligations by not giving the South Vietnamese the help in the form of arms and economic aid they need to survive.

History gives little hope for lasting peace in the Middle East either, but here the stakes are so high that we must not give up trying. No other region outside the territory of the major powers bears the combined geopolitical and economic significance of the Middle East, and, for this reason, it threatens to become an area of confrontation between the Soviet Union and the West. Any hostilities between local powers carry the danger of being the spark to set off a general conflagration. We cannot, therefore, either stand aside or take sides without endangering our national security. Nowhere is there a more compelling need for American diplomatic ingenuity. There are many who speak euphorically of miracles of American diplomacy in the Middle East, but I do not believe in miracles in foreign relations. Before we get too dizzy with success, we should reflect on whether our earlier diplomatic neglect of the region may not have been responsible for the crisis that many now want to believe was resolved by brilliant American diplomacy. We are the only major power that can deal with both sides in this festering enmity, and we have a solemn obligation to use our influence to create stability in the region. We have a long way to go and many serious hurdles to cross, and we had better count on hard work and prudent application of power to get the job done, not miracles or miracle makers.

When all is said, the future prospects of world order hinge on what emerges from negotiations between the Soviet Union and the United States. From that relationship, between the two leading superpowers, all others will derive. Dramatic changes have taken place, and others are no doubt in the offing. It remains to be seen whether they will mark the end of the cold war, the beginning of a generation of peace, or something else. The point I wish to drive home is simply this: if something good is to come from the new environment, we must keep our feet on the ground. Wishful thinking and idealistic euphoria will lead only to disaster.

I will illustrate with a specific. Although we have been negotiating on many fronts with the Soviets, they have consistently maneuvered to ensure that important political questions—such as strategic arms limitation and mutual force reductions—are not resolved until the Soviets have achieved what they seek from us and other Western countries. To put it bluntly, what they seek is primarily economic aid in the form of huge long-term loans and concessionary terms of trade. We, as a nation, can gain very little from such economic arrangements, whereas the Soviet Union stands to gain a great deal. The situation obviously argues for our providing economic benefits only in exchange for political ones. Above all, we must not delude ourselves that tribute is a substitute for defense.

Nor should we indulge in the fantasy that a cordial diplomatic atmosphere is any more than that. Speaking softly in polite discourse is absolutely essential if diplomacy is to do what it must to avert the potential catastrophe of confrontation. But it is the means not the end. A stable world must rest on a solid foundation of institutions that will endure beyond the prime of any single person, no matter how skilled he may be in diplomatic pyrotechnics. If the machinery of foreign policy, built by a mortal genius, is to function successfully for very long, it must be designed to be run by mortal idiots. It must be held together by sturdy institutions, not by a fragile web of old school ties. And it must be run by capabilities, not intentions. Perhaps Comrade Brezhnev is indeed a dictator who looks upon the outside world with benevolence, but we need more than words and smiles to be sure. And, however that might be, we would be mad to imagine that the kind of political system he now rules will never spew forth another of its Hitlers or Stalins to command the heights. What comfort shall we then take in the good old days of graceful encounter?

In brief, personal diplomacy and summitry are the absolutely necessary beginning of a civilized process of negotiation, but there is a very real danger that the shadow of détente may be mistaken for the substance of peace.

32

Foreign Policy
and Détente

"**D**étente is an imperative. In a world shadowed by the danger of nuclear holocaust, there is no rational alternative to the pursuit of relaxation of tensions." This was the choice offered to the American public by the newly appointed Secretary of State Henry Kissinger:[1] either his policy of détente as it had materialized or utter destruction of the world, one or the other.

If Kissinger were right, there would be nothing to argue about. But he is wrong: there are other ways of avoiding a nuclear holocaust that would be far less damaging to our way of life than détente, a term that I shall use to designate the particular configuration of policies and procedures associated with Kissinger's stewardship of foreign affairs. I do not have time today to spell out the alternatives, but perhaps they will be implicit in my critique of détente.

The basic trouble with détente is that it is designed to be a no-risk policy. It was an earlier Henry Kissinger who soberly warned against such a no-risk policy with these opening words from his first book.

This essay, which is based on G. Warren Nutter, *Kissinger's Grand Design* (Washington, D.C.: American Enterprise Institute, 1975), was read at the meetings of the American Association for the Advancement of Slavic Studies, St. Louis, Mo., in October 1976.

[1] In his speech to the Pilgrims of Great Britain, U.S., *Department of State Bulletin,* Dec. 31, 1973, p. 779.

Those ages which in retrospect seem most peaceful were least in search of peace. Those whose quest for it seems unending appear least able to achieve tranquillity. Whenever peace—conceived as the avoidance of war—has been the primary objective of a power or a group of powers, the international system has been at the mercy of the most ruthless member of the international community. Whenever the international order has acknowledged that certain principles could not be compromised even for the sake of peace, stability based on an equilibrium of forces was at least conceivable.[2]

Détente is a policy not merely of avoiding war but of eliminating all risk of confrontation that might generate a risk of war. To proclaim, as Kissinger has, that the United States has no choice but to follow a course in which no risks are taken is to ensure that American diplomacy has no leverage whatsoever vis-à-vis the Soviet Union.

But that is precisely what Kissinger intends, for he explicitly rules quid pro quo bargaining out of the diplomacy of détente. The object is to entice the Soviet Union to behave responsibly by showering her with gifts, and détente presents us with an opportunity to do so. Why? Because, Kissinger says, "the United States and the Soviet Union, after decades of profound suspicion, have perceived a common interest in avoiding nuclear holocaust and in establishing a web of constructive relationships."[3] Diplomacy need only take advantage of the relaxation of tensions to create, within the spreading environment of global interdependence, a web of mutual involvement and vested interest. The evolving order will acquire legitimacy because the great powers will recognize that they stand to lose more in the way of critical vested interests than they would gain otherwise if they defied the rules of international conduct and broke the bonds of interdependence.

The diplomacy of détente is based on the principle of linkage, which means something quite different from what one might think. Normally, linkage is used to describe a quid pro quo relationship: an action by one country is made contingent upon—is linked to—a reciprocal action by another. But to Kissinger linkage means an interrelationship among issues.

Our approach proceeds from the conviction that, in moving forward across a wide spectrum of negotiation, progress in one area adds momentum to progress in other areas. If we succeed, then no agreement stands

[2] *A World Restored: Castlereagh, Metternich and Restoration of Peace, 1812–1822* (Boston: Houghton Mifflin Co., 1957), p. 1.

[3] Speech to the American Legion, *Department of State Bulletin,* Sept. 16, 1974, p. 375.

alone as an isolated accomplishment vulnerable to the next crisis. We did not invent the interrelationship between issues expressed in the so-called linkage concept; it was a reality because of the range of problems and areas in which the interests of the United States and the Soviet Union impinge on each other. We have looked for progress in a series of agreements settling specific political issues, and we have sought to relate these to a new standard of international conduct appropriate to the dangers of the nuclear age. By acquiring a stake in this network of relationships with the West, the Soviet Union may become more conscious of what it would lose by a return to confrontation. Indeed, it is our hope that it will develop a self-interest in fostering the entire process of relaxation of tensions.[4]

In other words, one thing leads to another, and, once the network of relations is established, the Soviet Union risks losing it all if it renounces any part.

This approach is one of moving diplomatically "along a broad front" rather than step by step, settling one issue at a time. There is no reckoning of quid pro quo, either for each agreement or for the outcome as a whole. The only criterion to be met is that each arrangement should derive from mutual interest and dispense mutual benefit. There is no need for concern if the Soviet Union gains more than the West along the way since the fundamental balance of power will not be altered by such incidental marginal adjustments. What is important is that the Soviet Union, the unruly power being tamed, perceive sufficient gain from the ultimate network of relations to be induced, for fear of losing the gain, to behave in accord with agreed rules of international conduct.

While Kissinger attaches great significance to the diplomacy of détente, he also continues to emphasize that deterrence of aggression, so obviously important today, must remain an essential component of Western policy, new order or not, and that the foundation of deterrence must be built out of strong conventional forces. As in the past, he views SALT (Strategic Arms Limitation Talks) as the cornerstone of negotiations with the Soviet Union, having the purpose of stabilizing nuclear parity while preventing an arms race. Détente thus involves a mixed strategy: interdependency is the carrot, deterrence the stick, and arms control the rein.

Deterrence is obviously the key element, for without it the security of the West would depend solely on Soviet good will and self-restraint. By definition, effective arms control would reduce the level of Western

---

[4] Statement to the Senate Committee on Foreign Relations, *Department of State Bulletin*, Oct. 14, 1974, p. 508.

military strength required for deterrence, but the relation between deterrence and interdependency is far more complex. Greater gains from so-called interdependency might induce the Soviet Union to restrain its expansionist instinct. But the unilateral concessions yielding those gains will cause us to appear all the more weak-willed in the eyes of Soviet leaders, while the gains themselves increase Soviet power commensurately. Soviet leaders will consequently be tempted to seek even greater gains through power politics and to treat the United States as a weakling deserving contempt. Meanwhile, the atmosphere of détente is certain, as we now witness, to sway Western psychology toward downgrading the Soviet threat, cutting defense budgets, and disrupting alliances—the effect being a further tipping of the power balance in the Soviet Union's favor. The dynamics of this process can, as Kissinger once constantly warned, lead to demoralization of the West and Soviet victory by default.

Kissinger's grand design rests on the thesis that the dominating effect of greater interdependency will be to restrain Soviet behavior, but he has little backing from history. Economic interdependence is scarcely new: on the eve of World War I, Norman Angell argued in *The Great Illusion*[5] that the intricate network of world commerce had destroyed all possibility of gain from war. Yet the warring nations of Europe in the twentieth century, as in the nineteenth, normally were close trading partners. As Professor Gregory Grossman reminds us, "history provides little reassurance that trade ensures peace, and Russia's own history least of all. Germany was her largest trading partner just before each of the two World Wars, while China was her largest trading partner (and Russia China's) before the break between Moscow and Peking around 1960."[6]

It is doubtful in any case that the interdependency seemingly envisaged by Kissinger can grow out of normal trading relations, since there is no reason to believe that the Soviet Union is about to abandon its traditional policy of autarky. Soviet planners are, however, eager for a generous infusion of Western technology if the price is right—which

[5] *A Study of the Relation of Military Power in Nations to Their Economic and Social Advantage* (New York and London: Putnam's Sons, 1911).

[6] U.S., Congress, Joint Economic Committee, *Soviet Economic Outlook: Hearings,* 93rd Cong., 1st sess., July 17–19, 1973, p. 143. In each case, Germany accounted for 40 percent of Russia's foreign trade. On the general issue of trade and peace, see also Albert Wohlstetter, "Threats and Promises of Peace: Europe and America in the New Era," *Orbis* 17 (Winter 1974): 1112–15.

is to say, if available on cheap long-term credit or otherwise concessionary terms. The response called for is economic aid, which might
seem to weld a stronger bond of dependency than a network of trade.
But, historically, tribute has been no more successful than trade in
preventing conquest or domination by a foreign power.

Perhaps the weakest link in Kissinger's argument is the insistence
that any gains accruing to Soviet power from détente are irrelevant
"because when both sides possess such enormous power, small additional increments cannot be translated into tangible advantage or even
usable political strength."[7] This does not make sense, as Professor
Albert Wohlstetter succinctly demonstrates.

> The reasoning supporting this view of the present equilibrium proceeds
> from the notion that adding an increment of military power to the "over-
> whelming arsenals of the nuclear age" does not effectively change any-
> thing. But is it true that because both the Soviet Union and the United
> States have many thousands of nuclear warheads, it makes no difference
> at all if one of the superpowers adds to its arsenal wire-guided anti-tank
> weapons or surface-to-air missiles or laser-guided bombs or the like for
> use in limited contingencies? And, can neither gain some political end by
> transferring such weapons (or even some day a few nuclear weapons) to
> an ally? On the evidence of October 1973 the Soviet Union feels that
> one-sided gains are feasible. Statements about the sufficiency or stability
> of military balances cannot be derived from the mere size of the super-
> powers' nuclear stockpiles. "Power" is much more complex and varied
> than that. Neither military nor political nor economic power can be mea-
> sured by one simple scalar number.[8]

In other words, the power balance is still subject to infinite variation
through "marginal adjustments."

The issue, then, is how to make the best use of our assets in the
continuing struggle to defend Western civilization against the threat
from the East. Stripped of rhetoric, Kissinger's détente amounts to
giving the assets away without requiring any strategic benefits in return, this being done on the premise that the Soviet rulers will so
treasure what they are receiving that they will carefully avoid upsetting
the strategic equilibrium. But they will hardly need to do anything since
the power balance will steadily move in their favor anyhow. We should

---

[7] *U.S. Foreign Policy for the 1970's: Shaping a Durable Peace,* A report to the Congress by
Richard Nixon, President of the United States (Washington, D.C.: Government Printing Office,
1973), p. 232.

[8] Wohlstetter, "Threats and Promises of Peace," pp. 1116–17.

instead exchange our assets only for compensatory strategic benefits, achieved step by step. Such a diplomacy of reciprocal concession holds far more promise for meaningful peace than the drift of détente.

There is a grand design to Kissinger's détente, but the West is drifting all the same. Confusion reigns in Congress and the public, and it cannot be dispelled by consensus because diplomacy has become personalized. There is no way for the legitimate organs of government to guide the direction of American foreign policy as long as it conforms to Kissinger's grand design. The policy and his stewardship must both be accepted as a matter of faith.

What Kissinger promises in exchange is peace without risk: he will create a stability of forces and a legitimate international order while eliminating the risk of confrontation between the nuclear superpowers. He promises to do so by entangling the Soviet Union in a web of involvement that it will never wish to escape. The promise cannot be fulfilled.

Kissinger calls his diplomacy creative, but it is more aptly described as romantic. Such statesmanship is rare in the American tradition, which favors a foreign policy resting on idealism and realism, mixed in proportions appropriate to the times.

33

Foreign Policy as Public Policy

Democracy, Lord Bryce once observed, is government by discussion. That is the substance of the matter, the essence that distinguishes democracy from other types of government. There are many forms of democracy but only one process: popular discussion leading to consent.

Like all valid generalizations, this one cannot be taken literally. Democracy hardly means open discussion of everything or consent by everybody. Even if we could resolve the initial paradox of who "everybody" is to be (not infants, surely, nor some others, depending on standards of maturity and competence), it goes without saying that we could not govern ourselves by means of a huge town meeting, sitting in continuous session and reaching decisions only by unanimous agreement. Government must be both less and more than this, for freedom also requires order and progress.

There will always be important areas of disagreement in our society, no matter how open it may be, which is to say that there will always be social problems. These must be resolved through a less-than-perfect political process, which will be legitimate to the degree that it rests on

This essay, which was delivered as a speech at the Borah Symposium, University of Idaho, Moscow, in March 1976, is reprinted, with minor omissions, from the monograph of the same title (Washington, D.C.: American Enterprise Institute, 1976).

popular approval and democratic to the degree that it involves discussion and consent.

To avoid misunderstanding, I want to state clearly at the outset that I find no serious fault with our political system. On the contrary, it is, in my opinion, the best one yet devised by man for government by discussion. But an eminent historian once described history as "just one damn thing after another," and somewhere along the line in recent years our history has gone off the track.

Crises have erupted because complex social forces, sweeping across the globe, have brought powerful stresses and strains to bear on our established institutions and mores. Something had to give. However we might diagnose our basic social ills and whatever we might find as the ultimate cure, the first thing to do is to restore order and confidence.

Foreign policy is in a state of confusion, in no small measure because it has lost touch with the people. The doctrine of containment, once widely understood and broadly supported, has been displaced by the slogan of détente, which has at best only a negative meaning. Now even that slogan has been tossed aside, and we are left with an incoherent jumble of day-to-day diplomacy to comprehend. In the absence of basic concepts to orient thinking and debate, the legislative and executive branches of government have fallen to squabbling over who is to do what, when, and how in the ad-hocery of foreign affairs. We are muddling through.

There was a time in earlier days of the republic and even not so long ago when we could afford to muddle through until a new order was established. We cannot afford to do so today. We were once a minor power in the affairs of a world divided into many relatively self-contained regions, each with its own problems and conflicts unlikely to spill over automatically into other areas. Surrounded by an invulnerable moat of seas, we could attend to key relations, primarily in Europe and the Western Hemisphere, and ignore others. We could avoid entanglements and enjoy the blessing of isolation.

All that is gone. We are now a mighty nation, built by territorial expansion and the wonders of our political economy. Our territory extends far beyond the continental island into the vast reaches of the Pacific. Technology has made the world one, drawing together previously isolated regions and creating history in real time. Wars have long since become global, and in the nuclear age they have taken on the dimension of potential holocaust. Modern weapons combined with modern means of delivery have rendered obsolete the moat of seas surrounding the American island and made our heartland subject to attack without warning at any time. We are one of two superpowers in a bipolar world split by an epic and tragic ideological struggle. Unless we wish to undo our history, we have no choice but to be deeply and constantly involved in world affairs.

Why, then, are we muddling through? No doubt, for many complex reasons woven into the fabric of history. Yet one must begin somewhere in unraveling them, and I will start with the tragedy of Vietnam.

Go back some twelve years when President Johnson, newly ascended to office under tragic circumstances, confronted the question of really getting into the Vietnam War or getting out. With great expectations, the Great Society had been launched with the goal of transforming our domestic structure virtually overnight. The doctrine of containment still reigned over foreign policy, but its thrust had been shifted somewhat earlier by President Kennedy in the direction of a more active and interventionist policy of nation building and counterinsurgency.

The issue of Vietnam came to a head with the Tonkin Gulf incident, which occurred in the midst of a presidential campaign. The fundamental decision on our involvement was made when Congress, with only two dissenting votes, passed the Tonkin Gulf Resolution, abdicating its right to declare war by delegating to the president the power to make war or not, as he saw fit. Recall the sweeping words of that resolution.

> The United States regards as vital to its national interest and to world peace the maintenance of international peace and security in southeast Asia. Consonant with the Constitution of the United States and the Charter of the United Nations and in accordance with its obligations under the Southeast Asia Collective Defense Treaty, the United States is, therefore, prepared, as the President determines, to take all necessary steps, including the use of armed force, to assist any member or protocol state of the Southeast Asia Collective Defense Treaty requesting assistance in defense of its freedom.

Within less than a year, the president used that power to send American soldiers directly into battle, and Congress ratified the decision by appropriating funds and levying troops. The public was told not to worry: our mighty economy would funish both guns and butter. We would move the Great Society forward with our right hand while fighting the war with our left. We would create whatever extra resources were needed simply by speeding up economic growth.

Let me pause at this point to emphasize that the issue I want to talk about is not whether the decision on Vietnam was right or wrong, but whether it was made and implemented legitimately, in accord with proper process for our republic. Nor do I mean to point the finger of blame in any particular direction. It must be pointed all around. The executive branch must be blamed for being too reckless and ambitious, the legislative branch for being too irresponsible, and the public for being too greedy—at least at the start—about having its cake and eating it too.

War is the ultimate political act, and no nation such as ours, seeking as it does to live in peace and harmony, should take that fateful step except in defense or in protection of vital interests when all else has failed. Under the circumstances, we should not have gone to war without carefully deliberating the consequences and making sure through established constitutional procedures that there was a consensus in favor of doing so.

Instead we went to war too lightly and suffered all the dreadful consequences. The presidency lost credibility and respect by stretching the truth and exercising unprecedented power. Congress came under a cloud as well by shirking its responsibility to wield countervailing power while screaming about the way the war was being prosecuted. The war effort never having received the full sanction of law, unrestrained dissent and dissidence tore our society apart.

And so our next president was elected by the tiniest of majorities as the American people, confused and disunited, groped for a way out of this mess. Lacking a mandate and operating from a position of weakness, President Nixon quickly turned our foreign policy around while disengaging us from Vietnam. But he did so in obsessive secrecy, distrustful of public and congressional opinion. These two coequal branches of government, Congress and the presidency, instead of converging in their outlooks toward foreign policy, moved onto a collision course. In the ensuing struggle, President Nixon went for broke by seeking an overriding mandate at the polls, letting the end justify the means. He won the mandate but lost power when he reaped the harvest of Watergate.

That is, of course, not the end of the story, for the Nixon foreign policy has lingered on in style and content under the tutelage of Henry Kissinger, whom President Nixon elevated to the position of secretary of state in the fall of 1973. As Secretary Kissinger conceives and practices statecraft, it must be personalistic, secretive, and mysterious.

In his days as a scholar, Henry Kissinger revealed this attitude quite clearly. "It can never be the task of leadership to solicit a consensus," he said, "but to create the conditions which will make a consensus possible. A leader, if he performs his true function, must resign himself to being alone part of the time, at least while he charts the road."[1]

He developed this theme with an extended metaphor.

> The statesman is therefore like one of the heroes in classical drama who has had a vision of the future but who cannot transmit it directly to his fellow-men and who cannot validate its "truth." Nations learn only by experience; they "know" only when it is too late to act. But statesmen must act *as if* their intution were already experience, as if their aspiration were truth. It is for this reason that statesmen often share the fate of prophets, that they are without honour in their own country, that they always have a difficult task in legitimizing their programmes domestically, and that their greatness is usually apparent only in retrospect when their intuition has become experience. The statesman must therefore be an educator; he must bridge the gap between a people's experience and his vision, between a nation's tradition and its future. In this task his possibilities are limited. A statesman who too far outruns the experience of his people will fail in achieving a domestic consensus, however wise his policies; witness Castlereagh. A statesman who limits his policy to the experience of his people will doom himself to sterility; witness Metternich.[2]

To Kissinger, the successful statesman is a great man who creatively molds a new order, making use of history instead of being used by it. The creative statesman recognizes that reality is as much inside him, latent in his ability to create, as it is outside. He develops a supporting consensus by explaining what has already unfolded, not what the future holds. For the masses cannot possibly comprehend the merits of a novel order existing only in the mind's eye of the creative statesman.

If this conception of the role of the statesman meant merely that leaders should lead, there would be nothing to quarrel about. We govern ourselves through elected representatives, and we want them to exercise leadership. We choose them in large measure on the basis of trust in their judgment, and we do not expect them to seek advance approval for every action they take. But consent means more than

---

[1] Henry A. Kissinger, "American Policy and Preventive War," *Yale Review* 44, no. 3 (April 1955): 336.

[2] Henry A. Kissinger, *A World Restored: Castlereagh, Metternich and Restoration of Peace, 1812–1822* (Boston: Houghton Mifflin Co., 1957), p. 329.

ratifying the past. It means approving the design for the future as well.

If we have learned nothing else from the recent past, we surely have learned that no foreign policy can be sustained by this country without firm and lasting public support. It must rest on consensus. That consensus will come only if foreign policy becomes public policy—only if its grand design is subjected to open scrutiny, appraisal, and approval. There is no place for mystery, secrecy, and faits accomplis in formulating the grand design.

How do we get there from here? There is no easy way, no simple sequence of remedial actions that will put things right. There must be a change in mood and attitude as well as in ways of making policy, and trends must converge from several directions to bring that change about.

To start with, Congress and the president must—to use those hackneyed words—move from confrontation to negotiation and begin acting as partners in formulating foreign policy. The present display of one-upmanship is sheer madness. There is only one answer to the question of which branch of government should formulate foreign policy, and that is "both." The powers of Congress and the president are indeed separate but equal, and neither can proceed far without the cooperation of the other. Each needs to respect the power of the other and search for a joint policy through compromise. In this reposturing, the first move is up to the administration: it must dispel the aura of mystery enshrouding its foreign policy, reveal the grand design fully, and discuss it candidly. It is therefore encouraging to see that President Ford, a veteran of many years in Congress, has been reaching into the ranks of former congressional colleagues to fill high executive offices concerned with foreign affairs. He obviously has his eye on improving working relations with the legislative branch.

Restraint is required along with cooperation. Our constitutional doctrine of balancing powers holds that one power is to be checked and balanced by a separate power, not by the same one wielded elsewhere. Congress countervails the president through exercise of legislative power, not by trying to play the executive. In the domain of foreign affairs, the authority of Congress derives from four legislative powers: creation by law of offices within the executive branch, appropriation of funds, confirmation of appointments, and ratification of treaties. They permit Congress to play a formidable role in formulating the objectives, rationale, and process that are to guide foreign relations. Congress should have the good sense to confine itself to this role in formulating policy and to avoid meddling in the day-to-day conduct of foreign affairs. And the president should do everything in his power to protect the nation against legislative diplomacy. One sure way to chaos is to put a board of directors of 535 members in charge of diplomacy. Another way is to get executive authority so mixed up between the two branches of government that neither can be held responsible for how it is exercised.

While sorting out their roles in formulating and conducting foreign policy, our executive and legislative leaders have an obligation to search for a doctrine to serve as the foundation for policy. Consensus on policy derives from agreement on an underlying concept of world order comprehended by the public at large. Doctrine comes first and then some simple label to identify it, such as "isolationism" or "containment." As we witness from the short life of détente in our official lexicon, coining a word does not create a doctrine. Détente has been a posture in search of both a policy and a doctrine, and as such it could not survive.

In the present state of the world, it will not be easy to find a doctrine that will command broad support. The plain fact is that there is no achievable world order that is not fraught with dangers to our way of life and national survival, and anyone who promises a solution without risk is either a fool or a charlatan. But the choice before us is clear: either we try to shape the order as best we can, or we drift aimlessly wherever fate takes us. I believe the American public is in favor of trying.

The time has therefore come for straight talk that will candidly tell us where we stand, what courses are open to us, and what risks and promises they hold. At this juncture of history, nothing can endanger our future more than spoon-feeding the people and prescribing sugar-coated pills. The people must experience the bitter taste of truth. They have had enough of illusions, apologies, and self-fulfilling prophecies. The issue now testing our political system is whether the search for the right foreign policy can rise above the battlefield of partisan politics and, if it can, whether it will then command intelligent and dispassionate attention in the arena of public opinion.

And so my case is for an open foreign policy, openly arrived at. But, to avoid misunderstanding, let me say immediately that I am not arguing against secrecy and confidentiality in the conduct of diplomacy and affairs affecting our national security. If we are to defend ourselves and carry on any meaningful relations with foreign powers, there must be state secrets. The inescapable problem is to protect secrecy where it is legitimate and necessary, while preventing it where it is not. This problem resembles most social problems in that it has no easy or perfect solution. There are only better solutions and worse ones, and from recent behavior one might suppose that we have become addicted to the worse ones.

The need for state secrets is embarrassingly obvious. Start with our means and plans for defending the country. Should we publish everything we know about designing and producing nuclear weapons? The blueprints for our sophisticated missiles? The plan for defending NATO? The target list for our strategic nuclear forces? Our successes and failures in breaking secret codes of potential enemies? Our ultimate fallback position in SALT [Strategic Arms Limitation Talks]?

Protecting the country also depends on knowing the threat posed by hostile powers, and that task of intelligence requires us to penetrate their secrecy. Should we publicly reveal every means used to gain intelligence and every conclusion drawn?

The issue is not whether to have state secrets, as if secrecy must be either good or evil regardless of its nature. The issue is what purposes justify what kinds of secrets.

Since there are legitimate state secrets, there must be a legitimate authority to identify and keep them. Our Constitution clearly vests such authority first and foremost in the president as chief executive and commander in chief. He cannot escape the responsibility for keeping state secrets and should not seek to. We can imagine what fate would befall a president who, by negligence or dereliction of duty, let state secrets become known to an enemy.

The problem comes, of course, in safeguarding against abuse of the power to classify and keep secrets. The safeguard is the same as for all abuse of power: checks and balances. But once again it is a separate power that must do the checking and balancing, not the same power shared elsewhere. It is fallacious doctrine, leading to serious trouble, that a congressman or a newsman enjoys the right to determine whether a particular item of information is a state secret regardless of how the president or his designated authorities have classified it. If everybody has the right—the power—to classify or declassify state secrets, then nobody has the power or bears the responsibility to do so. Unfortunately, the law on this question is in disarray, and we would do well to give serious attention to the best way of improving it.

No freedom or right or power is absolute in our society. None is supreme over all others with which it may come in conflict. Conflicts are resolved through countervailing forces, including judicial processes and self-denying ordinances. Just as freedom of speech does not imply the right to shout "Fire!" in a crowded theater, so freedom of the press does not imply the right to publish the battle order of the day. Publishing state secrets is not the way to counter abusive secrecy.

All right, some will say, we need to keep secrets having to do with negotiations, intelligence, contingency plans, and the like. So how can we have an open foreign policy, openly arrived at? Well, we can in the relative sense in which any such concepts must be interpreted. The doctrine of foreign policy must be derived through public discussion, even though some facts about the state of the world are not known by all discussants. Similarly, the framework of foreign policy must be constructed in public view, even though the procedures contemplated for meeting contingencies are kept secret. Commitments made should be a matter of public record, even though negotiations are conducted confidentially. These are critical distinctions of substance and degree.

Woodrow Wilson once called for "open covenants of peace, openly arrived at." He was talking about another world, not ours. He should have asked for the best to be hoped for: open covenants of peace, period.

To call for an open foreign policy, openly arrived at, is not to make the same mistake, for the one cannot exist without the other. The call is simply for government by discussion.

Bibliography of Works
by G. Warren Nutter

Excludes testimony at congressional hearings, radio
or television interviews, articles in foreign-language
journals, and round-table discussions.

Adam Smith and the American Revolution. Washington, D.C.: American Enterprise
Institute, 1976.

"Aid to Vietnam: Keeping Our Word." *Washington Post,* March 4, 1975.

"Capitalism, Communism and the Average Man." *Philadelphia Inquirer,* May 4–15,
1968. Also published as *The Strange World of Ivan Ivanov.* New York: World,
1969.

Central Economic Planning: The Visible Hand. Washington, D.C.: American Enterprise Institute, 1976.

"The Coase Theorem on Social Cost: A Footnote." *Journal of Law and Economics*
11 (October 1968): 503–7.

"A Comment on Okun." In *Income Redistribution,* edited by Colin D. Campbell.
Washington, D.C.: American Enterprise Institute, 1977, pp. 43–46.

"Competition: Direct and Devious." *American Economic Review* 44 (May 1954):
69–76.

"Diminishing Returns and Linear Homogeneity." *American Economic Review* 53
(December 1963): 1084–85.

"Diminishing Returns and Linear Homogeneity: Reply." *American Economic Review*
54 (September 1964): 751–53.

"Diminishing Returns and Linear Homogeneity: Reply." *American Economic Review*
55 (June 1965): 539.

"Duopoly, Oligopoly, and Emerging Competition." *Southern Economic Journal* 30
(April 1964): 342–52.

"Economic Aspects of Freedom." In *Liberty under Law, Anarchy, Totalitarianism —
This Is the Choice.* American Bar Association Standing Committee on Education
about Communism and Its Contrast with Liberty under Law, 1969, pp. 45–49.

"Economic Developments in the Soviet Union." In *Recent Developments in the Soviet Bloc: Hearings*. U.S., Congress, House, Committee on Foreign Affairs. 88th Cong., 2d sess., 1964, pt. 2, pp. 179–85.

Economic Policy in the American Revolutionary Period. Washington, D.C.: American Enterprise Institute, 1977.

"On Economic Size and Growth." *Journal of Law and Economics* 9 (October 1966): 163–88.

"Economic Welfare and Welfare Economics." *Journal of Economic Issues* 2 (July 1968): 166–72.

"On Economism." *Journal of Law and Economics* 22 (October 1979): 263–68.

"The Effects of Economic Growth on Sino-Soviet Strategy." In *National Security: Political, Military, and Economic Strategies in the Decade Ahead*, edited by David M. Abshire and Richard V. Allen. New York: Praeger for Hoover Institution, 1963, pp. 149–68.

"Employment in the Soviet Union: An Interim Solution to a Puzzle." *Soviet Studies* 12 (April 1961): 376–93.

The Extent of Enterprise Monopoly in the United States, 1899–1939. Chicago: University of Chicago Press, 1951. Also in *Enterprise Monopoly in the United States: 1899–1958*, with Henry Adler Einhorn. New York: Columbia University Press, 1969.

Foreign Policy as Public Policy. Washington, D.C.: American Enterprise Institute, 1976.

"Freedom in a Revolutionary Economy." In *America's Continuing Revolution: An Act of Conservation*. Washington, D.C.: American Enterprise Institute, 1975, pp. 183–201. Also in *The American Revolution: Three Views*. New York: American Brands, 1975, pp. 91–122.

Growth of Government in the West. Washington, D.C.: American Enterprise Institute, 1978.

Growth of Industrial Production in the Soviet Union. Princeton: Princeton University Press for National Bureau of Economic Research, 1962.

"Growth by Merger." *Journal of the American Statistical Association* 49 (September 1954): 448–66.

"How Important Are Corporate Payoffs and Bribes?" In *The Attack on Corporate America: The Corporate Issues Sourcebook*, edited by M. Bruce Johnson. New York: McGraw Hill, 1978, pp. 66–70.

"How Soviet Planning Works." *New Individualist Review*, summer 1965, pp. 20–25. Also published under the title "The Best-Laid Plans" in *Barron's*, October 18, 1965, p. 1.

"On Independence of Utility of Product Groups." *Review of Economics and Statistics* 38 (November 1956): 484–86.

"Industrial Concentration." In *International Encyclopedia of the Social Sciences*. Macmillan and Free Press, 1968, vol. 7, pp. 218–22.

"Industrial Growth in the Soviet Union." *American Economic Review* 48 (May 1958): 398–411.

"Industrial Growth in the Soviet Union: Reply." *American Economic Review* 49 (September 1959): 695–701.

"Is Competition Decreasing in Our Economy?" *Journal of Farm Economics* 36 (December 1954): 751–58.

Kissinger's Grand Design. Washington, D.C.: American Enterprise Institute, 1975.

"The Limits of Union Power." In *The Public Stake in Union Power*, edited by Philip D. Bradley. Charlottesville, University of Virginia Press, 1959, pp. 284–300.

"Markets Without Property: A Grand Illusion." In *Money, the Market, and the State: Economic Essays in Honor of James Muir Waller*, edited by Nicholas A. Beadles and L. Aubrey Drewry, Jr. Athens, Ga.: University of Georgia Press, 1968, pp. 137–45. Also in *The Economics of Property Rights*, edited by Eirik G. Furubotn and Svetozar Pejovich. Cambridge, Mass.: Ballinger, 1974, pp. 217–24.

"On Measuring Economic Growth." *Journal of Political Economy* 65 (February 1957): 51–63. Also in *Readings in Economic Development*, edited by Theodore Morgan et al. Belmont, Calif.: Wadsworth, 1963, pp. 25–38.

"Monopoly, Bigness, and Progress." *Journal of Political Economy* 64 (December 1956): 520–27.

Translator and editor with Marie-Christine MacAndrew. *Planning for Economic Growth in the Soviet Union, 1918–1932*, by Eugène Zaleski. Chapel Hill: University of North Carolina Press, 1971.

Translator with Marie-Christine MacAndrew. *Planning Reforms in the Soviet Union, 1962–1966*, by Eugène Zaleski. Chapel Hill: University of North Carolina Press, 1967.

"The Plateau Demand Curve and Utility Theory." *Journal of Political Economy* 63 (December 1955): 525–28.

"Power and Peace." In *Peaceful Change in Modern Society*, edited by E. Berkeley Tompkins. Stanford: Hoover Institution Press, 1971, pp. 64–70.

"Rejoinder to Mr. Lebergott." *Review of Economics and Statistics* 35 (November 1953): 352–53.

"The Relative Size of Soviet Industry: A Comment." *Journal of Political Economy* 74 (October 1966): 526–28.

"Reply." *Journal of Political Economy* 86 (August 1958): 360–62.

"Some Observations on Soviet Industrial Growth." *American Economic Review* 47 (May 1957): 618–30. Also published separately as Occasional Paper 55. New York: National Bureau of Economic Research, 1957.

"Some Reflections on the Growth of the Soviet Economy." *Studies on the Soviet Union* 7, no. 1 (1967): 144–50. Also in *The Development of the Soviet Economy: Plan and Performance*, edited by Vladimir G. Treml. New York: Praeger, 1968, pp. 290–96.

"The Soviet Citizen: Today's Forgotten Man." In *The USSR in Today's World*, edited by Festus Justin Viser. Memphis: Memphis State University Press, 1968, pp. 19–44.

"Soviet Economic Policies Toward Afro-Asian Countries." In *New Nations in a Divided World*, edited by Kurt London. New York: Praeger, 1963, pp. 193–204.

"The Soviet Economy: Retrospect and Prospect." In *Fifty Years of Communism in Russia*, edited by Milorad M. Drachkovitch. Stanford: Hoover Institution Press, 1968, pp. 75–98.

"Soviet Industrial Growth." *Science*, July 31, 1959, pp. 252–55.

"The Soviet Stir: Economic Crisis and Response." In *Society and History*, edited by G. L. Ulmen. The Hague: Mouton, 1978, pp. 483–89.

Editor and compiler. *Statistical Abstract of Industrial Output in the Soviet Union, 1913–1955*. 5 pts. New York: National Bureau of Economic Research, 1956.

"The Structure and Growth of Soviet Industry: A Comparison with the United States." *Journal of Law and Economics* 2 (October 1959): 147– 74. Also in *Comparisons of the United States and Soviet Economies*. U.S., Congress, Joint Economic Committee. 86th Cong., 1st sess., 1960, pt. 1, pp. 95– 120.

With John H. Moore. "A Theory of Competition." *Journal of Law and Economics* 19 (April 1976): 39– 65.

"Trends in Eastern Europe." *Economic Age* 1, no. 1 (November-December 1968): 8– 12.

"The True Story of Russia's Weakness." *U.S. News and World Report*, March 1, 1957, p. 46.

Et al. *Vietnam Settlement: Why 1973, Not 1969?* Washington, D.C.: American Enterprise Institute, 1973.

"Where Are We Headed?" *Wall Street Journal*, January 10, 1975. Also published separately as Reprint 34. Washington, D.C.: American Enterprise Institute, 1975.

Biographical Note

Gilbert Warren Nutter (1923–1979) was a scholar and a teacher specializing in microeconomic theory, industrial organization, the Soviet economic system, and the economics of defense and international affairs. A native midwesterner, he earned his undergraduate and doctoral degrees at the University of Chicago. His studies were interrupted by service in the U.S. Army from 1943 to 1946 where he was awarded the Bronze Star with oak leaf cluster and the Combat Infantryman's Badge.

Before joining the faculty at the University of Virginia in 1956, Nutter taught briefly at Lawrence College and for six years at Yale University. In 1969 he was granted a leave of absence from Virginia to serve as assistant secretary of defense for international security affairs. When he resigned from that office in 1973 to return to teaching at Virginia, he was awarded the Defense Department's Distinguished Public Service Medal. He received an honorary degree of doctor of laws from The Citadel in 1978.

Nutter's major publications include *The Extent of Enterprise Monopoly in the United States, 1899–1939* (1951), *Growth of Industrial Production in the Soviet Union* (1962), and *Growth of Government in the West* (1978). He received the Gavel Award of the American Bar Association for the series of articles written for the "Philadelphia Inquirer," later published in book form as *The Strange World of Ivan Ivanov* (1969).

Index

307